Old Man Basking in the Sun
Longchen Rabjampa's
Treasury of Natural Perfection

Radical Dzogchen

Old Man Basking in the Sun
Longchen Rabjampa's
Treasury of Natural Perfection

Foreword by Chogyal Namkhai Norbu

Translation and Commentary
Keith Dowman

Vajra Books
Kathmandu, Nepal

Vajra Publications
Kathmandu, Nepal

Distributed by
Vajra Book Shop
Jyatha, Thamel,
Post Box: 21779, Kathmandu, Nepal
Tel/Fax: 977-1-4220562
e-mail: bidur_la@mos.com.np
www.vajrabooks.com.np

ISBN 99946-644-9-2

Cover design by Nicholas Liber

Printed in Nepal

Dedicated to freedom from all dogma
and to universal realization of natural perfection.

Other Titles by Keith Dowman

Eye of the Storm
The Flight of the Garuda
The Sacred Life of Tibet
Power-places of Kathmandu
Boudhanath: The Great Stupa
Masters of Enchantment
The Power places of Central Tibet: The Pilgrims Guide
Masters of Mahamudra
Sky Dancer: The Secret Life and Songs of the Lady Yeshe Tsogyel
The Nyingma Icons
The Divine Madman: The Life and Songs of Drukpa Kunley
The Legend of the Great Stupa
Calm and Clear: A Manual of Buddhist Meditation

Additional textural material relating to
Old Man Basking in the Sun can be found at:
http://www.keithdowman.net/dzogchen/naturalperfection/htm.

Contents

CONTENTS

Foreword by
Chogyal Namkhai Norbu

Ati Dzogchen is the inspired transmission Sakyamuni, buddha and master. Known as the yoga of the all-good nature of mind, it serves as a last resort and refuge to all beings in particularly degenerate times. When, increasingly, opinionated fundamentalism prevails and inner vision is dim, when coarse passion is rife and conflict and strife escalate, when time quickens and the body-mind is variously afflicted, it is this special yoga that provides freedom in our every act. At this time, insofar as we rely upon the all-inclusive compassion of the master Garab Dorje, Ati Dzogchen permeates our lives—the lives of the most fortunate of beings.

There are very many treatments of the extensive tantras, transmissions and precepts that elucidate Dzogchen instruction, but the quintessential meaning of it all was given by Garab Dorje to his chief disciple Manjushrimitra when the master achieved a body of light. That incontrovertible final testament consists of three incisive precepts: introduction to the nature of mind, conviction of the validity of the praxis and confidence in automatic release. Manjushrimitra, Garab Dorje's principal disciple, absorbed in the existential implications of those three incisive precepts of his master's final testimony, classified all the very many tantras, transmissions and precepts that he had received in person from his fearless master according to the rubric of mind, matrix and secret precept. Thereafter, in Oddiyana and the holy land of India, this great teacher's personal and lineal students, known as The Twenty-one, amongst others, followed and transmitted their master's teaching.

Second in status to Garab Dorje was the great master Padmasambhava who walked the valleys of Tibet and taught the profound pith precepts of the oral transmission of Dzogchen to those most fortunate students known as the Twenty-five, King and Court. Amongst his personal students were the supreme lotsawa Vairotsana and other translators, and in order that a last resort and ultimate refuge should be available to the people of Tibet he directed them to travel to Oddiyana to bring back all the tantras, transmissions and secret precepts of Dzogchen that they could find there to the Land of the Snows and to translate them into the Tibetan language. Vairotsana and his friends went to Oddiyana and heard all the very many Ati Dzogchen tantras, transmissions and secret precepts from the great master Sri Singha and others and thereafter gradually translated them into Tibetan. It was at that time that the celebrated Dzogchen master Vimalamitra came to Tibet and taught innumerable pith Ati Dzogchen precepts, and he and his students translated similar texts into Tibetan. Thus it was through the translation of texts that the sacred teaching, widespread in the land of Oddiyana, came to be transferred to Tibet.

At a much later time, the omniscient Longchen Rabjampa (Longchenpa, AD 1308-63)—renowned as an emanation not only of Garab Dorje, the source of the Dzogchen tradition, but also of Garab Dorje's eminent successor the scholar Vimalamitra—composed many extensive treatises such as *The Seven Treasuries* (*Mdzod bdun*) and *The Trilogy on Relaxation* (*Ngal gso skor gsum*), which clearly elucidate the mind-set and intention of Ati Dzogchen. Thereby, he gave the precious yoga of the all-good nature of mind a broad and high profile. Amongst Longchenpa's works there is one outstanding treatise that distills the meaning of the three series of Dzogchen instruction (Mind, Matrix and Secret Precept), and that is *The Treasury of Natural Perfection* (*Gnas lugs mdzod*), which is translated herein. Currently, when the teaching of Ati Dzogchen is spreading in the West, if we can obtain a popular translation of this extraordinary text, particularly in the English language, then immeasurable benefit will undoubtedly accrue in terms of direct perception of the nature of mind.

Kusho Keith Dowman, the translator of this text, has spent many years living in India and Nepal in communion with many great masters who have realized the Dzogchen view. Studying within their purview, fully immersed in the sacred teaching, he has fortuitously absorbed the realization of Ati Dzogchen. Now he has translated this extraordinary text, *The Treasury of Natural Perfection*, and if it can become part of the lives of fortunate Westerners, its inestimable value will become immediately apparent. I congratulate him for overcoming the deep problems of translation of both words and meaning and producing a straight-forward English rendition. It is my hope, therefore, that the translation of this text may draw the vision and meditation of the yoga of the all-good nature of mind into the mindstream of many people, so that through the realization of the nature of things just as they are all beings may be quickly released from the ubiquitous clutches of samsara.

With all good fortune,
the Dzogchenpa Chogyal Namkhai Norbu
on the 10th day of the 9th month of the wood-bird year 3723.

Translator's Introduction

Dzogchen was a secret tradition in Tibet. It remained so during the lifetime of the grandfather lamas who were the bearers of the tradition and who became refugees in India and Nepal. Today, recognized increasingly as the final analysis and apotheosis of Tibetan Buddhism, translations of Dzogchen texts are freely available in the market place and tulku-lamas teach atiyoga to all-comers throughout the world. Its popularity may be attributed to a single basic tenet which is contained in the notion 'non-action'. The buddha-nature is immanent in every moment of experience and simply by recognizing the moment and relaxing into it that realization is achieved. Relaxation is the imperative need of our stressed-out culture and relaxation is the key to buddhahood here-and-now. The materialism, rationalism and goal-oriented ambition that mark our contemporary societies is undermined by Dzogchen with its promise of optimal awareness and recognition of a natural state of perfection. Tangentially, the message of Dzogchen provides a functional approach to the medical ills of the age, a redemptive approach to sexuality and a positive, joyful vision of death and dying. These popular effects of Dzogchen, however, should not obscure its fundamental purpose—to recognize the unity of all things in a nondual universe of full awareness, harmony and compassion.

It is unfortunately true that a heavy seriousness tends to pervade texts on the Dzogchen view; but perhaps that is inevitable in works that purport to resolve our every existential quandary. Yet evidently in the work of providing meaningful commentary and translation of Dzogchen texts something crucial in the heart of Dzogchen is being forfeited. This essence of Dzogchen may be characterized as a lightness of being, humor and laid back detachment, spontaneous joy and an uninhibited freedom of expression. Perhaps these qualities will emerge here through an understanding of the author's intent, but we need to apologize, immediately, for any failure to share this cosmic joke full of joyful laughter, to induce a dance of cosmic energy involving all life and work, and a pacific play of light that is free of all pain and anxiety. The exemplar of Dzogchen may be anonymous, but he is also the divine madman—or the urban yogi—jumping through decisive moments in life as easily as through the most trivial dilemma, gleefully shouting the absurdity of existence from the rooftops and asserting the essential beauty of the human predicament. This Dzogchen text should be read as a paean of joy that loosens every knot, opens up every attenuation and softens every hardening of the psychic arteries in a resolution of the anxiety that marks human embodiment.

Indeed, *The Treasury of Natural Perfection* belongs to a class of Dzogchen literature that promises to induce the awakened state of awareness that it describes. The difficulties of the text arise from an absence of an equivalent vocabulary in English to render the self-evident truths of Dzogchen's 'natural' language, a language that constantly refers back to its own empty nature, that is the way of natural perfection. A close reading of the root text, and the repetitions of the commentary, is required to allow the magic of the words to act reflexively in returning the reader to the natural state of perfection. It constitutes, therefore, an introduction to the nature of mind, which in the threefold root precept of the founder of the Dzogchen lineage is the initiatory phase of Dzogchen praxis, succeeded only by the phases of conviction and resolution. Baldly stated, this 'introduction to the nature of mind' may precipitate the crumbling of all mental constructs and intellectual concepts and projections, like the collapse of a house of cards or a complex system of directories in a computer, and the initiate's mind is left free of emotivity and motivation in the free and easy spaciousness of the natural state of reality. This purpose and outcome, of course, depends not only upon the craft of language but presupposes a ready and willing mentality, a condition that may limit the number of readers who will gain the optimal benefit, for this book is directed at those who already possess an intuition of the nondual nature of mind. Those readers who require an overview of Dzogchen and information about a system of yoga should look elsewhere. Those who seek a philosophical treatise will not only be disappointed but they may be left confused and rejective.

In a wider purview Dzogchen, the Great Perfection, is Tibet's principal tradition of gnostic mysticism, commensurate to the Chinese Taoism of Lao Tsu and the Indian Advaita Vedanta of Shankaracharya and Ramana Maharshi. Without reference to similar and parallel Tibetan schools of yoga such as Mahamudra and Lamdre, it describes itself as the pinnacle of attainment of the Buddhist yogin, yet at the same time it maintains a distance from conventional Buddhism. Moreover, insofar as the ancient Bon school of Tibetan religion traces its own Dzogchen tradition back to its pre-Buddhist, shamanic roots, it may be surmised that the vision of Dzogchen is innate in any soteriological culture, or indeed in any human society. If a perfect nondual state of being is indeed the inescapable intrinsic state of all our being, as Longchenpa, the author of *The Treasury of Natural Perfection*, intimates, then we should expect to see traces of the idea around the world in poetry and historical religious literature, which surely is the case. Yet it is the Tibetan Dzogchen tradition that addresses the mood of our Western cultural moment which we find enmeshed in egregious materialism and the dichotomies of Judeo-Christian fundamentalism. It is in the lived Tibetan tradition founded upon a mellow oral transmission and a vast library of literary sources—most particularly in the revelations of Longchenpa—that we can find immediate access and inspiration.

Within the Tibetan arena of Dzogchen exegesis, there are many variations on the theme of natural perfection developed over 1200 years. The principal tradition of Dzogchen taught by lamas both in the West and in Tibet today is derived from Jigme Lingpa, an eighteenth century mystic, an incarnation of Longchenpa and founder of the Longchen Nyingtik tradition. This later-day Dzogchen praxis is embedded in the vajrayana Nyingma tradition and at first sight cannot be differentiated from it and is evidently an integral part of a Central Asian cultural form and lifestyle. The current exigencies of parts of Western societies, and indeed of any community that feels itself on the edge of time, demand an immediate, simple, formless, entry into the authenticity of the natural state of mind, and that is provided by what we may call radical Dzogchen. Here, as analogy, with full confidence that the human body can float in water, rather than extending a timorous toe into the pool, we jump into the deep end and either sink or swim. Knowing that awareness of radiant reality is the natural state of mind, there is no need of an extended preparatory phase, no need to modify lifestyle or moral conditioning: radical Dzogchen requires only an intimation of the nature of mind for a rainbow body to be imminent. The precepts of 'radical' or 'pristine' Dzogchen are contained in the sources of Longchenpa's philosophical poem and commentary.

Basic Assumptions

Although the origins of Dzogchen are lost in a hoary past, it appears to have come to light in the cultural nexus of the valleys of the Hindu Kush in present Pakistan and the contiguous plateau of Western Tibet. This was in the seventh and eighth centuries when the culture of Zhangzhung dominated the area. Here shamanism, Hinduism and Buddhism were mixed, but we assume that the Indic religious ethos permeated the culture. Simplistically stated, the people of this culture believed that living beings are bound to suffering on the wheel of time. Ritual worship and appeasement of the gods may alleviate that suffering and bring relief from capricious fate, and such undoubtedly was the belief of the common people; but for those with a superior karmic destiny the practice of personal moral discipline and social virtue would lead through a series of rebirths to the attainment of liberation from samsara into nirvana, or, in the case of Hindus, release (*moksha*) into union with the godhead. For those with the best karma and with the capacity to practice meditation and techniques of yoga, a path was defined through which the succession of rebirths leading to nirvana could be radically reduced. 'Liberation', synonymous with happiness, whatever the method, is thus the purpose of life. Dzogchen assumes a stance not only outside and beyond the innumerable schools of Buddhism and Hinduism that provide methods of attaining that release, but by default beyond all religious systems whatsoever, including the Judeo-Christian and Muslim, and all secular systems of belief including nihilist, atheist, hedonist and humanist.

Within the context of tantric or vajrayana Buddhism, which was the dominant form of Buddhism in the area where Dzogchen appeared and which eventually prevailed in Tibet, types of religious endeavor with final nirvana in mind are classified as eight 'progressive' approaches. These vehicles—yogas and lifestyles—include monastic discipline, solitary ascetic retreat, altruistic (bodhisattvic) social involvement, ritual activity to modify the spiritual environment, techniques to alter or transform the state of mind, and meditations and behavior designed to heighten awareness. Although all such religious practices—a different approach for every personality type—are distinguished by varying degrees of subtlety and sophistication, they are all goal-oriented, and as such a conceptual distinction is implicit between what is and what should be, between samsara and nirvana, sentient beings and buddha. Striving to attain a spiritual objective is implied in all these approaches and it is here that Dzogchen defines itself outside the frame of religion and tantra-yoga. Dzogchen stresses the undeniable fact that any goal-oriented conscientious endeavor assumes a result in a future that by definition never comes and thereby precludes attainment in the present moment. Thus there can be no liberation until the drive to attainment is relinquished. In this important sense, every path of religious striving is a dead end and represents a deviation from the natural gnosis of pure mind, 'the heart of the matter'. 'Nonaction' is the salient key term in the evocation of the reality of natural perfection.

Reality—the 'reality' that is evoked on every page of Longchenpa's text—is the light of the mind that shines equally and inescapably in every moment of existence. Much of the difficulty of Dzogchen translation into English arises from the multiplicity of expression, the fine nuance of terminology, employed to evoke this fundamental luminosity. It is the single most important, unique, assumption of Dzogchen that this light is self-existent and self-aware and in fact the sole ingredient of all our experience. This light is the great mystery of nondual mysticism. When we comprehend that Dzogchen is based upon the assumption that all and everything, consciousness and every form of experience, is naturally composed of this light, then we are able to read without let or hindrance the technical exposition of its revelation that allows the light to shine out in all its brilliance. The innate awareness of this pristine nondual brilliance is called *rigpa*, which herein is translated as 'gnosis'.

The Dzogchen view insists that there is no prescriptive practise in which to engage to attain gnosis, that there is nothing that we can do to induce that view. Dzogchen 'nonmeditation' is a spontaneous noncontingent continuity—a timeless synchronicitous awareness. Yet many people enter the arena of Dzogchen by consciously placing themselves within the reach of transmission, and then, receiving an introduction to the nature of mind from a human guru, enter the praxis of the 'hyper-yogin', which is called *atiyoga* or *maha-ati*. Identifying the Dzogchen view as the attitude of the hyper-yogin, still there exists a dichotomy between the timeless state of natural perfection and the mind that is bent on divesting itself of temporal and spatial confines. The process through which resolution of this apparent dichotomy is reached can only be a momentary synchronicitous event, yet in the Tibetan tradition two phases are identified. The first is the mind's spontaneous function of disengagement from sensory and mental objects of attachment and simultaneous self-identity with the light of which they are made. This is called Breaking Through, or Cutting Through (*trekcho*), into the original purity—or alpha-purity—where natural perfection lies. In the spacious luminosity of alpha-purity there may still be a gap between the mind of the hyper-yogin with its all-suffusing light and this last vestige of self-consciousness, and this is eliminated by the natural flow of nonmeditation upon the brilliance of the light through its apparent nuclear components known as 'holistic nuclei' which may be compared to the pixels of light in a hologram. This phase of hyper-yoga is called Jumping Through (*togel*) and implies entry into the state of spontaneity that belies causality.

The distinction between these two phases of praxis, although prominent in the contemporary mainstream Nyingtik tradition, may appear an invidious invasion of a nonverbal state by an obdurate intellect, and indeed we can only find bare traces of this distinction in *The Treasury of Natural Perfection* (see canto 122ii). The tendency to consider the difference purely academic and an indication of a concretization of Dzogchen in its recent history, however, is vitiated by the definition of two modes of final resolution. The culmination of Breaking Through is a body of light called a 'rainbow body' which presages corporeal dissolution leaving only hair and fingernails behind. The culmination of Jumping Through on the contrary is the so-called 'body of great transformation' that betokens visible longevity. To onlookers the first may appear as a dissolution at death, whereas the body of light or great transformation appears as an ongoing corporeal illusion. But again this mythos is a development later than the tantras of *The Collected Tantras of the Ancients* allow and Longchenpa only makes a distinction between the natural perfection of the here-and-now within a body and the natural perfection of the bardo state, in the process offering a pure vision of death and its aftermath.

Errors and Answers

The Great Perfection does not entail an attitude of boundless optimism, although that is a possible spin-off; it is not a perpetual intellectual perception of a silver lining in each and every experience, although that too is not precluded; it is not an altruistic ambition to save all beings—and the environment—through a positive and loving attitude, although that also may eventuate. Dzogchen provides a deconstructive view that allows automatic access to the spaciousness of the intrinsic complete and perfect reality that is the nature of mind. This lurch from a reliance upon the rational mind to an existential understanding of reality occurs in the light of deep initiatory experience, which is known technically as an introduction to the nature of mind. The praxis of Dzogchen is not an intellectual exercise, despite the evidence of scholarly exegesis in which the intellect mimics and usurps the pre-eminence of pristine awareness. The intellect is redundant in the momentary insight into every experience of the flow of experience as compassionate emptiness and light. It is therefore an error to assume that one is 'not ready' for Dzogchen because of a lack of study and intellectual preparation.

Initiatory experience is present in this very moment and nothing can be done to facilitate its advent. Any kind of preparation or fore-practice muddies the waters in its assumption of a goal to be reached. Access to the clarity and the zing of reality, on the contrary, is more likely to be found in an innocent pristine mind that has not been conditioned by the cultural and religious assumptions of a 'sophisticated' tradition. Purity of karma, putative rebirth, guru-relationship, degree of meditation-concentration, facility in visualization, levels of attainment, and so on, are all issues pertinent to acceptance and success within a hierarchical cult wherein a particular ideal form of social and psychological behavior is a goal to be achieved; but to the formless experience of Dzogchen such considerations have no relevance. Striving in any kind of preparatory endeavor is an exercise in shooting oneself in the foot, or at least running after a mirage. In fact, to reach the point of relaxation in the moment that provides intimation of gnosis, non-action is the sole precept. This perspective in radical Dzogchen is exclusive to those who have no need or inclination to exchange their inbred cultural norms and mores for those belonging to a more exotic or 'spiritual' tradition, or to reject their cultural legacy and educational conditioning in an effort to change their psychological make-up. Recognition of our lived experience, just as it is, in its miraculous immediacy and beauty, without any yen for change, is the praxis of radical Dzogchen, and belief in personal development and improvement, progress towards a social ideal, moral evolution of the species, and so on, is deviation from the pure pleasure of the unthought timeless moment.

It is an error of interpretation, however, to believe that Dzogchen requires abandonment of religious devotions or ritual practice. The sacred and the profane have the same weight in the Dzogchen view, and the temple or church and the beer-hall or gymnasium are equal. Insofar as the form or shape or color of experience in the moment is immaterial to its potential for transfiguration or recognition of the nature of mind, whatever physical verbal or mental habits prevail in the stream of one's life provide the stuff of buddhahood. Evidently, Dzogchen precepts such as those Longchenpa discloses in *The Treasury of Natural Perfection* are available primarily within the vajrayana tradition of Tibetan Buddhism, and it is to be expected that the majority of Dzogchen yogis and yoginis will have assimilated an intellectual understanding of that tradition, if not a daily practice of meditation, yoga and devotions; but no Buddhist conditioning, ritual worship and lifestyle, nor even Christian or Jewish devotions, provides any more or less fertile ground for recognition of the nature of mind than the lifestyle of an agnostic professional, for example, or a self-indulgent hedonist. On the other hand, the recognition of the light of the mind, the emptiness and clarity of mind, that signals Dzogchen initiation, may loosen attachment to conventional forms and mundane obsessions and habits and galvanize any renunciant tendency.

The here-and-now is the receptacle of the nondual reality that is the matrix of mind where gnosis inevitably fires in the very moment of every experience. If this matrix of intrinsic gnosis sounds like God to some people, then they are definitely on the right track. But the nondual state of gnosis is personified as Samantabhadra, a naked and blue seated buddha, whose name appears in the text as 'the supreme source' and who is the principal interlocutor in one of the seminal and most oft-quoted tantras herein. It would be a mistake, however, to approach 'Samantabhadra' as anything but a label for something that is quite beyond language and symbolism. If we look closely, it appears that this 'God' has no kind of existence or definable attributes whatsoever and can only be spoken of—if at all—in terms of gnosis, luminosity, emptiness and nonduality. For this reason Buddhists with a conformist predilection prefer to call it 'buddha'. Even this is unacceptable in the Dzogchen view. 'Buddha' is primordial cognitive awakening that happens only in a moment of experience of the here-and-now and, therefore, can never be distanced and objectified. It is an egregious mistake to understand 'buddha' or 'the nature of mind' as something infinitely subtle yet indicative of a state that may be attested and attained. Assimilating Samantabhadra's transmission of 'I am nothing at all!' pre-emits the error of reification.

To take Longchenpa's exposition of Dzogchen as mere philosophical speculation, it must be emphasized, is a futile error, along with the corollary of mistaking *prima facie* theoretical understanding of the Dzogchen view for existential realization. To the top end of recipients of the Dzogchen transmission, merely by its assimilation, an immediate dissolution of samsaric dichotomy is assured, and whatever validity such a promise entails it indicates the nature of the transmission and the Dzogchen dialectic as a functional tool. Insofar as its language is self-referential, its letters, sounds and meanings always pointing at their luminous, joyful, essence, its dialectic relentlessly and consistently referring back to the unstructured light of gnosis, and insofar as language is inseparable from our experience, we are constantly thrust into the reality that the Dzogchen exposition evokes. Its incessant self-reference, giving not an iota of validity to the perceptual and intellectual functions of our ordinary rational mind, dissolves all concrete points of reference and leaves us in the spaciousness of ineffable being. Its language establishes the recipient of the transmission in the timeless reality beyond linguistic conditioning which we call 'nondual', in a dynamic condition that we call 'nonaction', in a state of consciousness that we call 'gnosis', with a feeling tone we call 'pure pleasure', in an unmotivated space that is 'unconditional compassion'. This self-referential language induces the nonreferential state of natural perfection where causality has ceased to function. Thus natural perfection implies the immanence of a nonverbal reality and Dzogchen is nothing at all. Far from being an objective philosophical description of the world at large, or a soteriological blueprint, this exposition is a magical psychotropic poem.

More specifically, for the magic of the poem to kick in, it is crucial to understand the text to be what the tantric tradition terms 'definitive', as opposed to 'provisional'. There is no time lag between the momentary perception of the words of the poem and its consummation. We are not instructed to change our evil ways, to cultivate virtue and forsake vice, to do a hundred thousand prostrations, or to persevere in contrived meditations. On the contrary the imperative voice is rarely used and when infrequently it appears we are told simply to relax, to let go and let it all be, and even in such formulations the advice is not actually prescriptive but descriptive of the moment (although grammatical forms may indicate otherwise). Any tendency to interpret the Dzogchen precepts as a consummation to strive for is an indication of misunderstanding. The precept 'nonaction', for example, if taken literally may precipitate the undiscerning reader into a state of couch-potato indolence rather than allowing the magic of the Dzogchen dialectic to dissolve all motivation— including the tendency to idleness—allowing dynamic spontaneity to prevail. Likewise, the precept 'nonaction' should not be understood as cause to cease and desist in any discipline whatsoever, particularly on the progressive paths of spiritual aspiration, although the habit of the rational mind demanding the identification of a cause reliably efficient in producing an effect through time will be detected there. The Dzogchen transmission taken as the cause of some future benefit indicates a mind at work at the lower end of the spectrum of its recipients.

Moreover, it is a dangerous error to interpret the precept 'nondiscrimination' as licence to indulge the peculiar personal weirdnesses that genetic and personal karma engender. *In the moment, in the here-and-now,* the originally pure mind of natural perfection makes no discrimination between right and wrong, good and bad, high and low, and between the poles of any dichotomy that social conditioning and intellectual idealism have inculcated, and it gives no positive reaction to the good nor any denial of the bad. Acceptance of the totality of human potential may expand to infinity the horizons of our experience, but if the self-serving rational mind takes hold of the notion that all and everything is permitted and uses it as a principle to act upon through time, then the expectation that karma will perform its worst will not be disappointed. Karma may not exist in the timeless moment of nondual awareness, but it is certainly lethal in the credulous rational mind in which a frame of moral conditioning is taken to be incontrovertible and in which moral causality is operative.

As to the charge of antinomianism—a disdain for moral law, where the atavistic maxim 'Do what thou wilt shall be the whole of the law' is elevated to sacred dogma—in Dzogchen evidently it is a non-starter. In the mind of natural perfection, certainly, moral discrimination and moral causality do not exist, yet what remains is nondual 'bodhichitta', both the ground and the emanation of pure mind, which can only ever be pure vision and perfect conduct. What begins as pure mind exists and ends as pure mind. Here, bodhichitta, which in Dzogchen means the pure gnostic mind of nondual perception, reaffirms its mayahana definition of compassion. Here and now compassion is all. It is true that in the progressive left-handed, yogini path of tantra-yoga antinomian principles may be employed to induce intimation of the nature of mind and as skillful means to eradicate intractable mental habits— but that is another story. In Dzogchen, 'taking the position of consequence' (as Yogi Chen would have it), there is no fall from grace, and there never has been a fall, and in the realization of that reality where the golden age lies just beneath an insubstantial, fragile surface of dualistic belief, any moral dualism becomes the problem rather than the solution. Judeo-Christian dualism served—and continues to serve—the Roman empire and its successors as a method of taming the barbarians; but it becomes morally and existentially oppressive when the natural perfection of being becomes gloriously evident as in the sixties' efflorescence of soteriological consciousness.

The insecure mind that relies upon religious dogma and moral dualism will feel threatened by these ethical considerations and tightening up it may become unreceptive to Longchenpa's sublime poem. Everyone who partakes of a moment of awareness in the here-and-now, everyone without exception is a candidate for the revelation of natural perfection because Dzogchen is all-inclusive by definition; but it is a mistake to believe that Dzogchen, open to all, is accessible to all. If it were so, then the samsaric world would have vanished long ago. 'Secret' Tibetan texts such as Longchenpa's are useful only to those people whose time has come. To most others—perhaps less so in Tibetan society than others—although the words are familiar, the choice and order of the words are incomprehensible. Those whose faith has been placed in a goal-oriented progressive path will find their receptivity occluded by a rejective emotional response induced by attachment to investment of time and energy in a dogmatic sadhana and devotion to a personal mentor. Some will be unable to approach due to socially conditioned blockage, for many in Tibetan society consider Dzogchen heterodox and hazardous, and in Western society the Church's historical condemnation and persecution of nondual mysticism has been unremitting and unforgiving. Others will be unable to accept a human guru as the mouthpiece of Samantabhadra. The majority will be so caught up with the concerns and affairs of this life, with love and social acceptance, with profit and shopping, that they have no time for Dzogchen. Thus the candidates for Dzogchen transmission are few and far between and an aspect of Dzogchen's 'self-secrecy', its natural hermetic character, is disclosed. In pre-revolutionary Tibet, to this natural protection was added a veil of secrecy contrived by a self-protective priesthood, the custodians of the wish-fulfilling gem; in its transmission to the West many teachers have forsaken the old conventions, and in order to serve the spiritual thirst and fill the spiritual vacuum left there by a moribund religious establishment take the risk of teaching Dzogchen openly.

In Western society the message of Dzogchen may come as a relief particularly to those who feel that much of vajrayana Buddhism is culturally alien, or that the cultishness of Lamaism is akin to *Animal Farm*, or that the great gains of the Protestant Reformation and the move towards nondogmatic humanism seem to have been thrown away in a fascination for oriental ritualism and dogma, or that the distinction between Buddhism and Christianity rests on fashionable conceits. It is an error, however, to believe that Dzogchen can be taken ready-made from a book (see canto 24). A cogent semantic or poetic statement of Dzogchen—any of Longchenpa's innumerable verses of precept— has the potency to induce an incipient realization of natural perfection; but lacking a contexturalizing lineal tradition and a mentor and exemplar who can assist in short-circuiting rationalistic mental habits, it is likely to fast fade. It is the personal mentor speaking in the final stanzas of the text:

So stay right here, you lucky people,
let go and be happy in the natural state.
Let your complicated life and everyday confusion alone
and out of quietude, doing nothing, watch the nature of mind.
This piece of advice is from the bottom of my heart:
fully engage in contemplation and understanding is born;
cherish non-attachment and delusion dissolves;
and forming no agenda at all reality dawns.
Whatever occurs, whatever it may be, that itself is the key,
and without stopping it or nourishing it, in an even flow,
freely resting, surrendering to ultimate contemplation,
in naked pristine purity we reach consummation.

The Origins of the Text and its Structure

According to the Buddhist Dzogchen tradition, the root guru, *adiguru*, of Dzogchen, Garab Dorje, received the 1,084,000 verses of Dzogchen scriptural poetry from the visionary being Vajrasattva whose embodiment he was. Everything relevant to the Dzogchen view was exhaustively composed in those verses that Garab Dorje was heir to and nothing can be added to that; the multitude of commentators' work simply represents the old truths in contemporary language and in an order appropriate to the needs and priorities of the time. It is the opinion of contemporary Western scholars that Garab Dorje lived in the seventh century in the Swat Valley (or thereabouts), presently in Pakistan, ironically now the base of the Muslim fundamentalist Taliban. Garab Dorje's verses, orally transmitted, were finally written down as the Nyingma tantras in the Indic languages of the region and then translated into the Tibetan language by eighth century masters such as Vairotsana and Vimalamitra. Insofar as Tibetan is the only language that we know of in which written Dzogchen is extant, to all intents and purposes Dzogchen is the prerogative of Tibet and Tibet may be considered its origin and its home.

Fourteenth century Tibet saw a renaissance of the Nyingma School, the tradition of the Ancients, which was the medium and protector of Dzogchen and its scriptures, and it also saw the birth of Longchen Rabjampa Drime Wozer. Longchenpa lived with and traveled with the great masters of his age, later spending years in the snow-line hermitages of Central Tibet. Not only was he a yogin and master of Dzogchen but out of his own realization and vast learning he revealed a synthesis of Dzogchen in a series of literary masterpieces that made him a nexus of the tradition upon which subsequent generations were to depend. Perhaps the greatest composition of Tibet's greatest literary mystic and master of prose is *The Treasury of Natural Perfection,* which has remained the best known and most renowned exposition of the Dzogchen view and Dzogchen dialectic until the present day. The treatise as the matrix of ineffability demonstrates the mystery of language; it is the immutable here-and-now as the source and scene of our linguistically created reality, a field of mystery that cannot be described but only felt and inhabited. The very name Longchenpa, suggests that the author was someone who made this cosmic matrix his home.

The Treasury of Natural Perfection is the title of only the 127 root verses of this work. These root verses are derived from the ethos of the Nyingma tantras and restated in Longchenpa's immaculate verse and prose. In his auto-commentary to this seminal work, which comprises the bulk of this translation, he provides the specific tantric sources of his inspiration. Long after Longchenpa passed away the Nyingma tantras were collected into the large compendium of seminal Nyingma texts called *The Collected Tantras of the Ancients* (*Nyingma Gyubum*). His sources are identified in the annotation to the translation and a list is appended (Appendix I). Some sources remain unlocated and may have been casualties of the Chinese cultural revolution.

The auto-commentary to *The Treasury of Natural Perfection* begins with a prologue (cantos 1-3) in which the essence of the work is laid bare. The first canto, under the heading of Vajra-Homage, evokes the quintessence of Dzogchen, and shows the method of self-referential language. The second canto reveals Longchenpa's purpose, which is nothing less than to induce, experientially, the natural state of gnosis in the minds of his readers. He has high expectations, however, of only the brightest of minds; the rest can familiarize themselves with the principles so that gnosis can be arrived at with greater facility at a later date. The third canto, called "The Concise Exposition" provides a powerful poetic presentation of Dzogchen that constitutes an introduction to the nature of mind and thus to nondual gnosis itself. That should be adequate to Longchenpa's purpose, but in the event of malfunction "The Extensive Exposition" follows.

The body of the text comprises four themes—absence, openness, spontaneity and unity—all of equal weight, each providing a complete description of, and by default, access to, buddhahood. The four themes are the samaya-commitments of Dzogchen, aspects of reality that are intrinsic to our everyday experience and which are naturally observed through our participation in being.

It is easy to lose sight of this principal meaning while engaged in the subtleties of the text. Although equality of value is maintained between them in the exposition, as Longchenpa admits and as is evident in the increasing complexity and paradoxical method of his argument, absence forms the basis of a leap into nonduality, openness and spontaneity define the method, and unity is the consummation.

In this regard, there is an important structural division implicit in the work that is not treated by Longchenpa. This neglect may be due to the lack of any strong formulated tradition of Cutting Through and Jumping Through in fourteenth century Tibet, although the involuntary 'carefree contemplations' (*chojak*), the visions of diminishing substantiality (*nangwa zhi*) and the windows into the nature of mind (*semdzin*) are present in germinal form. It may be useful, however, to consider the division of the four themes as two pairs, the first pair, absence and openness, treating Cutting Through, and the second pair, spontaneity and unity, treating Jumping Through. In short, the first focuses upon the alpha-purity of all experience while the second treats its spontaneous manifestation as light. These two may usefully be distinguished by the characterization of their culmination as either a 'rainbow body' or 'the body of transformation'.

Each of the four samaya themes is divided into four sections—disclosure, assimilation, the bind, and resolution—again each constituting a discrete exposition of a facet of the particular theme. Yet therein development can be traced in the progress from the disclosure of the nature of the theme, through the description of the manner in which experience is instantaneously integrated and bound to reality, to the finality of resolution. If it were not for Dzogchen's denial of the applicability of the traditional four descriptive categories of every approach to reality, the first section could be characterized as view, the second as meditation, the third as conduct and the last as fruition.

There is a fifth theme, unmentioned by Longchenpa in his description of the structure of the text (in canto 3), entitled "Advice to Recipients of the Transmission". This theme may be viewed as an addendum, placing the Dzogchen teachings in the context of the mainstream vajrayana tradition, particularly of the Longchen Nyingtik, and within the Tibetan cultural context. At the end of canto 122, however, this theme is described as 'the key to the four storey treasury' of the four samaya-commitments and canto 122 certainly provides an extraordinary epitome of the Cutting Through and Jumping Through precepts, yet with a different didactic slant, as if it had been orally delivered, whereas the foregoing was a literary composition. We have no information about the history of the text, how or when it was compiled, or by whom.

In its entirety, the auto-commentary to *The Treasury of Natural Perfection* consists of 127 chapters, which in deference to the poetic nature of the content—at least in the original Tibetan and despite the disparate elements that compose each chapter—we have called cantos. The title of each canto indicates the topic that it treats and in translation is a pithy summary of Longchenpa's introductory sentence. The root verse, composed by Longchenpa in his root text, then follows. A few sentences of prose commentary elucidate the meaning of the root verse, which is then illustrated by quotations from the Nyingma tantras interspersed with sentences of commentary. The identity of the tantras from which the quotations are derived evinces fulfilment of the promise in the title of the auto-commentary to elucidate the meaning of the three series of Dzogchen instruction—Mind, Matrix and Secret Precept—which subsume the entire body of Dzogchen texts and precepts. (Appendix I: The Tibetan Text and Quotations categorizes the source tantras according to these three series.)

Regarding the classification called 'the three series', Manjushrimitra (Jampal Shenyen), Garab Dorje's heart-son, categorized the innumerable precepts gathered by his teacher into three classes—Mind (pure mind or bodhichitta), Matrix (or 'Space') and Secret Precepts. The Tibetan literature gives great importance to Manjushrimitra's classification revealed particularly in the structure of *The Collected Tantras of the Ancients*, yet beyond some variations in vocabulary any more profound distinction is difficult to discern. Some seemingly contrived didactic analysis may, however, be useful. The Three Series can be associated with the three incisive precepts of Garab Dorje, for example: the Mind Series as introduction to the nature of mind; the Matrix Series providing conviction in the praxis and the Secret Precept Series to confidence in release. Dudjom Rimpoche associates each of the three series with a psychological type: the Mind Series for those who abide in the mind, the Matrix Series for those who are free of activity, and the Secret Precept series for those intent upon the innermost essence. That is in accord with Manjushrimitra's professed criteria which emphasized 'presence of mind', 'nonaction' and 'the crucial point' respectively. A Bon analysis recommends that the Mind Series cultivates clarity, the Matrix Series cultivates emptiness and the Secret Precept Series cultivates both appearances and emptiness equally.[1] It seems probable, however, that the three series were derived from three discrete lineages with slightly variant approaches, or that they represent three layers of temporal presentation. Anyway, Longchenpa avers that the meaning of these three series is contained within the four themes, and finding no evidence of it in the structure of the text nor any allusion to them, we must assume that the meaning he refers to is a synthesis, or a distillation, of Dzogchen.

At the end of the work, Longchenpa refers to a further set of categories, under which all Dzogchen precepts, like the three series, may be subsumed, and this is the categorization of the nine matrixes (listed in canto 126). It would seem to be an impossible task to place the verses from *The Treasury of Natural Perfection* within these nine categories according to the subtle distinction of existential exegesis indicated by the nine matrixes of the here-and-now, and again we assume that the four themes subsume the ninefold distinction.

The translator's commentary elucidating technical terms and sometimes providing another cultural context for aspects of the Dzogchen view is appended where necessary to each canto, appearing in diminishing quantity in the latter themes.

The title of the book, *Old Man Basking in the Sun,* is taken from canto 20.

The Translation

The difficulties of translation of the technical Dzogchen terminology are immediately apparent. To avoid strings of turgid jargon that have tended to become the hallmark of such works we have attempted to make the translation interpretive and literary without losing any grammatical force or technical meaning. In this regard although we have appropriated a few technical terms, we have resisted the temptation to employ a vocabulary derived from quantum physics where scientific theory appears to intersect the thrust of Dzogchen's meaning. Some readers may consider that the motivation adhering to any scientific formulation is so at odds with the ethos of Dzogchen that its evocation inevitably inhibits the mind's receptivity to the Dzogchen view.

The difficulty of translating the one single term that distinguishes Dzogchen texts, the word *rigpa*, has yet to be fully resolved. It is tempting to use the Tibetan word itself, but '*rigpa*' lacks any connotation for the English reader and provides no adjectival form. Insofar as *rigpa* denotes both cognitive and ontological aspects of nondual reality, establishing the intrinsic cognitive nature of all experience, mere 'awareness' is inadequate;

'knowledge' is an option yet its primary current denotation is the horrible 'data'; and 'presence' or 'total presence' has been usefully employed, but the word is unable to hold the weight of the meaning of reality. If *rigpa* is to be defined at all, it is brilliant radiance, a constant experience of pure pleasure, lightness and clarity, the soft silence in every moment. The apposite English equivalent has yet to emerge: herein we have introduced the word 'gnosis', a strong word of Greek extraction with a long history in Christian mysticism, which brushed off and refurbished, through usage may help to assimilate this sublime Central Asian mysticism into post-Christian culture.

As praxis, *The Treasury of Natural Perfection* may be understood as a transmission of the realization of all phenomena, all experience, as light, light being the common factor of cognition and the intrinsic spaciousness of experience. The three words 'brilliance', 'radiance' and 'clarity' have been used as synonyms of 'light'. Emptiness is the essence of things, light is their nature and compassion is the medium of indeterminate manifestation. Rest in the nature of being and we understand ourselves as beings of empty light in which the three existential dimensions or buddha-bodies manifest spontaneously as a unitary gnostic envisionment of outside and inside, a momentary luminous gestalt. The totality of this gnostic vision is light. The Newtonian universe of matter and energy is light. We know it through the light of the mind—our prosaic everyday experience is light—and insofar as the field of light is unitary, complete and all-inclusive, it is natural perfection. We know it through its absence, openness, spontaneity and unity.

The 'cauldron' or 'crucible' of the here-and-now is both the vast expanse and a point-instant of that gnostic vision which we have called the 'matrix'. Its unstructured nature that is pure mind is boundless extension; a total perspective knowing no center or circumference, without spatial or temporal distinction, with no limitation, fragmentation or partiality, without gaps, lacunae, fissures or interruptions. It never materializes or crystalizes as anything at all, but remains an unimpeded natural flow of light. The matrix describes the totality of a moment in the nonspatial, atemporal here-and-now and so contains the 'dynamic' that is the all-inclusive mind of Samantabhadra and that dynamic, without intent or movement, is denominated 'contemplation'—the nonmeditative contemplation that is the natural state of all our minds, to which we are bound through the natural samaya-commitments of absence, openness, spontaneity and unity.

Acknowledgments

We offer our deep gratitude to the lamas of the various Dzogchen lineages, particularly to Dudjom Rimpoche and Kanjur Rimpoche and to Trulzhik Rimpoche, the principal contemporary embodiment of Dudjom Rimpoche's Dzogchen tradition, for their transmission; and to Chogyal Namkhai Norbu, a great teacher and treasure-finder for a later generation whose generosity has opened the doors to Dzogchen for innumerable Western aspirants, for his generous foreword, for his heart, for his inspiration and encouragement. We are indebted to Richard Barron (Chokyi Nyima) and the Padma Translation Committee under the auspices of the late Chagdud Tulku Rimpoche for their brilliant ground-breaking work in the first translation of this difficult text. Dr Tamas Agocs of the Buddhist College in Budapest, Hungary, provided vital impetus, and collaboration in the first draft of the translation and part provision of references in the annotation and appendixes—a beneficent grant from Steven Landsberg funded that work. Thanks also to Tony Duff of the PKTC, Jim Valby and Erik Padma Kunzang for their generous provision of textural material and translation tools.

May all beings be happy!

Keith Dowman
at the Great Stupa of Boudhanath,
Kathmandu, Nepal. 2005 AD

The Treasury of Natural Perfection

Homage to Glorious Samantabhadra, the All-Good!

To timeless buddhahood, basic total presence,
to unchanging spontaneity, the spacious vajra-heart,
to the nature of mind—natural perfection,
constantly, simply being, we bow down.

This unutterable space that is the nature of things,
the apogee of view that is natural perfection—
listen as I explain my understanding
of this sole immanent reality.

The conclusive meaning of Mind, Matrix and Secret Precept
lies in absence, openness, spontaneity and unity.
These four are treated each in four aspects:
disclosure, assimilation, 'the bind' and resolution.

The First Theme: Absence

The Disclosure of Absence

First let me tell you about 'absence',
the absence that is essentially emptiness:
in the super-matrix of pure mind that is like space
whatever appears is absent in reality.

In the universal womb that is boundless space
all forms of matter and energy occur as flux of the four elements,

but all are empty forms, absent in reality:
all phenomena, arising in pure mind, are like that.

Magical illusion, whatever its shape,
lacks substance, empty in nature;
likewise, all experience of the world, arisen in the moment,
unstirring from pure mind, is insubstantial evanescence.

Just as dream is a part of sleep,
unreal gossamer in its arising,
so all and everything is pure mind,
never separated from it,
and without substance or attribute.

Experience may arise in the mind
but it is neither mind nor anything but mind;
it is a vivid display of absence, like magical illusion,
in the very moment inconceivable and unutterable.
All experience arising in the mind,
at its inception, know it as absence!

Just as the objective field is absent in reality,
so 'the knower'—in actuality pure mind,
in essence an absence, is like the clear sky:
know it in its ineffable reality!

In the heart-essence that is self-sprung awareness,
the absence of causality closes the abyss of samsara,
the absence of discrimination integrates samsara and nirvana,
and in the absence of glitches and veils the triple world coalesces.

In total presence, the nature of mind that is like the sky,
where there is no duality, no distinction, no gradation,
there is no view nor meditation nor commitment to observe,
no diligent ideal conduct, no pristine awareness to unveil,

2

no training in the stages and no path to tread,
no subtle level of realization, and no final union.

In the absence of judgement nothing is 'sacred' or 'profane',
only a one-taste matrix, like the Golden Isle;
the self-sprung nature of mind is like the sky,
its nature an absence beyond all expression.

The actual essence, pristine gnosis,
cannot be improved upon, so virtue is profitless,
and it cannot be impaired, so vice is harmless;
in its absence of karma there is no ripening of pleasure or pain;
in its absence of judgement, no preference for samsara or nirvana;
in its absence of articulation, it has no dimension;
in its absence of past and future, rebirth is an empty notion:
who is there to transmigrate? and how to wander?
what is karma and how can it mature?
Contemplate the reality that is like the clear sky!

Constantly deconstructing, investigating keenly,
not even the slightest substance can be found;
and in the undivided moment of nondual perception
we abide in the natural state of perfection.

Absent when scrutinized, absent when ignored,
not even an iota of solid matter is attested;
so all aspects of experience are always absent—
know it as nothing but magical illusion!

During the empty enchantment of dream
ignorant babes are entranced,
while the wise, disillusioned, are undeceived;
those unaware of the truth of absence,
clinging to their identity, wander in circles,
while the wise yogin, fully present,

knowing the zing of reality,
convinced of the absence in that very moment,
is liberated in the non-contingent reality-matrix.

In total presence, the indeterminate nature of mind,
lies the timeless pristine awareness of nondual perception;
in sheer naked, non-contingent, gnosis,
lies the nondiscriminatory holistic seed;
in the holistic transparence of zero-dimensional gnosis,
lies the contemplation of Dharmakaya Samantabhadra;
in essential absence, the intrinsic gnosis of total presence,
nonreferential, immaculate contemplation is shining.

In the yoga of enchanting illusion, the play of gnostic vision,
empty experience arises as evanescent, uncrystallizing, display,
and convinced of absence in the moment of its inception,
without the least urge to control, to cultivate or reject,
we remain open, at ease, carefree and detached.

A fool deceived by magical illusion is like an animal
pursuing a mirage in his thirst for water;
expecting his delusive hopes to be realized,
trusting in his dogma, he is trapped;
losing his way on the eight-fold gradation of intellect,
he fails to see the real meaning.

The spaciousness within and beyond the atiyoga precepts
is a complete absence, nothing whatsoever, like the sky:
in the very moment, in the natural disposition of pure being,
as the original hyperspace that we cannot abandon,
the natural state of pure pleasure is spontaneously arisen.

If secret gnosis, the actual buddha-dynamic, eludes us,
to attain release by any purposeful action is no option.
'Everything is impermanent and bound to perish'—

4

how can a tight mesh of body, speech and mind
reach out to touch its own indestructible core?

So if we aspire to the supreme state of being
we should cast aside all childish games that fetter
and exhaust body, speech and mind;
and stretching out in inconceivable nonaction,
in the unstructured matrix, the actuality of absence,
where the natural perfection of reality lies,
we should gaze at the uncontrived sameness of every experience,
all conditioning and ambition resolved with finality.

In the absence of outside and inside, subject and object,
intrinsic gnosis, being out of time and space,
supersedes all finite events that seemingly begin and end;
pure as the sky, it is without signposts or means of access.
Any specific insight into gnosis is always deluded,
so that any spiritual identity, always delusive, is abandoned;
and convinced that the space of undifferentiated Samantabhadra
is the all-encompassing super-emptiness of all samsara and nirvana,
the natural state obtains as the reality without transition or change.
Breaking out of the brittle shell of discursive view
into the hyperspaciousness that is nowhere located,
in the experience of absence the crux of the matter is fully disclosed.

Assimilation of All Experience to Absence

Once the existential crux of absence has been disclosed,
in the gnosis of carefree detachment, in nonmeditation,
the nondiscriminatory space of whatever occurs is assimilated,
gnosis congruent with the nondual super-matrix of mind.

Pure pleasure left alone in vajra-spaciousness,
gives uncultivated, spontaneous, hyper-concentration;

5

with the yogin settled in uncontrived sameness,
it shines forth easily, a constant, like a river's strong current.

Authentic sky-like reality in its utter simplicity,
unchangeable, admits no gradation,
and its ineluctable all-suffusing spaciousness
has no language to express itself.
Yet insight bursting through, gnosis self-arising,
uninhibited by his learning, without any pedantry,
the yogin in whom mental silence supersedes ideation
gains conviction in signlessness, without sign or no sign,
and since there is no meditator nor object of meditation,
lethargy and agitation need not be confronted as foes.

Essential absence has already released dualistic perception,
so delusion falls naturally into the matrix of sameness—
we live without interruption in pure being.

Inception and release are simultaneous
entwining in the single blissful matrix:
whatever arises appears spontaneously as its pure nature,
as it abides it exists spontaneously as its pure nature,
when it vanishes it dissolves spontaneously as its pure nature.

Whatever arises in the reality-matrix, release is reflexive,
always a play of pure being, never shifting into anything other,
a timeless vision, another form of emptiness—
we live in nondiscriminatory essential reality.

Whatever occurs in the mind, quiescent or proliferating,
as one of the five 'poisons' or any other gnostic potency,
in the very peculiarity of its arising and in that very moment,
it recognizes itself, fully potentiates, and vanishes without trace:
the crucial carefree detachment at the subject/object junction,
the crucial self-sprung awareness as a bird's traceless trajectory,

the crucial all-inclusive spaciousness as a unitary billowing ocean,
and even the crucial focus upon the sublime mystery itself,
are assimilated from the beginning in every experience,
and mere recognition of this crux is the reality of release.

In the intrinsic gnostic dynamic of the super-matrix,
everything the very same at inception, in existence and upon release,
nothing unequal, nothing fixed, nothing unreleased,
total integration in the ultimate total-presence matrix is assured.

Involuntarily, in spontaneous gnosis
the free buddha-dynamic is naturally present,
and the pure mind that supersedes moral conditioning
is one with unchanging reality.

The Ineluctable Bind of Absence

The dynamic of space that is the nature of absence
binds all experience without exception;
just as matter and energy are bound by elemental space,
so all events, self-imaged, are bound by super-emptiness.

Samsara merely a label, goal-oriented endeavor is undermined;
and in the emptiness that cannot be improved or impaired,
freedom is just another word, and there is no nirvana:
striving in the ten techniques accomplishes nothing.

Exhausting exercises exacting struggle and strain,
with short-lived product, like a child's sand-castle,
and, moreover, all moral endeavor,
all experience is caught from the beginning in the bind of absence.

Now, the ati-yogin, the yogin of essence,
forsakes all provisional techniques
designed for straight cause and effect babes

on the lesser, laddered, path,
and binds the gnostic dynamic
that supersedes all clever technique
to the yoke of the nonactive sky.

Deliberate action deceives—look at treacherous samsara!
Diligence corrupts—consider the vicious cycle of suffering!
Neither virtue nor vice can stop the turning of the wheel,
and accumulated karmic propensity may lead up or down
but it gives no chance of release from existence.

For the person in whom the flow of good and bad ceases
there is no duality of union with and separation from reality,
and that hyper-yogin, certain in the great mystery,
effortlessly reaches the natural state of original perfection
and abides forever in the royal citadel of pure being.

In the very moment, therefore, of an event occurring,
whoever recognizes the language of biased projection
and morally discriminating goal-directed endeavor
as unreal, like the nonactive sky,
he catches all experience in the snare of absence.

Resolution in Absence

Resolution in absence is the very heart of the matter:
all the various events of samsara and nirvana
in their inherent absence belie their existence,
in their unceasing appearance belie their nonexistence,
neither existent nor nonexistent, being both is belied,
and since both are absent, being neither is also denied.
In the intrinsic absence of assertion and negation,
reality, indefinable, cannot be indicated as any one thing.

8

So reality is alpha-pure,
yet the babes who are careless of that
stay attached to their various ideas and opinions.
What mania to believe in concrete ideas!
How sad to believe in an 'I' that is actually absent!
How disheartening to make an argument out of nothing!
How we love those fervent believers, eternal migrants in samsara!

White or black, virtuous or vicious,
all clouds equally obscure the sun of intrinsic gnosis.
Stressed by the lightening of frustrated discriminating endeavor
an incessant downpour of delusive satisfaction and grief
waters the seeds of samsara, ripening the harvest of the six realms,
and we love all the tormented beings!

In the ultimate definitive analysis
just as golden chains and hempen ropes are equally binding,
so the sacred and the profane do both enslave us;
and just as white and black clouds are equally enshrouding,
so virtue and vice alike veil gnosis:
the yogin or yogini who understands that
fosters release from moral conditioning.

As self-sprung awareness arises from within
and the dark night of causality dissolves
the clouds of moral duality melt away
and the sun of nondual truth dawns in the field of reality.
This is final, ultimate resolution,
induced by the absence of the ten techniques,
exalted above all progressive approaches.

The intangible samadhi that lacks any field of meditation,
pristine, simple, intrinsic gnosis,
consumes all events in consummate resolution,
and all experience spent, itself is consumed.

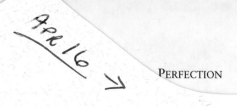

A single fiel...
integrating past, p...
an unbroken holistic ,
that is the arena shared v.

The unchanging and indivisible,
the matrix of self-sprung awareness
the ineffable matrix where labels are a jo...
this is the nonactive space of Samantabhadra,
where everything is the spaciousness of Samantabhadra,
where empty appearances are neither good nor bad.

Absence reified as some 'thing' is delusive projection;
but in the very moment of projection
there is neither delusion nor non-delusion
and everything is resolved in hyper-namelessness:
that is the way of natural perfection.

In all experience of samsara and nirvana, inner and outer,
convinced of the absence of both delusion and freedom from delusion,
we do not seek to abandon samsara to attain nirvana;
with conviction in the absence of birth and birthlessness
belief in life and death, existence and nonexistence, is suspended;
with conviction in the absence of right and wrong,
there is equanimity in the absence of value judgement,
and all experience is resolved in Samantabhadra's matrix.

The first theme of *The Treasury of Natural Perfection*, showing conclusively that all experience is beyond thought and expression, is concluded.

The Second Theme: Openness

The Disclosure of Openness

Now that you have sussed absence as the natural way of being
I shall show you the nature of openness.

The transmission of atiyoga, the apex approach,
like space, is without center or boundary;
higher than the highest, it is Samantabhadra's vast mind,
an immense seamless super-sameness.

All inner and outer experience manifest
and unmanifest pure mind,
unstirring from unstructured reality,
ineffable, zero-dimensional,
remains open, constantly, without interval.

In the moment, all things in the objective field,
in the absence of any substantial aspect, are open to infinity,
and intrinsic gnosis, wherein past and future are indivisible,
likewise is open wide to sky-like infinity;
the past closed, the future unbegun,
the present is indeterminate pure mind,
and signless, rootless, without foundation or substance,
it is an untrammeled openness at the boundless center.

In essential reality, which lacks all bias and partiality,
view, empowerment, mandala and mantra-recitation are absent,
and levels, paths, commitment, training and progress are unimaged;
all are wide open, unfounded, boundless vastness,
everything embraced by pure-mind reality.

All experience, however it may appear,
is hallowed in its unoriginated nature;

11

arising spontaneously, never fixed or crystalized,
immaculate in its ontological indeterminacy,
it opens infinitely into the reality of natural perfection.

Gnosis, the essential reality of total presence,
with a 360 degree perspective, free of quantitative bias,
unsubstantiated by language or logic,
unsigned, neither eternal nor temporal,
subject to neither increase nor decrease,
without directional movement or pulsation,
immaculate in the immensity of immanent hyper-sameness,
it is seamless openness unconfined by space and time.

The gnostic dynamic lacks any intrusive hope or fear,
so nothing can happen to rupture seamless openness;
in such autonomous, genuine, unrestricted freedom
we can never be caught in a cage of belief.

All and everything reverted to openness,
its nature is beyond denial or assertion;
just as all worlds and life-forms open into interior space,
so emotion and evaluating thought
melt into hyperspaciousness.

Now here, now gone, thoughts leave no trace,
and opened wide to seamless gnosis
hopes and fears are no longer credible,
the stake that tethers the mind in its field is extracted,
and Samsara, the city of delusion, is evacuated.

Whosoever recognizes the events appearing in the external field
and the internal mental emanation, all that play of energy,
all alike, as utterly empty openness,
to him is disclosed everything as this key—this crucial openness.

Assimilation to Openness

The endless facets of reality are now assimilated
to the brilliant emptiness of intrinsic gnosis
which is the pristine awareness of openness;
the perceiver unloosed, the field of perception dissolved,
with nothing to hold on to, yet with full awareness,
this is the contemplation of consummate undistracted mindfulness:
open like the sky, neither meditation nor nonmeditation,
it is the super-matrix of Samantabhadra's contemplation.

In the vast gnostic super-matrix of brilliant emptiness,
no matter what evanescent particularity shows itself,
the direct sensory perception of gnosis illuminates its reality
and the image unconfined, cognition is pure pleasure;
the six sensory fields relaxed in the pristine-awareness matrix,
clear light, unobstructed, without outside or inside,
in artless super-relaxation—spontaneity!

With the carefree mind of an idler,
neither tight nor slack, we rest easy;
here gnosis is infinitely open, like a crystal-clear sky,
and we linger gratefully in spaciousness without anticipation.

With spacious intuition of the brilliant emptiness of reality,
unconfined gnosis is a seamless infinite openness,
and free of belief, all ideation dissolving,
all things converge in the matrix of the gnostic dynamic.
The blissful ground and a happy mind blended,
inside and outside is the one taste of pure mind:
this is the vision of reality as the consummate way of being.

At the moment of engaging with a sensory object,
the mind is opened to infinite, blissful vision,
and free of belief, as its luminous expression, its natural clarity,
it is assimilated to super seamless openness.

13

The Bind of Openness

In the clear sky wherein dualistic fixation has dissolved,
free of the turmoil of compulsive thought,
gnosis is bound in naturally luminous openness:
the vajra-dance of seamless unconfined reality,
pristine awareness of the hyper-sameness of the here-and-now,
enjoys the natural seal of Samantabhadra's timeless dynamic.

Sleep entraps our dreams
as unreal and empty images;
experience of samsara and nirvana is caught in mind,
evanescent in the pure-mind super-matrix.

Just as all worlds and life-forms in the matrix of elemental space
are a seamless openness without center or circumference,
so all dualistic appearances within the gnostic matrix
are bound as empty images, open inside and outside.
This is the bind of pure mind that embraces all things
revealed as nondiscriminatory openness free of perceptual duality.

The pure mind that binds all things is also bound,
bound by nonspatial, atemporal, super-openness;
like the vast space that binds all matter and energy,
it is without extension, utterly ineffable.

In gnosis, inclusive nonspatial sameness,
experience of samsara and nirvana never concretizes;
in the very moment no mind nor event can be specified:
everything is bound by wide open reality.

Out of time, the unbreakable pure-mind seal
is affixed for all in Samantabhadra's hyper-expanse;
reinforced by the dynamic of the lama, master of beings and truth,
it is naturally confirmed in the timelessly purified vajra-heart.

14

Accessible only to the most fortunate—not for all,
the sublime mystery of definitive truth,
the bind of the vajra-point beyond transition or change,
the dynamic super-matrix of gnostic clear light,
though innate, is difficult to keep in mind:
recognized by the grace of the lama, master of beings and truth,
it is known as 'the all-inclusive bind of seamless openness'.

Resolution in Openness

Here is the essential meaning of resolution in openness:
coming from nowhere, abiding nowhere and going nowhere,
external events, unoriginated visions in empty space, are ineffable;
internal events, arising and released simultaneously,
like a bird's flight-path in the sky, are inscrutable.

Mind in its field, just as it is, is surely self-sprung gnosis,
beyond any identity in its ineffable simplicity;
like the sky lacking any dynamic, it is an empty scope;
in the absence of deliberate action, it is beyond moral distinction;
and in the absence of causality, it is unattainable by the ten methods.
This ineffable matrix of vast untrammeled openness,
neither something nor nothing, utterly empty,
an inconceivable and ineffable reality,
this is resolved in no-mind natural perfection.

The second theme of *The Treasury of Natural Perfection*, showing conclusively that all experience is seamless openness, is concluded.

The Third Theme: Spontaneity

The Disclosure of Spontaneity

Timeless spontaneity,
forever present, is created by no one;
it is the pure mind that like a wish-fulfilling gem
is the origin of all our samsara and nirvana.

Just as all environments and beings float in space,
so samsara and nirvana never crystallize in pure mind;
just as a variety of dreams occur in sleep,
so the six realms and the triple world manifest in mind:
all events, at their arising, within the scope of gnosis,
are the cosmic gestalt of empty spontaneity.

The gnostic ground and its gestalt emanation,
neither identical nor different from each other,
occur in the medium of timeless gnostic spontaneity;
as the potency of the display samsara and nirvana
appear impure or pure, respectively,
but in the moment—nondiscriminatory spaciousness!

In the unimpeded diffraction of a crystal's spectrum
the five colored lights are separately distinguished,
yet the potency of the one crystal prism is undiscriminating:
basic intrinsic gnosis diffracts like the crystal.
Its emptiness is the dimension of pure being,
its intrinsic brilliance is the dimension of perfect enjoyment,
and as the indeterminate medium of its emanation
it is the magical dimension of gnosis:
these are the gnostic dimensions of spontaneity
in the spacious ground.

Even while gestalt imagery arises in that ground—
whether as the masters' pure three dimensional display,
or as impure experience of samsaric worlds and life-forms—
as empty essence, clarity and unimaginable diversity,
it is the play of pure being, enjoyment and magical being:
all display is the gestalt imagery of the potency of the three dimensions
which is nothing but spontaneous gnostic envisionment.

With a clear understanding of these fine distinctions,
all experience of samsara and nirvana is realized
as the three dimensions of spontaneity in pure mind.

The pure being and pristine awareness of buddha,
the creatures of the three realms' physical, energetic and mental complexes
and the karmic-emotional tangle of their inner and outer worlds—
there is nothing but pure mind!

The matrix of spontaneity is the source of all and everything:
insofar as all external and internal, animate and inanimate forms
occur as unpatterned buddha-body, a circle of ornamentation,
and insofar as all frequencies and volumes and qualities of sound
occur as unpatterned buddha-speech, a circle of ornamentation,
and insofar as all unrealized mind and realized pristine awareness
occur as unpatterned buddha-mind, a circle of ornamentation,
and insofar as ideal conduct and quality are also unpatterned,
spaciousness is the precious wish-fulfilling gem,
and because it is unsought, everything arising by itself,
it is called 'the spontaneous creativity of self-sprung awareness'.

Multifarious events in their ground of spontaneity
are pure mind, perpetual spontaneity,
so the three gnostic dimensions, unsought, are naturally present;
since moral discipline is thus redundant,
relax into the authentic yoga of nonaction—
the matrix of spontaneity requires no discipline
so do not try to gild the lily.

17

The total presence of buddha past, presence and future
is achieved spontaneously in natural pure pleasure;
so eschewing low level, graduated, causal techniques,
watch the nonactive sky-like nature of mind!

Uncontrived, timeless, magical super-spontaneity,
just as it is in the here-and-now, cannot be contrived;
jumping through all the hopes and fears of the strobe-like mind,
recognize unsought super-spontaneity in spaciousness.

Every experience, whatever it may be,
is the uncontrived triad of essence, nature and compassion,
the display of pure being, enjoyment and magical emanation;
since samsara and nirvana are the three-dimensional matrix of pure mind,
spontaneously perfect in uncontrived hyper-sameness,
samsara is not to be rejected here, nor nirvana attained.
All evaluation silenced, we abide at the heart of reality
where every experience is pure mind,
and timeless spontaneity is disclosed as the key.

The Assimilation of All Experience to Spontaneity

All experience is assimilated to spontaneity:
the five elements, matter and energy, all appearance,
arise to demonstrate timeless, unthought, spontaneity;
self and other deconstructed, as pure intrinsic clarity
the elements are assimilated autonomously as ordinary mind.
Let the six senses relax in the amorphous perceptual field!

Gnosis, the universal source, is luminous spontaneity,
and unmodified by the five senses, by projection or concentration,
the empty gnosis of pure being is spontaneously perfect contemplation.
With incisive recognition, just leave things alone in simplicity!

In the fertile unconfined super-matrix of intrinsic gnosis,
whatever appears in the field of mind through sensory perception,
as a crucial locus of seamless sameness, is assimilated
to spontaneity's natural concentrated absorption.
Always, incessantly, like a great river's flow,
uncultivated spontaneously-arising awareness uninterrupted,
all things, in essence self-sprung in the primordial matrix,
reach fulfillment in Samantabhadra's contemplation.

All experience is grounded in pure mind,
and pure mind is like space, that universal simile.
Just as everything is contained in the matrix of space,
through the very lack of exertion, naturally pure,
so all inner and outer experience is spontaneously assimilated
in the crucial nonaction that supersedes all intention and ideation,
and with the vital zero-attachment to whatever appears.

Timeless—unborn and unceasing,
motionless—without coming or going,
the master's contemplation is all-inclusive,
so spontaneity is a pure unwavering samadhi
and all events are assimilated to nonaction.

The Bind of Spontaneity

All and everything is caught in the bind of spontaneity:
all inner and outer worlds are spontaneously imaged,
the whole of samsara and nirvana is a spontaneous display,
and pure mind is primordial spontaneity—
there is nothing other than spontaneous perfection.

Since the nature of mind is timeless spontaneity,
pure mind contains the ground, the source and the essence:
because spontaneity is unattainable through the ten techniques,
forced concentration upon view and meditation is redundant,

extraneous support, like goal-oriented technique, is superfluous,
and egoistic ambition and apprehension is dispensable,
spontaneity is alpha-pure being here and now!

In the unchanging sky of the matrix of mind's nature,
in the matrix of the three gnostic dimensions,
samsara and nirvana indeed occur adventitiously,
yet they never move from this threefold matrix—
the display is a treasury of equivocal, compassionate magic.

Since all and everything at once is Samantabhadra's spontaneity,
samsara and nirvana are overwhelmed by their own spaciousness;
since everything is all-good, including the bad,
all is spontaneous perfection, the spaciousness of the vajra-essence;
and all experience is held in its ineluctable bind.

Resolution in Spontaneity

Resolution is spontaneously accomplished:
within nonspatial spontaneity, lacking inside or outside,
all experience is indisputable, motionless, auto-envisionment;
an all-embracing matrix, without top or bottom,
it is utterly ambiguous, nowhere restricted,
beyond indication, inconceivable and ineffable.

Since experience is alpha-pure in essence,
and spontaneity is its very nature,
free from the four extremes—
existence, nonexistence, eternity and annihilation—
it is nondual pure mind.

Alpha-purity, in essence, is nowhere attainable,
its sky-like nature primordially pure;
spontaneity, in essence, can be contrived by no one,
its emanation never crystalizing, it can appear as anything;

20

the source of all samsara and nirvana,
it is without past or future, beginning or end.

Unborn spontaneity is the indeterminate ultimate ground:
its timeless emanation is inexorable,
its empty empirical mode is nonreferential,
its intangible mode of release is uninterrupted;
in the place of its arising, its resolution is inevitable,
and that is dissolution into pure being,
the all-consuming spaciousness of the ground.

Like clouds evaporating into the sky from which they emerged,
like colored light retracting into a crystal prism,
the archetypal imagery of samsara and nirvana
that arises in the ground of spontaneity
recoils into the alpha-purity of the essential ground.
This convergence in the spaciousness of spontaneity,
this is the ultimate super-resolution of all experience,
all structure deconstructed, naturally dissolving into spaciousness.

In the here-and-now, whatever appears,
all objective appearances, melt into pure being,
into the natural disposition of the six sensory fields;
thereby outside and inside are instant by instant resolved
in the interfusing spaciousness of spontaneity.

Similar to resolution in manifest buddhahood
as total presence of the ambiguous gestalt of samsara and nirvana,
when the flicker of inner-outer imaging
naturally settles in the matrix of clarity
in an unthought, unstructured, natural state,
immediate resolution in the crystal clarity of brilliant emptiness
is known as 'settling in the cavern of jewels'.

Resolution in natural spaciousness occurs in the moment—
there can be no subsequent liberation into the present ground;
obsessive concentrated absorption imprisoning basic space
provides no occasion for freedom from divine trance.
Cherish, therefore, every instant of resolving intrinsic samadhi
in the interior spaciousness of the here-and-now!

Each and every experience resolved in the spontaneity of gnosis,
spontaneity resolved in the natural state of original hyper-purity,
and alpha-purity resolved in the inconceivable and ineffable
that is the ultimate resolution of spontaneous perfection.

The third theme of *The Treasury of Natural Perfection*, showing conclusively that all experience is timeless spontaneity, is concluded.

The Fourth Theme: Unity

The Disclosure of Unitary Self-sprung Awareness

And now let me tell you about unity:
gnosis alone the experiential ground,
'appearing as multiplicity yet unmoving from unity',
self-sprung awareness is the unitary source.

In the one cat's eye gem, under different conditions,
distinct images of fire or water appear;
just so, in the one source, intrinsic gnosis,
illusions of both samsara and nirvana appear,
one of recognition, the other of ignorance,
both based in the single nondual pure mind.

Samsara and nirvana, all gnostic vision,
as it appears, is one in its empty face;

like dream, enchantment, reflection of the moon in water,
like the four visions and evanescent celestial space,
one in ultimate emptiness, total emptiness, it is simplicity itself.
Since everything is a single field, pure from the beginning,
there is no 'duality', everything contained in a single seed
that is zero-dimensional pure being. Ho!

The five elements manifested in pure mind,
unoriginated, cannot escape unitary sameness;
though appearing to exist, the six types of beings are empty form,
they are archetypal images, unstirring from the gnostic scope;
though pleasure and pain are surely felt, they do not move
from essential total presence, sole self-sprung awareness:
know all experience as the one spaciousness, as emptiness,
the same unborn reality of pure mind!

Actual spaciousness is the super-matrix of intrinsic gnosis
where lies the sole dynamic of all buddha;
multiplicity unimaged, without any fragmented structure,
it is the unshakeable palace of total presence:
it is nothing but self-sprung awareness.

A wish-fulfilling gem, a cornucopia of precious experience,
the three gnostic dimensions of spontaneity are the buddha-fields.

Within the sole holistic matrix, made by no one,
the entire gamut of multifarious experience is projected;
yet causality reverted, experience is one in its projective base
as the brilliant emptiness of the vastness of reality
shining in the timeless, nonspatial, pure sky.

All of samsara and nirvana is created spontaneously,
but basic gnosis itself, uncreated by anyone,
like the sky, lies beyond endeavor;
in accord with that simile

unitary spaciousness, the vast super-matrix,
stills the concretizing exigencies of multiplicity.

At the heart of the matter, beyond affirmation and negation,
the display of indeterminate events, whatever they may be,
are the matrix of the ineffable nature of mind
that lies beyond all conventional words and expression.

In total presence, the essence where everything happens,
there is no duality, yet an incalculable multiplicity;
buddhas and sentient beings, matter and energy, are resplendent
all unmoving from the one immediate reality.

Interconnected in unity, everything is perfect and complete
and that is the exalted quality of pure mind;
whatever manifests, in that very moment,
all conventional imputations are resolved.

As luminous expression of the empty nondual nature of mind,
both external phenomena—objects of knowledge,
and all internal phenomena—bare pristine gnosis,
in the reality that is neither one nor many,
are disclosed here as a single field of gnostic realization.

Assimilation of All Experience to the Singularity of Self-sprung Awareness

The assimilation of all experience to the one taste:
in the imaged field of empty delusive appearances,
whatever appears, let it rest in its uncontrived singularity,
and in that moment it dawns only as brilliant emptiness.

In the empty scope of myriad self-dissolving thoughts and visions,
whatever moves, relax and let it alone, just as it falls,
and contemplation of reality arises within the movement.

24

In the moment when mind and objective field are seamless sameness,
relax into its aimless, traceless, natural purity,
and internal luminosity shines as heightened pristine awareness.

When those three key functions are assimilated to a single essence,
realization and non-realization are always the same,
mind and its field are one in pure being,
glitches and veils are one in the dynamic of sameness,
and without intermission, we enter upon the natural state,
without tightness or looseness, we discover the definitive essence,
without a break, we abide in the reality-dynamic,
and willy-nilly there's no transition or change.

Vast! spacious! the mind of the masters is the same as the sky;
ineluctable! it is the matrix of the holistic seminal seed;
released as it stands! with neither realization nor non-realization;
experience consummate! no mind! it is open to infinity.
On the pinnacle of the forever-unfurled victory banner
the rising sun and moon illuminate the microcosmic realms.

The Bind of Unity

The one intrinsic gnosis binds all experience:
environments and life-forms, infinite and unconfined,
whether of samsara or nirvana, arise in spaciousness;
spaciousness, therefore, embraces all experience at its origin.

Whatever multifarious appearance arises in the moment,
inalienable, it is never anything other than gnosis,
bound in the matrix of self-sprung awareness.

Even in simultaneous inception and release,
fading into spaciousness,
since it does not become anything other than pure mind,
it is bound by the one all-consuming original reality.
Thus, all events are bound by unitary gnosis

and indeterminate gnosis, the essence of total presence,
is bound by the heart of reality without transition or change—
instantaneous unconditioned fulfilment!

Resolution of All Experience in Self-sprung Awareness.

There is only one resolution—self-sprung awareness itself,
which is spaciousness without beginning or end;
everything is complete, all structure dissolved,
all experience abiding in the heart of reality.

So experience of inner and outer, mind and its field, nirvana and samsara,
free of constructs differentiating the gross and the subtle,
is resolved in the sky-like, utterly empty field of reality.

And if pure mind is scrutinized, it is nothing at all—
it never came into being, has no location,
and has no variation in space or time,
it is ineffable, even beyond symbolic indication—
and through resolution in the matrix of the gnostic dynamic,
which supersedes the intellect—no-mind!
nothing can be indicated as 'this' or 'that',
and language cannot embrace it.

In the super-matrix—unstructured, nameless,
all experience of samsara and nirvana is resolved;
in the super-matrix of unborn empty gnosis
all distinct experiences of gnosis are resolved;
in the super-matrix beyond knowledge and ignorance
all experience of pure mind is resolved;
in the super-matrix where there is no transition or change
all experience, utterly empty, completely empty, is resolved.

The fourth theme of *The Treasury of Natural Perfection*, showing conclusively that all experience is basic gnostic awareness alone, is concluded.

The Fifth Theme: Advice to Recipients

The elixir of this most profound approach
should be offered only to the most favored and brightest,
not to adherents of the lower approaches,
to those caught up in their moral conditioning
or to unfortunate narrow-minded people.

It should be concealed from those who revile the teacher,
who are hostile to their brothers and sisters,
who violate secrecy in gossip,
who are faithless, avaricious and dishonest,
and who are preoccupied with mundane affairs.

Only the brightest and best receive the Great Perfection:
those who respect the teacher and possess deep insight,
who are open-hearted, even-minded and most generous,
who have little critical thought and little concern for it,
who do not care about this life but aim for supreme awareness,
who have faith and perseverance, and can maintain secrecy.

The student pleases the master with gifts,
and having previously made his commitment
he requests the teaching with deference;
granted the transmission, he accomplishes it appropriately,
and finally surrenders to the natural state of being.

The master is learned with high qualities.

The teacher, knowing his students,
gives the keys appropriately;
to conceal them from the unsuited,
he should affix the seals of ban and entrustment.

Entrust the essential teaching of definitive meaning
to talented and favored heart-sons.

They, in return, should keep this eternal truth
in their hearts, without dissemination;
if secrecy is violated, retribution will follow,
and ensuing criticism will diminish the heart-teaching;
so cherish the mystery with a quiet and easy mind
and attain the kingdom of pure being in this very life.

The fifth theme of *The Treasury of Natural Perfection*, showing conclusively to whom the teaching should be entrusted, is concluded.

Concluding Verses

The meaning of natural perfection, the ultimate secret,
is no longer hidden—its message here fully revealed:
may all migrant beings of the triple world, without effort,
find their intrinsic freedom in original spaciousness!

Shattering the encasing shell of conventional views—gliding high,
in the apex approach—the space of the great garuda king,
may the message of atiyoga—exalted above all,
spread everywhere as an eternal victory banner!

The three series and nine matrixes contained within the four themes,
its definitive meaning structured in sixteen sections,
this exegesis of The Precious Treasury of Natural Perfection,
was carefully composed by the good Longchen Rabjampa.

May the definitive meaning of the five themes
in this treasure-house of natural perfection,
finely adorned by its pearls of breadth and depth,
elegant in its structure of finely tuned meaning,
bring joy to hosts of the fortunate!

The Treasury of Natural Perfection, composed by Longchen Rabjampa, a yogin of the supreme approach, is concluded.

Thrice good fortune!

The Commentary to
The Treasury of Natural Perfection:
An Exposition of The Inner Meaning of Dzogchen Instruction

Prologue

Homage to Glorious Samantabhadra, the All-Good!

To the matrix of primordial, spontaneous perfection,
to the original lord, the glory of samsara and nirvana,
and to the masters and magi, mystics and lamas,
we bow down with a thousand shimmering petals of lotus-faith.

I shall now elucidate The Treasury of Natural Perfection,
the quintessential truth, the final, definitive teaching,
distilled from the enigmatic heart-drop of direct experience,
the apogee of attainment that is existential pre-eminence.

The glorious Samantabhadra, manifestly and totally present in the fundamental ground of the here-and-now, abiding in the immutable vajra-space that is hyper-sameness, turns the wheel of unsurpassable, definitive revelation. The sublime fruition is the profound mystery of natural perfection. This is the indisputable and unchanging reality of pure gnostic mind and pure being revealed directly and effortlessly, ineluctably present in the moment. This treatise of secret instruction called *The Treasury of Natural Perfection* is a summation of the incontrovertible truths of natural perfection.

29

The nondual reality that is the natural state of being is the timeless and nonspatial experience of the here-and-now. The naked blue adibuddha Samantabhadra represents that pre-existent buddha-reality, the all-good reality whose pure and total presence never had a beginning and will never cease. He is a personification of the immutable nature of mind recognizing itself. Moment by moment Samantabhadra reveals the conclusive, definitive meaning of the nature of reality without prevarication, ambiguity or tantric metaphor, without provisional instruction, but directly in the manner of Dzogchen Ati.

'Pure mind' is bodhichitta; 'pure being' is dharmakaya; 'spaciousness' or 'hyperspace' is the dharmadhatu; and gnosis is rigpa.

At one and the same time Longchenpa expresses the unalterable perfection of the here-and-now and the source of his inspiration for the composition of the work which is the vast reservoir of secret teaching contained in The Collected Tantras of the Ancients (see Appendix I).

In this elucidation of the lodging places of reality, I begin with the verse of homage:

1. Vajra-Homage

To timeless buddhahood, basic total presence,
to unchanging spontaneity, the spacious vajra-heart,
to the nature of mind—natural perfection,
constantly, simply being, we bow down.

This verse of homage evokes the essential immutable spaciousness, the vajra-space, of this treatise. This spaciousness is the essence of self-sprung awareness, the ground of the spontaneity—the perfection and creativity—of pure and total presence. It is the unchanging field of reality, clear light as the nature of mind, the original face of natural perfection.

'Vajra' homage is rendered in and to that unchanging space without any attempt to alter anything, without focusing on anything, and without stirring from the disposition of pure being.

Natural perfection is the self-sprung awareness that precludes any specific bias or partiality, rendering any training or endeavor redundant.

Ho! The atiyoga of natural perfection! Dzogchen Ati!
The Great Perfection, in its unbiased inclusivity,
actualizes the meaning of self-sprung awareness;
as the lion overawes all other beasts with his roar,
so the language of Great Perfection commands the gradual approaches;
speaking a tongue of its own, it engenders its own ultimate meaning.

The land of natural perfection is free of buddhas and sentient beings;
the ground of natural perfection is free of good and bad;
the path of natural perfection has no length;
the fruition of natural perfection can neither be avoided nor attained;
the body of natural perfection is neither existent nor nonexistent;
the speech of natural perfection is neither sacred nor profane;
and the mind of natural perfection has no substance nor attribute.
The space of natural perfection cannot be consumed nor voided;
the status of natural perfection is neither high nor low;
the praxis of natural perfection is neither developed nor neglected;
the potency of natural perfection is neither fulfilled nor frustrated;
the display of natural perfection is neither manifest nor latent;
the actuality of natural perfection is neither cultivated nor ignored;
and the gnosis of natural perfection is neither visible nor invisible.

The hidden awareness of natural perfection is everywhere,
its parameters beyond indication,
its actuality incommunicable;
the sovereign view of natural perfection is the here-and-now,
naturally present without speech or books,
irrespective of conceptual clarity or dullness,
but as spontaneous joyful creativity
its reality is nothing at all.[2]

31

In the verse of homage, the first, second and third lines reveal the self-sprung natural essence while the fourth line shows familiarity with that unchanging space of reality. The fruition of natural perfection is distinguished from our ordinary disposition by nothing more than an indication about the existential ground (the starting point that is 'basic total presence' adduced in the first line of the vajra-homage). All experience, therefore, is revealed as perfect and complete in the gnosis of pure mind.

There is no imperfection anywhere:
perfect in one, perfect in two, perfect in all,
life is blissfully easy.

Unity is perfect as unitary pure mind,
duality is perfect as the mind's creation,
and multiplicity is abundant completion.

In the transmission of the perfection of unity
lies the pure buddha-dynamic;
the teaching on the perfection of duality
reveals everything as perfect projection;
and by virtue of the perfection of multiplicity
everything turns whole and splendid.

Abiding here, doing nothing,
embodied as man or god,
our dynamic is buddha-reality;
here sentient beings are cared for,
and without any exertion we live in ease.[3]

So homage is given to the nature of mind itself, self-sprung awareness, the projective base of samsara and nirvana:

Homage to the sole nature of mind, the seed of all and everything,
to the mind that creates the sense of existence and release from it,
to the mind that fulfils all our desires like a wish-fulfilling gem![4]

32

The act of vajra-homage, a ritual verbal gesture, is recognition of the primordial perfection of the nature of mind. The language of the Great Perfection is the natural expression of gnosis, empty and joyful, that establishes its own nonreferential reality. Inducing self-sprung awareness, the totality of experience, its language evokes a timeless reality beyond linguistic—and also social and moral—conditioning.

The famous line 'perfect in one, perfect in two, perfect in all' could be rendered 'unity is perfect, duality is perfect, plurality is perfect'—everything is necessarily perfect. The 'perfection' of Dzogchen carries with it the notion of completion. The final verse of that quotation is an introduction to the notion of nonaction, that nothing at all need be done to attain natural perfection since everything is perfect as it is. Yet, transmission is required—one pure mind accomplishes all:

2. The Promise to Compose

This unutterable space that is the nature of things
the apogee of view that is natural perfection—
listen as I explain my understanding
of this sole immanent reality.

The matrix of inconceivable and ineffable reality is pure gnostic mind, which is natural perfection. It is unique and beyond illustration in that it is without any substance or attributes, marks or signs. I have understood it well enough through the grace of the true guru, and here in this treatise, I promise to reveal it for the sake of future generations.

By revealing here what is not realized in the gradual, progressive approaches to buddhahood, namely that the nature of mind cannot be intuited on a causal path of endeavor, the understanding that everything is nominal illusion is taught, and that glitches and veils, pure in their evanescence, are not to be rejected.

The super-matrix of nonaction, unbegun and unending
like the Golden Isle, is all-inclusive and undifferentiated,
and without outside or inside, the sun of pure mind
ever dawning, never setting, dispels the shadows of polarity.
Pure mind does not spurn the four extreme beliefs
but it is unaffected by them, and glitches are in effect eliminated.
In the pure nature of mind, uncleft, where no abyss can be,
the three gnostic dimensions are spontaneously complete and perfect,
samsara and nirvana mere labels imputed by conditioning.[5]

My primary intention in composing this treatise elucidating Garab Dorje's meaning is to benefit those most keen minds that are able to gain instantaneous release into reality just as it is by listening to these words or by reading them. In order to fulfil this undertaking I shall teach the four themes of the Great Perfection definitively and conclusively.

He who loves others and serves them
does not slacken his effort when his life is endangered;
the fearless sage with true sense of responsibility
never forsakes others' desperation.[6]

The following four factors will further clarify my intent: firstly, the subject matter of the work is pure gnostic mind, beyond causality, inconceivable and ineffable; secondly, the primary purpose of the work is to induce the brightest minds to intuit the reality of pure gnostic mind; thirdly, the secondary purpose of the work is to induce people to familiarize themselves with this intuition and arrive at the natural state of mind; and the fourth factor is the synchronicitous conjunction of the three preceding aspects.

That given, everything lying within the scope of gnosis, by realization of this gnosis that lies beyond both causality and directed effort, all progressive approaches are superseded:

34

I am pure mind, the supreme source:
realize my nature
and all events that occur, whatever they may be,
shall be revealed as nothing other than me.
If you give this transmission of mine to others,
your entire audience gathered around
will realize my nature,
the nature of the supreme source,
and they will become one with me.

Then whatever happens, whatever appears,
relinquish the dualistic discipline of rejection and inhibition,
forsake the grace of the three types of ritual purity,
and no longer strive to develop samadhi and a compassionate mind.
Since everyone is created in me, the supreme source,
everything and everyone is the same as me;
I am sameness, so I need not promote sameness.
I reiterate: identity with me need not be cultivated![7]

So to what purpose is this understanding?

To reveal the purpose and necessity:
Innumerable aeons ago
some ati-yogins with good fortune and karmic connection,
with faith in me, the supreme source, and in my total presence,
perceived that there was no view to cultivate, no commitment to keep,
no ideal conduct to strive in, no path to tread,
no climbing spiritual levels, no karmic cause and effect,
no duality of ultimate and relative truth,
and nothing to cultivate in meditation,
and seeing that there was no mind to develop and no remedy
they saw the nature of my mind:
this revelation is necessary for those like them![8]

The 'matrix' is the here-and-now. Nothing can ever escape it; it is all-embracing. It is the unitary wholeness of pure mind; it is a nondual totality. It may be called 'the vajra-space of reality', or simply 'the vast expanse'. It is ultimate intimacy. As the source of all experience, and thus language, it is a field of mystery. (See canto 126.)

The three gnostic dimensions are the three buddha-bodies, that may be imaged as interpenetrating spheres. They are, of course, one in reality (see cantos 69 and 70). But as a primary conceptual aid they provide both the method of release for body, speech and mind and a key to altruistic pure pleasure in the dimensions of emptiness as essence, radiance as nature, and indeterminate emanation as compassion.

The four extreme beliefs are the rigid attitudes about reality arising from belief in existence, nonexistence, both or neither (see cantos 36 and 37).

The supreme source is the original, all-inclusive adibuddha, Samantabhadra (Tibetan: Kuntuzangpo), known by that name particularly in the great root tantra of the Mind Series precepts, *The Supreme Source*. In an uncompromising statement of radical Dzogchen, to forsake the gradualist approaches with their heavy baggage that precludes an open mind is a condition sine qua non of receiving the transmission of Samantabhadra.

Here at the outset I have told you the reason for writing this treatise; now I shall continue with a concise exposition of its substance.

The Concise Exposition

3. The Short Exposition of the Four Ineluctable Vajra-Binds

The conclusive meaning of Mind, Matrix and Secret Precept
lies in absence, openness, spontaneity and unity.
These four are treated each in four aspects:
disclosure, assimilation, 'the bind' and resolution.

The entire teaching is contained in the elucidation of the ultimately significant four hyper-commitments of natural perfection, to wit the samaya of the intrinsic absence of all experience, the samaya of primordial spontaneity, the samaya of impartial and unrestricted openness and the samaya of the integral unity of self-sprung awareness.

The entire corpus of Dzogchen scripture, the tantras of the Great Perfection, including the aphorisms of Garab Dorje, are classified according to Manjusrimitra's categorization as Mind, Matrix or Secret Precept Series. Mind and Secret Precept, but no Matrix Series tantras, are quoted herein, no categorical distinction made between them. The four hyper-commitments, the four samayas, the 'four ineluctable vajra-binds or themes'—absence, openness, spontaneity and unity—reveal the timeless meaning of all three series.

The natural samayas of wondrous spontaneity,
absence, unity and openness,
all of which are beyond any observance,
all are aspects of each other.[9]

My hidden samaya is intrinsic gnostic awareness
where the commitment and the observance are the same

and where the keeping and the breaking are the same,
and therein are the four commitments that need no heeding,
confidently observed, inviolable, from the first:
the contrived commitments of the eight lower approaches,
I deny, and I call that 'absence';
liberated from lesser obligations, uncommitted,
the media of awareness—body, speech and mind,
are vastly spacious and I call that 'openness';
the way of keeping an inviolable commitment,
a pledge that cannot be observed,
is through holistic, intrinsic gnostic awareness,
that alone, and I call that 'unity';
that intrinsic gnostic awareness,
maintained effortlessly, doing nothing,
that I call 'spontaneity'.[10]

I, the supreme source, have no samaya commitment to keep,
for in the absence of cause and condition, endeavor is redundant.
I am spontaneity itself, so analysis is futile;
I am timeless awareness, so knowledge is vanity;
I am self-sprung, so causes and conditions are unavailing;
I am undiscriminating, so renunciation and self-discipline are pointless:
I am unreal and 'Absence' is my name.

Never becoming concrete, pristine awareness is never reified,
and thus 'openness' is defined;
all is one in pure mind, and thus 'unity' is defined;
all and everything, whatever happens,
as mental events in pure mind
is always complete and perfect,
and thus 'spontaneity' is defined.[11]

Each of the four samaya commitments is first disclosed here as the heart of immediate reality ('disclosure'); secondly, each is shown to be assimilated to the self-sprung awareness of the actual here-

38

and-now ('assimilation'); thirdly, each is shown to be bound as unoriginated and unintentional ('the bind'); and fourthly, the resolution of each is shown beyond any deliberate, goal-oriented endeavor ('resolution').[12] Each of the four samaya commitments is thus treated under four headings, and the entire exposition is presented in sixteen sections. That is a concise presentation of the structure of the work.

Understanding the four sections, respectively, as the timeless, natural way of being ('disclosure'), the atiyoga of abiding there ('assimilation'), detached activity therein ('the bind'), and the spontaneity of pure being ('resolution'), what previously has been hidden is revealed as 'the zero experience wherein the individual intellect is superseded and all sense of dualistic unreality is surrendered'.

The four headings under which the four samayas are elucidated should not be understood as the conventional categories of view, meditation, conduct and fruition, although 'disclosure' or the natural way of being as the view, 'assimilation' or the yoga of abiding there as meditation, 'the bind' or careless relaxation as conduct, and 'resolution' as spontaneous fruition, is a tempting analysis. In the 'zero experience', the dualizing intellect desists, and 'no mind!' and simultaneously the mental thrust to image and dualize and so create the phenomenal world is spent (see canto 94). These verses constitute an introduction to the nature of mind:

Rather than time or no time,
measurement of time now redundant,
a single unbroken flow,
without beginning, middle or end,
we call 'hyper-sameness'.

In such sameness appearances are ambiguous
and thoughts are indiscrete and unknowable
and the universal significance of natural perfection
insinuates itself into the poor intellect;

the conceptual process, objectless,
involuntarily stops in its tracks.

Without ever knowing delusion
root ignorance is automatically cut,
eradicated from the first without trying—
but surely we all know that!

All coarse materiality, besides,
evanesces by itself in the moment,
and with no place to go simply vanishes:
in fact, the body has never existed;
there is only gnosis without past or future.

Everything, outside time or even in time,
as unity, duality or multiplicity,
visible, invisible, or evanescent,
invisible but resonating or vibrating,
everything holds its place but transcends it—
surely everyone knows that everything is timeless!

The pathless path
is the path always under our feet
and since that path is always beneath us,
if we miss it, how stupid!

The dynamic of involuntary concentration,
irrespective of meditation, is always present—
but surely we all know that!

Surely we all know that our selves
and the things we want and cling to,
from the very first, in reality,
are all images of intrinsic gnosis.

40

The five passions, self-imposed shackles,
from the first occur together with gnosis—
surely we all know that!

The four material elements,
earth, water, fire and air,
constitute the body—
surely we can all see that!

The distilled elixir of the most secret instruction
resounds spontaneously in every ear—
surely we can all hear it!
Or don't we have ears to hear?

The tang of natural spaciousness and gnosis
indelibly surrounds us—
surely we can all smell it!
Or are our noses blocked up?

The three elixirs rolled into one secret precept
have always been the flavor of body-mind—
surely we can all taste it!
Or have we lost our tongues?

The phantasmagoria of pure vision
is always with us, day and night,
like a shadow, a part of the body—
or are we shadowless corpses?
Surely we can all feel it!

Happiness, hand in hand with suffering,
inexpressibly, is intrinsically present—
or are our minds too dull to notice?
The build-up of samsaric propensities,

primordially, is the pure dimension of being—
pity him who has not noticed!

In the field of sense organ, object and consciousness
every recollection and apperception, every flicker of the mind,
arises as the dimension of perfect enjoyment—
how can we fail to see it!

All goal-oriented conventional activity
and all chatter, gossip and laughter,
is the dimension of magical emanation—
surely we all know that! Or are we so dull?

Every impulse and stirring of the mind,
seamless, like a flowing stream,
our constant mental enchantment,
is effortless, natural meditation—
surely we can't miss that!

Looking closely at matter and energy,
and at thought, sound and form,
it is all insubstantial projection,
and this view that empties our urban samsara
has always been with us, though unseen—
surely our doors of perception are now open![13]

In short, all outer and inner experience of samsara and nirvana is decisively and crucially disclosed in the view of natural perfection as an absence, as only the potency, display, and ornamentation of the natural gestalt of self-sprung awareness. All experience is assimilated to the natural disposition of self-sprung awareness by a free and open natural contemplation. Originating spontaneously in self-sprung awareness, whatever happens is caught in the bind of inherently awakened, transparent activity. And since experience is nothing other than self-sprung awareness, fruition is resolution in unitary spontaneity.

In this way, although the four aspects are treated separately, their various meanings are all contained within self-sprung awareness. The meaning of self-sprung awareness itself is established through illustration, definition, and evidence:

To understand my nature with certainty,
take the sky as the illustration,
'unoriginated reality' as the definition,
and the elusive nature of mind as the evidence.
As 'sky-like reality'
it is indicated by the simile *of sky or space.*[14]

All experience is pure mind,
which is likened to the sky (that same simile):
the nature of pure mind is like the sky.[15]

Pure mind is the spaciousness, the origin, of all experience. Although forms of matter and energy appearing in that space seem to be either samsara or nirvana, they are actually all gnostic vision. Everything appears in pure mind as the work and projection of mind, but pure mind itself is uncreated:

Pure mind, uniquely uncreated, creates all;
everything made has the nature of pure mind
and the unique uncreated cannot be contrived.[16]

Thus all and everything is shown contained within the scope of self-sprung awareness which is the vajra-body.

The Extensive Exposition

The First Vajra Theme: Absence
'All things material and their qualities are absent'

I.1 The Disclosure of Absence

4. The Absence of All Concrete Reality

First let me tell you about 'absence',
the absence that is essentially emptiness:
in the super-matrix of pure mind that is like space
whatever appears is absent in reality.

Gnosis itself and everything appearing in its scope is utterly empty, lacking any identity, so with all proliferating projection and elaborating concepts undermined nothing ever comes into existence.

In the nirvana of indeterminate gnosis,
there is no proliferation, no substance or attribute.[17]

Despite appearances, form is emptiness and emptiness is form and there is no center inside nor any point of focus outside. The gnostic state is unoriginated and there is no dualistic mind that proliferates ideas and creates an objective universe full of specific things.

The super-matrix of pure mind is the spaciousness of absence, likened to elemental space, in which material phenomena appear as intangible images of light:

5. A Definitive Simile for Absence

In the universal womb that is boundless space
all forms of matter and energy occur as flux of the four elements,
but all are empty forms, absent in reality:
all phenomena, arising in pure mind, are like that.

Though all phenomena of all worlds seem to come into existence and perish in the sphere of elemental space, their appearance has no basis and thus, insubstantial, they are said to be absent. The four elements (earth, water, fire and air) that comprise whatever appears, because they are not composed of discrete particles, never actually come into being and, therefore, never cease to exist. Neither the supported phenomena therefore, nor the space that underlies them are actually established as existent. Likewise, both gnosis and all experience appearing within its scope are absent in reality.

Just as all worlds, inner and outer,
all forms of matter and energy,
the animate and inanimate,
all contained in space, are absent,
so is the vast field, the super-matrix of pure mind,
with its buddhas and sentient beings,
its crucible and contents, environment and life-forms:
in immaculate reality everything is nondual,
free of inflating or deflating conceptual projection.[18]

The hologram is a salient simile for our worlds and galaxies projected into cosmic space. Atoms, elemental components of matter, construed as 'supports' of materiality are said to be 'absent' insofar as their indivisibility precludes their application as building blocks of more complex structures. Once the fundament is discovered to be absent, 'supported' material structures—planets, continents, animate and inanimate, flora and fauna—must also be absent.[19] The absence of the material realm is employed as a simile for the status of all phenomena in the moment. The fundament, 'the support', is the pure space of gnosis, while the 'supported' is all experience appearing in its scope. The ontological status of absent phenomena is nondual, free of all evaluation in terms of existence or nonexistence. This existential indeterminacy is termed 'absence' or 'ineffability'.

Rather than referring to the utter nonexistence of all and everything, absence implies the lack of any exterior or interior identity:

6. Appearances in the Nature of Mind are Inherently Absent

Magical illusion, whatever its form,
lacks substance, empty in nature;
likewise, all experience of the world, arisen in the moment,
unstirring from pure mind, is insubstantial evanescence.

All experience of the world and our outer environment and the beings that partake of its energy, the crucible and its contents, no matter what the form, all is as empty of inherent existence as an hallucination of a world with illusory inhabitants— nothing can move outside the space of pure gnosis.

No experience of the world, inner or outer, no matter or energy,
no event in samsara or nirvana, ever leaves pure mind.[20]

Pure gnosis is our original face of awareness where phenomena appear up-front like empty reflections on the surface of a mirror. Things seem to be there; but actually they are not. Everything is a momentary illusion in the nature of mind; nothing whatsoever stirs from or differs from the nature of mind.

Pure mind is the all-inclusive space-time of the dream—of both samsara and nirvana:

7. Insubstantial Appearances Never Stir from the Scope of Gnostic Spontaneity

Just as dream is a part of sleep,
unreal gossamer in its arising,
so all and everything is pure mind,
never separated from it,
without substance or attribute.

Just as the places and the people seen in our dreams cannot stir from dream-space, so no experience imaged in any of the six realms can ever stir from gnostic space. Likewise, since it is pure display of the three gnostic dimensions, no experience can move even a hair's breadth from gnostic space free of dualistic perception.

The six types of being, womb-born, egg-born, moisture-born or lotus-born,
also arise in that field of reality and dissolve into the same spaciousness.
Though the poles of dualistic perception are seemingly different,
the field of reality is both the object and the perceiver,
and within that field's spaciousness there can be no dualistic perception.

Everything cognized by buddhas of the past, present and future
arises in the spaciousness of reality and is cognized by it;
this spaciousness is the indeterminate medium of cognition,
and this is the self-arising, self-released matrix at the three dimensions' junction.[21]

In the Tibetan tradition, all experience of samsara is subsumed, inclusively, within the psychological categories of human beings, long-lived gods, power-tripping demons, frustrated hungry ghosts, alienated hell-beings, and fearful animals. Experience of nirvana includes the pure visions of buddha-realms in the three gnostic dimensions of pure being, perfect enjoyment and magical emanation.

Pure mind is identified here with the spaciousness of reality (the dharmakaya and the dharmadhatu) which is a definition of gnosis. The source, the imagery and the destination of all life-forms is a nondual field of experience. The last line of the quote identifies spaciousness with the matrix—the junction of the three gnostic dimensions as a self-arising focus of reflexive release (see canto 21). The four types of birth are by womb (mammals), by egg (birds), by moisture (insects) and by miraculous birth (Padmasambhava).

Yet a distinction must be made between the ordinary mind and the phenomena that arise as experience within it:

8. The External World is Neither Mind Nor Anything But Mind.

Experience may arise in the mind
but it is neither mind nor anything but mind;
it is a vivid display of absence, like magical illusion,
in the very moment unutterable.
All experience arising in the mind,
at its inception, know it as absence!

All seemingly material forms and the energy of the universe, the five types of sensory object, like visual objects for instance, all appear in the mind and therefore are not other than mind. They may seem to have separate existence, but intrinsically empty like dream or magical illusion, no separate existence can be established. Appearances are thus neither mind nor anything apart from it; they are 'vivid visions of absence', 'empty yet brilliant appearance', like the eight similes of magical illusion. If we examine whether they are composed of atoms or not, we find that they are all equally empty and absent. Any aspect of the gestalt imagery of the nature of mind should be known as the spaciousness that is unchangeable emptiness.

If we seek the essence in derivative phenomena,
each aspect, deconstructed, unfocused, is display—
the essence manifest is nothing other than pure being.
As we integrate with the unitary atom, utterly unpatterned,

awareness of nonspecific reality is self sprung,
the essence that is wide-open, direct, nonconceptual perception,
and sustaining that immaculate process sovereign sameness is attained.
Unchanging and unchangeable, nothing is there to desire,
and with nothing to hold on to, not even a mind.[22]

'But are you not defining everything as mind?' someone will ask. Let me make a clear distinction here. We frequently hear the statement that all inner and outer experience of samsara and nirvana is pure mind. In this context all experience is called 'mind' because consonant in its inability to move out of the one gnostic space it is recognized in its gestalt imagery as gnostic display, potency and ornamentation. In the same way, we call the sunshine 'the sun', when we say, 'we stayed out in the midday sun'. The logical refutation of the assertion of the actual identity of mind with phenomena, reducing it to absurdity, however, is twofold: since phenomena have color and spatial extension, the mind would also have color and spatial extension; and mind would be external and appearances internal and they would be interchangeable. Further, when we die, the whole environment with all beings would pass away at the same time.

Belief in the identity of mind and appearances is a deviation from me.[23]

Why do we say that everything is mind?
Mind is the source and multiplicity mind.
Can buddha arise as product
or sentient beings evolve into buddhas?
Take charcoal for example—we can polish it,
but try as we may it does not become white;
in the same way, deluded beings,
though they practice endless meditation,
can never become buddha.[24]

Babes unable to understand the definitive meaning,
say that appearances are their own mind,
which is like mistaking brass for gold.[25]

Nowadays some people conceited in their knowledge of the Great
Perfection, together with the adherents of some ordinary schools,
through lack of discrimination, loudly and ardently assert the
egregious error that phenomenal appearances are our mind.
Ordinary mind and pure mind, however, are not the same thing.
Ordinary mind consists of triple-world beings' adventitious
conditioned ignorance manifested as the eight types of
consciousness with their different functions. 'Pure mind' is self-
sprung gnostic awareness having no substance or attributes, the
spaciousness of all samsara and nirvana. Since all outer and inner
experience originates as the energetic potency, or display, of pure
mind, we sometimes call it 'pure mind'—which is a case of
imputing the name of the cause to the effect. While all appearance
as samsara or nirvana should be understood as gnostic potency,
gnosis itself, established as neither samsara nor nirvana nor
anything else, should be understood as the impalpable foundation
of inexorable, uncrystallizing emanation.

'Objective' appearances are vivid visions of absence, neither mind
nor anything but mind, and should be understood as timelessly
pure, baseless, brilliant emptiness. At the moment of release all
potency and display, being groundless, dissolves by itself, like the
waking from a dream, and thus since intrinsic gnosis never stirs
from the original disposition of original changeless pure being, we
should understand substance and attributes as immaculate. These
days, no one but me (Longchenpa) seems to make these distinctions—either they argue that appearances are mental or they aver
that they are something other than mind, but that is all.[26]

Even our own school (the Nyingma) is unsure, some proposing
that the potency and display of gnosis appearing as ornamentation

51

is the essence. In regard to that, *potency* is the energy of gnosis that manifests in the variable appearances of both samsara and nirvana, in the same way that the very same sunlight causes a lotus blossom to open and a white water lily to close. *Display* is the luminous expression of gnosis, which is like the incandescence of a candle-flame, or the display of the sun as light. *Ornamentation* is the adornment of the self-arisen face of gnosis, the momentary appearance of complex structured gestalt imagery like a rainbow, or the sun, moon, stars and planets, in the sky.

The essential quality of potency is its indeterminacy.

And:

I teach the essence of display
as indeterminate nondual union.

And:

Ornamentation is beauty.[27]

The digression elaborating 'mind only' and defining 'display', 'potency' and 'ornamentation' ends here.

Materialism, asserting the substantial existence of atomic components, runs into the paradox—existence independent of any perceiving consciousness and the infinite divisibility of spatial objects. Subjective idealism, asserting the essentially mental nature of all experience, if taken literally, entails many absurd consequences. Belief in the duality of mind and matter suspended, all we can say about phenomena is that they seem to be there, yet they are not— they are mere show, a display of absence.

The eight modes of consciousness are the five external sensory consciousnesses (visual, auditory, olfactory, gustatory and tactile) and the three internal consciousnesses (conceptual, emotional and the 'storehouse' consciousness of subconscious tendencies, susceptibilities and archetypal potential). Conditioned mind is comprised of mental functions as elucidated

52

in the Abhidharma literature. Pure mind is bodhichitta, the ultimate nature of mind, and the ultimate source of all manifestations of samsara and nirvana. It is like an invisible projector of every scene of delusory enchantment upon the mindscreen that is itself.

In pure mind all things are equal and buddhas and sentient beings are one. But in the world of duality where all mental images are processed by the relative mind, black charcoal cannot be made white, a dog cannot be changed into a cat, chalk cannot become cheese, and sentient beings cannot be turned into buddhas.

The essential fact of gnosis cannot thus be identified with any particular external or internal entity. It is the pure mind of absence:

9. Gnosis Is Not Any Particular Thing

Just as the objective field is absent in reality,
so 'the knower'—in actuality pure mind,
in essence an absence, is like the sky:
know it in its ineffable reality!

The essence of gnosis, the indeterminate, inalienable, ground of all outer and inner, samsaric and nirvanic, emanation, cannot be determined in any way—just like elemental space.

All experience is pure mind,
which is likened to the sky (that same simile):
the nature of pure mind is like the sky.[28]

Pure mind and its gnosis are self-aware existential space wherein all phenomenal experience of samsara and all noumenal possibility of nirvana occur; but gnosis itself cannot be located, it is indefinable, like the element space. It is ineffable—beyond verbal conventions, intentional thought-forms and modes of expression. It does not turn into anything specific; it does not become something other; it never transforms into anything else; so it cannot be defined as anything at all.

Though ineffable, the pure mind of absence has three remarkable qualities: it is unconditional, nondiscriminatory and unerring:

10. The Face of Absence

In the heart-essence that is self-sprung awareness,
the absence of causality closes the abyss of samsara,
the absence of discrimination integrates samsara and nirvana,
and in the absence of glitches and veils the triple world coalesces.

In the intrinsically clear, naked essence of pristine gnosis there is no causality or conditioning, so the possibility of falling into samsara with its abyss of reactivity and alternating pleasure and pain is precluded. The entirety of samsara may spring up unhindered as if in a causal process, yet the original face of gnosis that is the nature of mind certainly cannot be adduced as the cause or as an effect. Thus, because there is no causal process, there can be no glitch in it and because there is no goal there can be no deviation from the path leading to it and no distinction can be made between right and wrong or good and bad. Whatever appears, samsara or nirvana, the nature of mind remains in harmonious equanimity, all dualities resolved. In fact, nothing is experienced, so the mind rests easy.

Whatever emerges in nonspecific gnostic space is experienced as nothing but rest in complete freedom. 'Buddhahood' is imputed simply by the immediacy of the intuition of the nature of reality, but there is no quantum change for the better because there never is and never has been any departure from our fundamental space-like nature.

Sameness is neither an objective field nor a mental perception,
and body and mind reside intrinsically in its super-matrix;
whatever appears as an emanation of gnosis
can never stir from that matrix of equality.
The non-objective 'sacred vase' exists in an objective field
and since duality has never prevailed the two cannot be separated,

and neither can sentient beings and buddhas,
nor samsara and nirvana, be distinguished.

The material and immaterial are the same in the spaciousness of reality,
buddhas and sentient beings are the same in spaciousness,
relative and absolute truth are the same in spaciousness,
faults and virtues are the same in spaciousness,
high and low and all gradations are the same in spaciousness.

Thus, at their advent, they arise as the same, undifferentiated;
in their abiding, they exist as the same, undifferentiated;
at their dissolution, they are released as the same, undifferentiated.

Even though arising differently, all appear the same in their spaciousness;
abiding differently, all exist the same in their spaciousness;
released differently all vanish the same in their spaciousness.

There is never arising nor non-arising in that same spaciousness;
there is never abiding nor non-abiding in that same spaciousness;
there is never release nor non-release in that same spaciousness.

When they arise they appear spontaneously as their pure nature,
as they abide they abide spontaneously as their pure nature,
when they vanish they dissolve spontaneously as their pure nature.

Arising, abiding, dissolving is all uninterrupted 'release at inception':
uninterrupted, the gap between cause and effect is closed
and without cause and effect, the abyss of samsara is closed;
without a dangerous vulnerable body, how can there be any glitch?
In the super-matrix of unchangeable Samantabhadra,
in the space of immutable Vajrasattva,
simply recognizing our own true face,
that is what is called 'buddha'.[29]

Regarding the absence of glitches and veils:

Within the holistic seed of natural perfection
deviation and conformity are one;
all aberration is pure by nature,
nothing excluded from sole singularity.

Atiyoga is timeless nonduality
of view, meditation, conduct and fruition;
it is free of dualistic glitches and veils.

The view, meditation, conduct and fruition,
these four, are timeless pristine awareness,
and thus free of contingent glitches or veils.

The view, meditation, conduct and fruition
of natural perfection are spontaneity itself,
so calculated effort and any expectation,
all aberrations and obscurations, are intrinsically pure.

There is no other than me, Samantabhadra,
so I am forever-exposed brilliant awareness;
the eight approaches stacked beneath me,
all are functions of my compassion.

Undivided, wisdom always abides within
and pristine awareness is complete and unadulterated,
so the glitches that are 'downfalls' are immaculate.
The intrinsic clarity of undivided wisdom
resolves the dichotomy of glitches and veils.[30]

'Buddhahood' is the term we use to describe the sense of joyous pristine immediacy that attends the dawning of realization of the nature of mind. There is nothing new in this realization and no change or transformation is to be expected of it because it has always been with us. The word 'buddha' denotes an abiding intuition of sameness, the 'sacred vase' (the chalice or holy grail?) of nondual spaciousness, in which every image is recognized as our own true face. (See also canto 20.)

The original face of absence is nondual, ultimate equality, and there is no time so no process, development or evolution. The beginning, the middle and the end of an event are actually always a total, undifferentiated whole and thus in a manner of speaking the same event. In this super-matrix of Samantabhadra the rational mind is absent so there can be no value judgement, and the matrix itself is nondiscriminatory. In the timelessness of the here-and-now there is no causality or conditioning and no glitches or veils. The natural state is described in the section on Assimilation (see particularly cantos 25 and 27).

A glitch is a perceived downfall from gnosis into a goal-directed attitude while laboring under the assumption that the form of the moment can improve its natural perfection. A glitch is also a deviation, a side track, into belief in the content of thought as true, untrue, both or neither. A veil is an obscuration of self-sprung awareness caused by limited view, or blindness to the perfect totality of the moment. As 'faults' of meditation agitation and lethargy are such obscurations. See also canto 2.

The nondual reality of pure mind renders effete the ten techniques applied in the lower, progressive approaches:

11. The Lower Approaches' Techniques are Superseded by Absence

In total presence, the nature of mind that is like the sky,
where there is no duality, no distinction, no gradation,
there is no view nor meditation nor commitment to observe,
no diligent ideal conduct, no pristine awareness to unveil,
no training in the stages and no path to tread,
no subtle realization, and no final union.
In the absence of judgement nothing is 'sacred' or 'profane',
only a one-taste matrix, like the Golden Isle;
the self-sprung nature of mind is like the clear sky,
its nature an absence beyond all expression.

The nature of mind can be nowhere attested because it cannot be identified with any particular state, and for this reason it can afford no specific view, meditation, conduct or fruition, no path of purification to tread, no characteristic phases of generation and completion, no samaya commitment to observe, no ideal conduct to accomplish, and no pristine awareness to properly realize. In the absence of any judgement in the nature of mind, sacred and profane (the religious and secular) are not differentiated. In the utter conviction that whatever occurs is an absolutely free, pure vision of the nature of mind, just as no ordinary earth and stone can be found once one has arrived on the precious Golden Isle, so nothing can be found to either release or reject through deliberate practice of view, meditation, action and goal. Everything, then, is bound in a gnostic embrace, all motivation at an end, all envisioned appearances shining vividly in the unrestricted freedom of seamless gnosis. Thus the nature of mind cannot be sought and accomplished through the ten techniques.

This pure mind, the ubiquitous essence—
it is spontaneously, originally, perfect;
so strenuous engagement with the ten techniques
is unnecessary, superfluous.

My nature is like elemental space
(that all-applicable simile):
we exist in pure space, so we need not strive for it;
we exist as pure space, so space is all our striving;
and all-creating space transcends any exertion.
Pure mind, the ubiquitous essence, is like that,
so transcending all cognitive activity
I am inscrutable and cannot be cultivated.
All the ten techniques are likewise transcended,
so nothing can be done to affect me.
Those who try to approach me on a causal path,
desirous of catching a glimpse of my face,

seeking me through the ten techniques,
fall straight to earth like a tenderfoot sky-walker,
tumbling down due to deliberate effort.

I, the supreme source, I am the revelation,
and transcend every sphere of activity,
so a view of me cannot be cultivated,
and the ten techniques are meaningless.
If you still think that the ten techniques have purpose,
look at me, and finding nothing to see,
taking no view, remain at that zero-point.
Nothing ever separates us from unoriginated simplicity,
so vows and discipline are redundant;
the essence is always spontaneously present,
so any effort to find it is always superfluous;
self-sprung awareness has never been obscured,
so gnostic awareness cannot be generated;
everybody already lives on my level,
so there is no place to reach through purification;
I embrace all and everything,
so there can be no path that leads to me;
I am forever incapable of dualization,
so there is never anything to be labeled 'subtle';
my form embraces everything,
so there has never been any 'duality';
I am self-sprung awareness from the very beginning,
so I can never be nailed down;
since I am the heart of total presence,
there is no other source of secret precepts.[31]

'The ten techniques' (*rang bzhin bcu*) may be more literally stated as 'the ten essential attributes of tantrayoga' (or simply 'the ten attributes'), or 'the ten categories of tantric method', which may be taken to imply the essential methods of all the nine approaches and indeed of the principle of soteriological technique in general. The list of the ten varies in different contexts. A basic list may include view, meditation, conduct, spiritual levels, samaya-commitment, path, ideal conduct, subtle realization, pristine awareness and the goal. The most significant variation is the inclusion of empowerment and mandala in canto 30. The ten techniques are also formulated as the 'ten absences' as elements of the absence of goal-orientation.

The super-matrix of nonaction, unbegun and unending
like the Golden Isle, is all-inclusive and undifferentiated
and without outside or inside, the sun of pure mind,
ever dawning, never setting, dispels the shadows of polarity.
Pure mind does not shun the four extreme beliefs,
but it is unaffected by them, and glitches are in effect eliminated.[32]

We are not urged here to abandon vajrayana praxis or to change our lifestyle in any way. No form of conduct is prescribed in the Great Perfection and none is proscribed; there is no specific activity to perform and none to abandon. Rather, through nonaction, all intentions dissolve. And in Dzogchen Ati there is no need to cultivate gnostic qualities because all arise through spontaneity; but mahayana and vajrayana may, perhaps sometimes, provide a platform for access to Dzogchen Ati, where one stands like a tree waiting to be struck by lightening. The Golden Isle (Serendipity), made of gold, where nothing exists that is not gold, is a metaphor for the matrix of sameness and inclusivity, where there is no bias, no value judgement and no restriction. Inalienable so unattainable, it is a paradise that can be neither lost nor regained.

As all rigid categories dissolve in the sheer immediacy of pristine awareness, gnosis is seen to be free of karmic causality:

12. Gnosis Supersedes Moral Conditioning

The actual essence, pristine gnosis,
cannot be improved upon, so virtue is profitless,
and it cannot be impaired, so vice is harmless;
in its absence of karma there is no ripening of pleasure or pain;
in its absence of judgement, no preference for samsara or nirvana;
in its absence of articulation, it has no dimension;

in its absence of past and future, rebirth is an empty notion:
who is there to transmigrate? and how to wander?
what is karma and how can it mature?
Contemplate the reality that is like the clear sky!

As it is said:

Gaze persistently at actual gnosis
and are there any ten virtues there to practice?
is there any samaya commitment to observe?
any view, meditation, conduct or goal to realize?
is there any maturation, karma or hell?[33]

Pristine gnosis is naked, simple, pure being. How does virtue affect it? Certainly it cannot make it any better. Thus virtue brings no benefit. And vice? Vice does not change it for the worse or distort it and it is therefore harmless. Since the nature of mind is nowhere attested, it has no karma, and there is no possibility of an action ripening as happy or sad, or good or bad. In the absence of linear time there are no past and future lives and there is no karmic cause and effect, so 'samsara', a mere label, is ineffectual.

For those who lack an intuition of the nature of mind, samsara appears in all its dualistic pleasure and pain, but for the gnostic yogin or yogini there is the primal purity of emptiness in which all motivation—all existence—has ceased. Even though samsara and nirvana and virtue and vice appear dream-like in the gnostic scope, they do not cover the face of pure mind, which is thus free of moral conditioning. In the absence of causality there are no past and future lives, birth loses all meaning and the triple world flows in each moment into its alpha-purity. This is called 'emptying the depths of samsara'.

Through the yoga of intuiting gnosis, abiding in the gnostic nature of mind, when the yogin or yogini has become fixated on the nature of mind, no amount of virtue or vice brings the slightest advantage or disadvantage because he or she is integrated with the immediacy of what is. The most excellent hyper-yogin or yogini, therefore, lacks moral discrimination yet always acts harmoniously and appropriately. Recognizing all appearances as perfect images of gnosis there is no escape from pristine awareness.

Confidence in such a mode can be gained through the twelve vajra-laughters:

O Vajra Essence of the Speech of Buddha! Look through the perspective of self-sprung awareness and morality, philosophy and meditation are superseded! How marvelous! Regardless of any physical or verbal action, the immutable ground remains untouched by benefit or harm and free of profit or loss! Ha ha!

O Vajra Speech! Look at the basic nature of things and the world never sheds its skin nor changes its color! How marvelous! Regardless of positive or negative interpretation, there is no change in reality! Ha ha!

O Vajra Speech! Look through the pristine awareness that is the ubiquitous source, total emptiness, and regardless of the intention enacted it is all magical display! How marvelous! Whatever we do is immediately released in the unborn matrix! Ha ha!

O Vajra Speech, listen again! Look through all-embracing pristine awareness, the emptiness of reality—it has been with us from time without beginning! How wonderful! Even if one person kills many others with a sharp knife, at that time neither benefit nor harm would accrue to his nature of mind. Ha ha!

O Vajra Speech! Look through all-illuminating pristine awareness, our own empty cognition, and every appearance arises as a friendly helper! How marvelous! Regardless of whatever appears, nothing ever leaves the ground of being! Ha ha!

O Vajra Speech-Essence! Look through the self-released gestalt of empty gnosis and the nature of the poison is its most effective antidote! How marvelous! Every passion is self-liberating! Ha ha!

O Vajra Speech! Look through empty gnosis, the immaculate essence, and fruition is effortlessly accomplished of its own accord! How marvelous! Through unity, all samsara and nirvana dissolve into nondual being! Ha ha!

O Vajra Speech! Look into the secret abode of the ubiquitous ground, at the super-empty essence, and effortlessly the six types of beings appear in their three gnostic dimensions! How marvelous! They all become buddha at once without practicing even an instant of meditation! Ha ha!

O Vajra Speech! Look through timelessly perfected fruition, the super-emptiness of the three dimensions, and time is beyond differentiation! How marvelous! Without practicing the six perfections (paramitas), *the accumulations of virtue and awareness are completed at once! Ha ha!*

O Vajra Speech! Look through the homogenous super-emptiness of simple gnosis and all deliberate action arises as ornamentation! How marvelous! All discriminatory activity is released through this vision! Ha ha!

O Vajra Speech! Look through ultimate super-emptiness, at the emptiness of emptiness, and all buddhas exist in an abyss! How marvelous! They have fallen due to deliberate meditation! Ha ha!

O Vajra Speech! Look at matter, substantial emptiness—this is the stance where absence is believed to possess identity! How marvelous! We attain the unborn state through birth! Ha ha![34]

Since pure gnostic mind is free of any substance or attribute, it cannot be modified in any way. Since it cannot be identified with any particular causal action or effectuated state, whether high or low, belief in time is suspended and the spacious moment is revealed as free of all moral conditioning. In the absence of subject and object in bodhichitta, there is no one to wander in samsara, no one to seek release through virtuous conduct and no one to suffer in hell. The moral values of Judeo-Christian dualism, for example, are based on conditioned preconceptions about what actions lead to heaven and what lead to hell, thereby precluding the natural all-inclusive compassion of pure mind inherent in the moment. The ten virtues basic to Buddhist moral discipline are restraint from killing, stealing, sexual misconduct, lying, slandering, cursing, gossiping, coveting, harboring malice and holding destructive beliefs.

The absence of moral conditioning and discrimination is a recurrent theme (see particularly cantos 30, 39 and 122i). In the absence of causality, the unconditioned timeless moment of total absence subsumes all past, present and future experience:

13. 'There Is Only Ever Nonduality'

Constantly deconstructing, investigating keenly,
not even the slightest substance can be found;
and in the undivided moment of nondual perception
we abide in the natural state of perfection.

Absent when scrutinized, absent when ignored,
not even an iota of solid matter is attested;
so all aspects of experience are always absent—
know it as nothing but magical illusion!

The profound significance of the absence of moral causality and conditioning is the lack of any distinction between past, present and future. Insofar as we may repeatedly seek the inside, outside and middle of gnosis and find no distinction, and insofar as we cannot find an iota or particle of solid matter in the universe, and insofar as we search for a discrete moment of pure gnostic mind and find nothing, and insofar as we fail to separate past, present and future because the past has gone, the future never comes, and the present is lost in between, so far we can find no karma, no process of karmic maturation, and no moral conditioning.

If time and space are absent when scrutinized, then in the same way they are surely absent when they are not under scrutiny, for then the parameters of investigation are absent and the objective field has neither specific nor general characteristics (like shape, color, or moral quality). In the latter case time and space are absent also in the conventional sense, for a babe oblivious to the *zing* of reality, conditioned to time and space, loses the sense of the existence of an experience once it has vanished. It may seem to him that he has performed a conventional good or bad action, but no process of maturation is experienced because the nature of mind always remains unchanged. In truth, cause and effect cannot be distinguished because there is no change between one moment and the next. Therefore, moral causality is never true for anyone, and particularly not for the yogin or yogini, for whom it does not exist even as a lie—karmic maturation cannot be experienced!

Trust in the absence of causality may unfold through these seven wonderful quintessential principles:

Ho! O Vajra Speech-Essence, listen! I, Samantabhadra, teach that by virtue of the first principle—that intrinsic gnosis is unborn and undying—there is not the slightest difference between a person who kills millions of sentient beings and one who practices the ten perfections (paramitas).

O Vajra Speech! I, Samantabhadra, teach that by virtue of the second principle—that the nature of reality is unstructured—there is not the slightest difference between a person who is always meditating upon emptiness and one who has never even momentarily entertained the idea of emptiness.

O Vajra Speech! I, Samantabhadra, teach that by virtue of the third principle—that gnosis is unconditioned—as to the completion of the accumulations of virtue and awareness there is not the slightest difference between a religious person who has performed countless conditional virtues and a psychopathic killer.

O Vajra Speech! I, Samantabhadra, teach that by virtue of the fourth principle—that the nature of gnostic awareness is unmoving—as to the vision of the real nature of things there is not the slightest difference between a person whose body and language exhibits all the signs of understanding and one who has never cared even momentarily to listen or study the teaching or to think about it.

O Vajra Speech! I, Samantabhadra, teach that by virtue of the fifth principle—that the nature of being is unborn and deathless—as to accessing realization there is not the slightest difference between a person experiencing the torment of hell and one experiencing the bliss of buddha.

O Vajra Speech! I, Samantabhadra, teach that by virtue of the sixth principle—the immutability of gnosis—as to intuiting the natural condition there is not the slightest difference between a person who has restrained discriminatory mental functions and one who has a strong fixated ego.

O Vajra Speech! I, Samantabhadra, teach that by virtue of the seventh principle—the intrinsicality of pure being—as to potential for fruition there is not the slightest difference between a person who performs all kinds of external offerings, uttering praise and prayers, and one who lives free of all religious activity.

O Vajra Speech! A person who lives by these seven great self-sprung principles gains confidence thereby in effortless realization, conviction in the understanding of appearance as inseparable from the three gnostic dimensions and intuition that he or she is buddha.[35]

We may do extensive research in the laboratories of matter (physics) and mind (meditation), but we cannot produce anything like a smallest unit of measurement, a final particle (quark?) or a measure of mind. Likewise, we cannot measure the past or the future or discover any absolute measure of time. Once ultimate building blocks of both spatial and temporal objects are found absent, there can be no causes and effects anywhere in time, in neither 'mechanical' nor 'moral' causality. In the very act of experimentation however, a timeless moment of nondual perception may be discovered where the natural essence of reality is spontaneously revealed.

The idea of karma is tied up with our conventional notions of time and space, and causality. In our daily life, as we go about our business without giving any philosophical thought to its parameters, we seemingly perform good and bad actions and experience good and bad results or reactions. That perception is due to a mistaken belief in the validity of the content of thought, which is judgmental and discriminatory in its nature. Our tendency to get caught up in discriminatory thought entails separation of time into past and future.

Virtue and vice are just thoughts—they cannot be fixed anywhere in time and space;' they are nothing substantial, having neither specific nor general characteristics. And insofar as we believe in duality (due to our moral conditioning), we create a delusory personality in our heads that ought to behave in some specific way to avoid being chastised by society, punished by god, or to avoid karmic retribution. Such imaginary persons, however, never existed, never exist and will never exist in the spaciousness of gnosis, so there is never any karmic fruit to be consumed by anyone. The ordinary imaginary (morally conditioned) person is a victim of his own imagination.

Karma does not even exist on its own low level of existential understanding. It is part of the universal delusion, maya, self-delusion. Not even a crutch, it is always a glitch. Karma is not something to be tolerated provisionally; it is something of the order of the snake that is delusively projected upon the proverbial rope.

Like the entirety of radical Dzogchen, this uncompromising affirmation of the seven principles of the nature of mind is to be taken at face value and understood as a restatement of the natural samaya of absence. Intuiting the timeless moment of absence and awakening from the hallucination of samsara is liberation:

14. The Realization of Absence is Liberating

During the empty enchantment of dream
ignorant babes are entranced,
while the wise, disillusioned, are undeceived;
those unaware of the truth of absence,
clinging to their identity, wander in circles,
while the wise yogin, fully present,
aware of the zing of reality
convinced of the absence of that very moment,
is liberated in the non-contingent reality-matrix.

Enchanted by the play of illusion, children who do not know their own minds are bewitched. They take the show to be real and become attached to it, enwrapped in their imagination. Old people, on the other hand, who know the story, cannot get caught by such fascination. Likewise, fools who never question the validity of their experience and impute identity to those vividly appearing, enchanting, empty images, take the show to be real and restrict themselves to cyclical patterns of transmigration. Hyper-yogins and yoginis, however, are aware of the *zing* of reality, and their minds are released into the nameless matrix which is beyond both bondage and liberation.

All experience is immersed in pure bliss,
and if the babes who believe in concrete reality
would spring into the absence of the mundane world,
their eyes opened, they would feel it and know it.[36]

For the hyper-yogin or yogini who understands that everything is unreal, there is nothing that is not released and dissolved in the super-matrix of pure mind. What is disagreeable and unpleasant for those who strive to accomplish a material ambition by some causal means is perfectly acceptable to the hyper-yogin or yogini.

ABSENCE

The lived reality of freedom in nonduality is not feasible for those aspirants on the gradual approaches. A young musk deer springs sprightly up a cliff, a feat that other animals cannot emulate; the yogin or yogini walking the sky-like path of nonaction is readily liberated in the matrix of non-intentional gnosis, an impossibility for the disciple on a linear goal-oriented path.

With the nonreferential awareness of timeless buddhahood is it possible to wander in samsara? The little mind that believes in material reality is freed in space, released in the unsupported matrix!

The deluded mind, distinguishing between sameness and difference, is released in unity, released into the matrix of reality!
In the zero-dimensional holistic seed, can there be dualistic perception? The deluded mind distinguishing between sameness and difference is instantaneously released in unity, freed in the reality-matrix!

In self-sprung awareness, causeless, non-conditional, is it possible that the five poisons can arise? Blocks to total presence, desire in the material world, are instantaneously released, freed in the matrix of pristine awareness!

Can spontaneity, impartial and unlimited, be tainted by prejudice? The unbalanced mind, attached to its biased opinions, is released through ultimate tolerance, freed in the matrix of spontaneity!

Can indeterminate emptiness without substance or attribute show itself as appearance? Appearances are released in clear light, released in the matrix of ambiguity! all-inclusive and indivisible, released into the matrix of spontaneity! without uniting or separating, released in the nuclear matrix! arising in all possible ways, released in the matrix of ambiguity!

Appearance arising as form is released as light; vibration arising as sound, whatever is heard is naturally released; whatever appearance is seen, whatever sound is heard, whatever is perceived in the five doors of perception, is 'seen' by itself and there is nothing other than that.

In nonduality, object and mind are released as one; whatever emerges out of unitary sameness is a unitary field; all created qualities are the existential ground; everything whatsoever, liberated without deliberate action, is a matrix of total freedom.[37]

The matrix is the spaciousness of timeless freedom. It is a point-instant free of all time and space; identical to nothing yet it contains or subsumes all times and spaces. Herein lies the potential for psychic power; but liberation is attained in the recognition of the here-and-now as this point-instant. Being beyond causation, it cannot be attained gradually. Ambitious people fixated on a goal tend to fear this matrix.

Absence is the actuality of nondual perception, the holistic cosmic seed, or sphere, containing the dynamic of Samantabhadra:

15. Absence is the Heart of the Matter

In total presence, the indeterminate nature of mind,
lies the timeless pristine awareness of nondual perception;
in sheer naked, non-contingent gnosis,
lies the nondiscriminatory holistic seed;
in the holistic transparence of zero-dimensional gnosis,
lies the contemplation of Dharmakaya Samantabhadra;
in essential absence, the intrinsic gnosis of total presence,
nonreferential, immaculate contemplation is shining.

The nature of mind, brilliant empty gnosis, neither eternal nor temporal, integrates inside and outside, the knower and the known. Since it is free of moral conditioning, devoid of karmic maturation and any latent tendencies that are the potential for experience, it is holistic transparence, the sole dynamic of Samantabhadra.

Pure mind is inscrutable; what is its purpose?
What is stainless virtue?
We are yoked to the original source.[38]

The dynamic of Samantabhadra is his intention or 'pure will', his thoughtless thought or buddha-thought. It is revealed in the timeless point-instant beyond karmic conditioning in the transparent immediacy of the moment. It is pure meaning intrinsic to awareness as the spontaneity of empty light (canto 18). The key to effortless nonaction, this dynamic is actuated in the absence of personal will, karma or life-force (canto 19). It is the actual emptiness of free will and intention, inevitably binding all temporal experience to absence (cantos 28-29). It is a continuum of spontaneous creativity and synchronicity, pre-linguistic intent and meaning, the beginning and end of all and everything (canto 32). It is the thoughtless space of pure being where all is one as the zing of reality (canto 34), precluding the four extreme ontological postures of existence, nonexistence, both and neither (canto 36). It is a single field of pure vision integrating the past, present and future, the common space of buddhas and masters of gnosis, where thought dawns freely and unrestrictedly as the self-expression of 'a carefree mind unfolding as pure joy' (canto 41).

The holistic seminal seed, or light-seed, is the space of absence conceived as a receptacle of potentiality. It is the infinitely open reality-matrix, metaphorically called the bhaga of Samantabhadri (the female adibuddha), where all experience 'coils together' and is integrated (canto 49), where everything is forever in a latent state, nothing has ever happened and nothing has ever come into existence. It is the all-consuming openness of the original ground of being (canto 51) that is pure being without any set parameters, 'edges or corners' (cantos 88 and 94). The unstructured reality of all and everything as clear, empty light (canto 103), the matrix of the holistic seed is the dynamic space of pure will or buddha-thought (canto 107).

Realizing the dynamic of absence, intuiting buddha-intention, the mind is spacious, serene and detached:

71

16. The Point of Realizing Absence

In the yoga of enchanting illusion, the play of gnostic vision,
empty experience arises as evanescent, uncrystallizing, display,
and convinced of absence in the moment of its inception,
without the least urge to control, to cultivate or reject,
we remain open, at ease, carefree and detached.

For the yogin or yogini intuiting all experience as illusory, enchanting vision, every appearance dawns as a display of absence. For him or her every experience is impressed with the seal of carefree detachment and that is what distinguishes the freedom of the yogin or yogini from a regular complacent person too clever by half in explaining things away.

We cannot escape the triple world by clever self-deception;
but by leaving things just as they are, uncontrived and relaxed,
neither samsara nor nirvana can hold us.[39]

Atiyoga is not so much a yoking of two things, an image employed largely in tantrayoga, but recognition of pre-existent unity, in this case where the play of Maya Devi is light and easy. Nonaction implies making no directed effort, neither embracing nor endorsing anything but certainly not rejecting anything; rather, it is a letting go of everything equally and maintaining the inner spaciousness of a carefree, easy mind.

Absence endows us with 'carefree detachment', 'freely resting' at ease, which is central to the Cutting Through phase of natural perfection praxis (see also cantos 22, 26, 54, 55, 80 and 122i). Carefree detachment is contrasted here with the clever intellect that deracinates potential obstacles by subtle intellectualization that amounts to self-deception, through the Jesuitical pedantry that discerns ontological subtleties in samsara, distinguishing between degrees of truth and right and wrong. Such a mind falls into the trap of taking what appears to be existent as nonexistent.

The goal-directed orientation of the gradualist approaches of Buddhist practitioners precludes the spontaneous realization of absence:

17. The Gradual Approaches Err in Ignoring Absence

A fool deceived by magical illusion is like an animal
pursuing a mirage in his thirst for water;
expecting his delusive hopes to be realized,
trusting in his dogma, he is trapped;
losing his way on the eight-fold gradation of intellect,
he fails to see the real meaning.

Like animals tormented by mistaking a mirage for water, babes are tormented by their habit of grasping at illusion as concrete, and practitioners of the eight different gradual approaches are obsessed by attachment to the dogma that gives them identity, thus failing to realize the heart of the matter. Personal identity is composed of concepts of arbitrary positive or negative attachment in dualistic perception; spiritual identity is concocted by imputing dogma to a field of absence, particularly the obscenity of clinging attachment to our various philosophical views, modes of meditation, behavior and spiritual goals. Ordinary people, non-Buddhists, and followers of the eight lower approaches are identical in that they do not realize natural perfection.

Attachment to the pathless path as a goal
ensures that the place of release remains obscure;
light and darkness, existence and nonexistence,
permanence and transience, cause and effect,
all eight, are congruent with boundless space
and whoever seeks the parameters of emptiness fails,
like a blind bird trying to reach the end of the sky:
what is ineluctable cannot be contrived by man,
and knowledge without purpose is endless.[40]

The Dzogchen yogin or yogini is such insofar as he or she is free of spiritual identity or belief in any dogma. This natural freedom is intrinsic to doing nothing and allowing moment by moment autonomous deconstruction of his or her identity both personal and spiritual. Any and all beliefs are unwonted projections upon the tabla rasa of absence. The eight lower Buddhist approaches to pure mind, all of which maintain beliefs about the nature of reality, are to be understood as eight levels of spiritual acumen. But although it is Buddhists who are targeted here as victims of their beliefs, all religious believers in a hereafter fall into the same error, as well as secularists whose mental life is driven by notions of utopia or any ideal to be realized in the future. Indeed, insofar as we set ourselves goals and harbor expectations we deny ourselves the possibility of attainment, which is an insight utilized by Zen archers and motorcyclists, and the like.

In Buddhist terms, types of goal-oriented religious endeavor are classified into the 'eight lower approaches': the monastic approach, the solitary ascetic approach, the altruistic householder approach, the three exoteric approaches of the tantric yogin or yogini and the three esoteric approaches of inner tantra.[41] Atheist, hedonistic, agnostic, eternalistic (monotheistic) approaches are allotted the same category as the lower Buddhist approaches due to the dualisms present in their dogma. Insofar as present dissatisfaction and a bright future are differentiated, heaven and hell are distinguished, right and wrong and good and bad are polarized, a goal to attain is set up and so on, and there can be no recognition of natural perfection. A 'spiritual identity' (such as 'tulku', 'lama', 'dzogchen yogin' or 'hyper-yogin') is a certain obstacle to the realization of nondual reality (see cantos 37 and 107). Stress and striving itself precludes attainment, and thus there can be no integration until the drive to reach perfection is relinquished. In this important sense, every path is a dead end and represents a deviation from the natural gnosis of pure mind, 'the heart of the matter'.

Religion, dogma, meditation precepts, every dualistic mind-set is superseded by the spontaneity of reality:

18. The Actuality of Absence

The spaciousness within and beyond the atiyoga precepts
is a complete absence, nothing whatsoever, like the sky:
in the very moment, in the natural disposition of pure being,
as the original hyperspace that we cannot abandon,
the natural state of pure pleasure is spontaneously arisen.

The self-sprung awareness of natural perfection cannot be attested or defined; it is the spontaneous arising of brilliant emptiness, the alpha-purity of the primal spaciousness of being. It is called therefore, 'the dynamic space that is the natural disposition of pure being'.

In the wellspring that is the emptiness of absence
intrinsic space is the great mystery,
existing from time without beginning,
timelessly emitting the grand display.
There is nowhere to hide therein,
nothing to do,
no special qualities,
no stasis, no progress.
It is primal super-emptiness,
spaciousness rather than absence,
without inside or outside,
without sense of up or down,
no direction or destination known.
Whoever knows this unassailable reality
was buddha before me, Samantabhadra:
this is the indeterminate place of all-inclusive awareness,
the uncreated, primordial ground,
the place of the first, original, buddha.
Abiding here naturally from the first,
we are the locus of buddha's secret word
and the receptacle of essential total presence.[42]

Here is total conviction that pure mind, the essence of pure being, lies in the natural disposition utterly pure from the first.

The atiyoga precepts are a reflection of ineffable fruition, which is recognition of spaciousness or absence. Spontaneously perfected in timeless reality, no deliberate action or ambition leads us any closer to the fulfilment that lies at the heart of the matter:

19. Buddhahood Is Not Attained by Purposeful Action

If secret gnosis, the actual buddha-dynamic, eludes us,
to attain release by any purposeful action is no option.
'Everything is impermanent and bound to perish'—
how can a tight mesh of body, speech and mind
reach out to touch its indestructible core?

In the event of failure to intuit intrinsic gnosis, which is pure being, there is no chance that we can attain release in this lifetime by any deliberate physical, verbal or mental act. Religious practice becomes a tense constraining mesh constricting and veiling gnosis, and although some small satisfaction may follow, the product is conditioned and thus certain to fade away, perishing like an earthen pot. Such practice can never attain to the indestructible reality of pure being. Whatever is deliberately created is conditioned and transient, whereas its opposite, the uncreated, is imperishable. Since it is indestructible, pure being can only be seen by non-deliberate, unintended relaxation into the natural state; goal-oriented action is a mesh of constraint leading us closer to buddhahood by not so much as a hair's breadth. Such ambition may well be regarded as a futile samsaric trap.

In reality, nothing is to be done![43]

There is no such thing as a flawless idea:
in a strait-jacket of physical and verbal commitment
it is very difficult to encounter reality.[44]

A detailed rationale from the same source:

O great being, listen to me!
What I teach you is not goal-oriented mahayana;
take it as my conclusive, definitive transmission.

Every experience, whatever its shape or form,
and the nature of mind have ever been one,
so forgoing the constructs of the goal-oriented schools,
in simply focusing upon the mind just as it is,
our own total presence is revealed as the nature of appearances.

Failing to realize this, people attach labels,
calling the tangible 'relative' and the intangible 'absolute';
nondual absolute and relative are the one reality
although even I cannot truly express it.
The longing for happiness is a disease of attachment,
and happiness is attained through absence of desire;
buddhahood, unattainable by any striving,
is spontaneously accomplished by unstressed simple being.
Rest unthinking in the relaxed natural state![45]

Any kind of conscientious meditation or yoga, any physical, energetic or mental effort, precludes the possibility of liberation from samsara in this lifetime. Deliberate effort entails constructing imaginary mind-forms instead of relaxing into the only essential reality, which is gnosis. Personal will or ambition is the motive force behind the selfish actions of body, speech and mind that constitute a mesh—an intricate web of knots—in which we are entangled. Wearing such a strait-jacket of regulated behavior we may feel happy and safe for a short time, but any conditioning obscures pristine awareness.

Spontaneously and effortlessly, we never stir from our original disposition:

20. Advice to Abide in the Natural Disposition That is Absence.

So if we aspire to the supreme state of being
we should cast aside all childish games that fetter
and exhaust body, speech and mind,
and stretching out in inconceivable nonaction,
in the unstructured matrix, the actuality of absence,
where the natural perfection of reality lies,

we should gaze at the uncontrived sameness of every experience,
and all our conditioned responses dissolving, we surrender!

By forsaking any deliberate, patterned, physical, verbal or mental action in which we have been immersed like innocent children in their uncertain, never-ending and pointless games in the playground, we may stretch out in the pure pleasure of immense relief like an old man basking in the sun with no intention to do anything at all.

By the label 'buddha', a synonym of 'gnostic awakening',
I do not imply that any immaculate buddha exists:
whoever thinks that buddhas visibly exist
can never find buddhahood in the spaciousness of reality.
Whoever knows buddha as unmanifest can intuit the nonactive mind;
knowing buddha as absent, the original face of mind shines forth;
never appearing concretely, 'buddha' is all-embracing,
and the essence of his being shows!

Conversely, in the gradual approach of the mahayana,
through the diverse blessings of discriminate lifestyles,
the nonactive reality of the mind is lost,
and what lies within cannot be found at a distance.

Nonaction, easily discovered and apprehended,
for the gradualists is no less than a terminal disease;
yet it is the stake that tethers unwavering samadhi,
timeless samadhi, that can never be lost or distracted.

The singer of false hope for contrived concentration
provides morbid inspiration for the causal approach:
what has always existed can never be lost or forsaken
and it supersedes all remedies based on goal-obsession.

Yet if this transmission of the supreme source were taught
to followers of a teacher of the causal approach,
they would denounce it from their limited viewpoint:
'Every product has a cause; every tree has a root.'

The yogin who aspires to buddhahood through concentration
spurns artless integration due to his very desire for samadhi;
the uncontrived natural state is universal reality,
and buddhahood is inseparable from that reality.

So 'buddha' is just a label, a verbal designation,
and 'reality' is nothing other than our own mind,
which left as it is, is called pure being, dharmakaya,
where 'left as it is' means unborn from the beginning,
and where 'unborn' means unsought and unfound:
nonaction cannot be realized by any endeavor.[46]

The image of an idle old man stretched out basking in the sun covers nonaction as instruction for nonmeditation and contrasts to the frenetic activity of super-achievers on the mundane stage or rather, to babes in the playground of life acting out their pointless games with body, speech and mind (see canto 31). All ambition is based on discrimination and is a futile attempt to change or recondition things. The nonaction of Samantabhadra in contrast is relaxation into the natural perfection of nondual reality that is our original disposition without stirring or departing from it. (The manner of 'gazing at the uncontrived sameness of all experience' is presented in canto 25.)

By the same token that the word 'buddha' presents a goal to strive for and forms a glitch in the process, in the Dzogchen view 'Buddhism' and 'Buddhist' are likewise dysfunctional nominal counters.

In brief, 'absence' is nothing less than gnosis disclosed by effortless relaxation in the natural state:

21. Disclosure of Absence: the Trailer

Without outside and inside, subject and object,
intrinsic gnosis, being out of time and space,
supersedes all finite events that seemingly begin and end;
pure like the sky, it is without signposts or means of access.
Any specific insight into gnosis is always deluded,
so that any spiritual identity, always delusive, is abandoned;
and convinced that the space of undifferentiated Samantabhadra
is the all-encompassing super-emptiness of all samsara and nirvana,
the natural state obtains as the reality without transition or change.
Breaking out of the brittle shell of discursive view
into the hyperspaciousness that is nowhere located
in the experience of absence the crux of the matter is fully disclosed.

Thus it is determined that every dualistically-perceived experience of the environment and life, samsara and nirvana, inner and outer, however substantial it may appear, in the moment is an image of absence, a pure form of emptiness in unconditioned sky-like gnosis. In as much as it appears, it is empty light; the appearance of empty gnosis, which is the empty brilliance of the luminous self-expression of self-sprung aware-ness, is revealed here crucially as baseless, rootless, vivid shine.

In my emptiness, there is no structured field,
and my radiance cannot be asserted or negated;
my presence of mind is infallibly retentive,
my appearances a process of direct perception;
I cannot be evoked by verbal elaboration,
and engendered by mantra, I am already perfect;
I am completely free of any cause or condition,
and free of dogmatic and experiential distortions
I am nonreferential, zero-dimensional.

ABSENCE

I have no representation or symbolic object,
no visualization, nor mantra,
no dogma, beyond all designation,
and I have neither friends nor foes.

Imperceptible, I have no body,
no religion, no doctrine;
no one is here, no one to perceive:
I do not exist and nor does my retinue.

No spaciousness, no gnostic dimension,
no virtue, no ripening of sin;
no life and nothing to lose,
no accumulation and nothing to gather.

Here is no buddha nor sentient being,
no place to stay nor even emptiness itself;
no method to teach, nor anyone to hear,
no space, no time,
nor any timeless moment.

Therefore, I am nothing at all,
undivided and indivisible,
my scope beyond gradation,
the conception and the act identical,
and in the identity of past, present and future,
there is no field nor its ineffable ground.[47]

The section on the disclosure of all experience as absence is here concluded.

81

I.2   The Assimilation of All Experience to Absence

22. The Congruence of Absence and Gnosis

Once the existential crux of absence is disclosed,
in the gnosis of carefree detachment, in nonmeditation,
the nondiscriminatory space of whatever arises is assimilated,
gnosis congruent with the nondual super-matrix of mind.

Knowing whatever happens as absence, freely resting in nonmeditation regardless of what arises, without attempting to change it, relaxing without endorsing or rejecting it, it is instantaneously assimilated to all-embracing translucent gnosis, and in the absence of dualistic perception it is congruent with, or synchronicitous with, utter emptiness.

The utter purity of all seemingly concrete attributes in the sense fields is the ground of total release. In that ground effortless nonaction dissolves the obsessive intellectual focus that tends to concretize what is absent in reality. The display in the field of the threefold junction is then assimilated at the coincidence of mind and object, nothing repressed, nothing excluded.[48]

The vital assumption here is the intuition of absence, which induces a state of complete abandonment and allows gnostic awareness full play. All experience is then gnostic experience which is utter emptiness (see cantos 26 and 103).

It is as if the compulsion of gnosis to resume its natural status creates a locus or nub that can then be assimilated. This nub is the neutral 'point of focus' in nonmeditation that is spontaneously assimilated when the fact of absence is recognized. Upon the revelation of absence, gnosis is congruent or synchronicitous with it; its time has come; it is potential begging for actualization. Thus the imperative focus, or locus, may be conceived as a dam that must burst, a seal that must be broken, allowing assimilation to the greater scope of indeterminate spaciousness. This instantaneous process may be described as 'giving up completely'.

Mental defenses dissolve in the gnostic ground, and since gnosis is the essential nature of all specifics or attributes of experience such a process allows total release. The threefold junction refers to the synchronicitous conjunction of a sensory organ, its field and consciousness. When nonaction kicks in, accepted without reservation by the rational mind, the luminous display in 'the field of the threefold junction' is assimilated to the mother matrix.

In the immediate process of assimilation of what is always present and inalienable, first, intrinsic concentration is recognized as the medium and its indwelling in pure being as a given (cantos 23 and 24). Then the habitual focus upon appearances is assimilated to pure being (canto 26) and all experience is assimilated to the greater matrix (canto 27), and finally, all conditioning is assimilated to pure mind (canto 28).

Assimilation, unlike the collapse of a house of cards, is not a temporal process; it is a spontaneous effortless instantaneous non-event in the moment:

23. The Natural Spontaneity of Concentrated Absorption

Pure pleasure left alone in vajra-spaciousness
gives uncultivated, spontaneous, hyper-concentration;
with the yogin settled in uncontrived sameness,
it shines forth easily, a constant, like a river's strong current.

Gnosis naturally contains concentrated absorption, which is like a great river's flow, and when the yogin or yogini rests in the complete uncontrived satisfaction of the natural state, he or she knows it intimately.

I reveal nondual, self-sprung, pure pleasure,
free from the extremes of meditation and nonmeditation;
powerful insight that intuits intrinsic gnosis,
resolves the dichotomy of meditation and nonmeditation.

Nondual pure pleasure abides naturally,
and through detachment, without need to do anything,

it is uninterrupted, like the river Ganges:
this I reveal to the most talented![49]

The perfect spontaneous concentrated absorption of gnosis is concomitant with the pure pleasure of natural ease and satisfaction as in sexual consummation (see also cantos 18 and 20). As such it is spontaneously accomplished without acting or striving in meditation. Conversely, recognition of natural concentrated absorption is accompanied by the pure pleasure that is the feeling tone of vajra-space.

Concentrated absorption is a natural function of mind:

24. Unerring Assimilation to Intrinsic Concentration

Authentic sky-like reality in its utter simplicity,
unchangeable, admits no gradation,
and its ineluctable all-suffusing spaciousness,
has no language to express itself.
Yet insight bursting through, gnosis self-arising,
uninhibited by his learning, without any pedantry,
the yogin in whom mental silence supersedes ideation
gains conviction in signlessness, without sign or no sign,
and since there is no meditator nor object of meditation,
lethargy and agitation need not be confronted as foes.

When the yogin or yogini has seen that there can be no stirring from the original gnostic disposition and while staying that course discovers intrinsic concentration, without attempting any deliberate mental technique whatever arises is held in concentrated absorption. At that time, because inception is coincident with clear perception, and concentrated absorption is intrinsic to a relaxed state, tranquil absorption is coupled with perfect insight, and glitches and veils of concentration such as lethargy and agitation dissolve of their own accord, and there is no need to fight them.

This natural concentration cannot be discovered by studying texts and listening to explanations, but it is realized in the moment—without any process of uniting or separating—by four types of yogin or yogini: those in whom insight wells up spontaneously from within due to the praxis of previous lifetimes; those who have received direct introduction to the nature of mind through the guru's grace; those who have perfectly mastered the essence of the teaching; and those whose minds are naturally quiet and relaxed. It is inaccessible for most others.

In natural, sky-like reality, resting in the natural state,
lacking potential for change, gnosis admits no distraction,
and that all-suffusing spaciousness, never lost nor regained,
remains beyond the possibility of verbal articulation.
With insight efflorescing, gnosis naturally dawning,
with learning but no pedantry,
the yogin who has realized the unspoken matrix,
gains conviction neither with nor without signs
and lacking any meditation and any object of meditation
he need not purge worries about lethargy or agitation.[50]

Concentrated absorption is like the sun in so far as all obscuration dissolves under its power (see also cantos 2 and 10), and once natural concentration in the space of absence has been discovered the yogin or yogini does not need to do any mental exercise involving deliberate focus (semdzin exercises) because his or her experience never stirs from the natural place of concentration. Insight into the nature of reality is integrated with meditative absorption in the moment (shamatha is joined with vipashyana) and there is no need to eliminate the glitches and veils of laziness and excitement.

Through immediate release of all thought and sense impression in the space of absence, the Dzogchen yogin or yogini always remains in pure being:

25. Living Constantly in the Spaciousness of Pure Being

Essential absence has already released dualistic perception,
so delusion falls naturally into the matrix of sameness—
we live without interruption in pure being.

Inception and release are simultaneous,
entwining in the single blissful matrix:
whatever arises appears spontaneously as its pure nature,
as it abides it exists spontaneously as its pure nature,
as it vanishes it dissolves spontaneously as its pure nature.

Whatever arises in the reality-matrix, release is reflexive,
always a play of pure being, never shifting into anything other,
a timeless vision, another form of emptiness—
we live in nondiscriminatory essential reality.

External phenomena originate, abide and cease in the gnostic
matrix, nothing stirring from that empty scope just as images
reflected in a mirror can never slide off the face of the mirror or,
more precisely, they do not even exist since they are the surface
itself. Internally, thought, in the same way, cannot stir from the
gnostic scope at its inception, during its existence or at its release,
just as ocean waves always remain within the ocean throughout
their rising, billowing and falling. Thus nothing can ever escape
the natural disposition of pure being, the medium of brilliant
emptiness that can never become reified, the matrix of the three
gnostic dimensions of spontaneity.

Whatever exists is only its own nature;
and whatever ends is only its own nature:
there is no movement at all in pure mind
and that stillness is the body of buddha.

Every word that is uttered is only its own purity;
and every vibration is only its own purity:
nothing is spoken or uttered in pure mind,
which is the speech of buddha.

Every thought and intention is entertained only as its own spaciousness,
and every intuition is realized only as its own spaciousness:
nothing at all is thought or intuited in pure mind,
the mind of buddha past, present and future.

Absence as emanation is the dimension of magic,
its innate pleasure the dimension of perfect enjoyment,
and its utter insubstantiality the dimension of pure being;
the totality is the matrix of these three dimensions.[51]

Reality is the sameness of whatever arises, abides and subsides. Or to say it
another way, neither sense impressions nor thoughts—nothing whatsoever—
stirs from the spaciousness of pure being as they entwine in the matrix of the
three gnostic dimensions of spontaneous creativity (see cantos 7 and 10, and
also 69 and 70). The matrix is always still and silent. The media of body,
speech and mind partake of that stasis.

There is no movement in pure mind, no process, no development, no flow,
no continuum, no transformation, no change of any kind. Each moment is
complete and perfect in itself and always released at its inception.

Reflexive release of thought and sense impression is maintained without any
trace of duality by instantaneous potentiation of emotionally charged
experience:

26. Traceless Assimilation of Dualistic Perception at its Junction

Whatever occurs in the mind, quiescent or proliferating,
as one of the five 'poisons' or any other gnostic potency,
in its particularity, and in the very moment,
it recognizes itself, fully potentiates, and vanishes without trace:
the crucial carefree detachment at the subject/object junction,

the crucial self-sprung awareness as a bird's traceless trajectory,
the crucial all-inclusive spaciousness as a unitary billowing ocean,
and even the crucial focus upon the sublime mystery itself,
are assimilated from the beginning in every experience,
and mere recognition of this crux is the reality of release.

Whatever occurs externally as the manifold appearance of the five types of external objects (forms, sounds, smells, tastes and tangibles) or internally as some mental activity, at the very moment of its inception as a field it is seen just as it is, and by the force of its advent it is fully potentiated and then vanishes by itself—how could it possibly remain?—released without trace, and in that moment the three crucial functions—carefree detachment in whatever arises, access to wide-open spaciousness, and easy relaxation into the appearance upon its inception—are assimilated. Thus we capture the citadel that is the natural disposition of pure being.

Moreover, if there is no recognition an ordinary oblivious state of mind results; if it vanishes upon observation before its full potentiation an insuperable threshold has been reached; and if it does not vanish automatically then it has not been directly perceived. For these reasons the three aspects of complete perception are crucial.

Furthermore, in naturally-occurring gnosis, without any concern for happiness, without striving, we let go, unfocussed, in the here-and-now:

Forsaking the dangerous yearning for happiness
and just watching the natural flow of the mind as it is
both samsara and nirvana are neutralized,
the 'self' and 'other' tricks of dualistic perception
and the hindrance of fascination and obsession dissolve,
and conceptual structures collapse in carefree detachment;

every mental and intellectual trick is stilled
assimilated at the coincidence of the conception and the act.[52]

Acknowledgment, or recognition, of thoughts and emotions in the very moment of their occurrence potentiates them, and having reached their fullness they dissolve of their own accord, leaving no trace. Recognition occurs at the 'junction' of an appearance with mind. Recognition exhausts its potency (as in psycho-analysis?). In this way appearances are assimilated to their absence in pure being.

The door to the sublime mystery of gnosis has three keys. The first is the key of detachment from dualistic experience by holding attention at the coincidence of the mind and its object, at their 'point of union'. The second key is the indeterminate space of pristine awareness where all experience (thoughts, emotions, sense impressions) is left without trace like a bird's flight-path in the sky. The third is the key of the unitary or holistic spaciousness of being where every movement, occurrence or stirring is just another wave in the ocean (see also canto 50).

The all-inclusive, total non-focus has three key points: recognition, actualisation of potency and automatic dissolution.

The notion of linear time dissolved in reflexive release, all and everything is assimilated to the unbounded gnostic matrix:

27. Assimilation to the Immense Gnosis of the Super-Matrix

In the intrinsic gnostic dynamic of the super-matrix,
everything the very same at inception, in existence and upon release,
nothing unequal, nothing fixed, nothing unreleased,
total integration in the ultimate pure mind matrix is assured.

Just as matter and energy appear, exist, decay and vanish by themselves in the matrix of elemental space, never departing from that space, so all experience happens in the matrix of mind, abides in the matrix and finally is released in the matrix, never divorced from pristine gnostic emptiness, and inevitably assimilated to that matrix of realization.

Thus, at their advent, they arise as the same, undifferentiated;
in their abiding, they exist as the same, undifferentiated;
at their dissolution, they are released as the same, undifferentiated.

Even though arising differently, all appear the same in their spaciousness;
abiding differently, all exist the same in their spaciousness;
released differently all vanish the same in their spaciousness.[53]

There is no differentiation in the matrix so there is no distinction between the three temporal phases of beginning, middle and end (see also cantos 10 and 27). The rational mind is in abeyance so all experience is assimilated to the timeless realization where bare gnosis is congruent with the matrix of total equality. This realization is called in Sanskrit ekarasa, 'the one taste' (see also cantos 56 and 103).

Spontaneous assimilation of all experience to absence dissolves moral conditioning:

28. Assimilation to the Locus that Supersedes Causality

Involuntarily, in spontaneous gnosis
the free buddha-dynamic is naturally present,
and the pure mind that supersedes moral conditioning
is one with unchanging reality.

Because of the pollution of causality in conscientious meditation and such, goal-orientation prostituting this moment to the next, we are utterly convinced that unconditional gnosis is omnipresent in the here-and-now, and we let go completely, doing nothing at all.

I, the supreme source, supersede causality,
and beyond causality, there is no more activity;
this transcendent reality is pure mind,
and pure mind is at the heart of all experience.[54]

The simplistic idea that understanding of natural perfection effectuates no change in the rational mind is put to rest with the assimilation

90

of the idea that all causal thought processes might imminently cease. In the actuality of that event, after all experience has been realized as absence, and the locus of causality has been assimilated to pure mind, one of the primary results is the loss of karmic conditioning and particularly the replacement of moral conditioning with compassionate spontaneity.

The main thrust of the next section, that all experience is ineluctably bound to absence, all and everything entwined in an evanescent network of absence, is accompanied by the discovery of the gnostic dynamic of the nondual space of absence (see canto 18) which may be called pure will. Absence is a 'universal bind' in the sense that it forces all dualistically perceived (inner and outer, animate and inanimate, etc.) phenomena into ineffability, like the evanescent reflection of the moon on the surface of a lake. Illusory and insubstantial, all experience is predestined to disappear as soon as it arises. The gnostic dynamic (see canto 15) is pure meaning—clear light—present in the moment without any conceptual judgement, thought or intention. It can in no way be concretized, always inherent in momentary realization of absence. It is the nature of mind and reality:

I.3   The Ineluctable Bind of Absence

29. The Alpha-Pure Bind of Utter Emptiness

The dynamic of space that is the nature of absence
binds all experience without exception;
just as matter and energy are bound by elemental space,
so all events, self-imaged, are bound by super-emptiness.

Just as all worlds and life-forms, matter and energy, are bound together by the same elemental space, so the five self-imaged external fields (of vision, sound, taste, smell and sensation), together with the immediately released mental images and ideas arising internally, are bound by the same self-sprung awareness, which in turn is bound by the natural hyper-purity of emptiness. Nothing escaping that baseless total emptiness, it is called 'Samantabhadra's integrated matrix'.

Let me show you, verbally, the definitive meaning of natural perfection!

All body, speech and mind of buddha are the manifestation of Samantabhadra's immaculate nature, and because that is demonstrated to the migrant beings of the six realms in the sameness of time, indistinguishable from my own image, sentient beings are 'integrated in the matrix of diversity'. All events, all experience, free of any negative interpretation, dissolve into this unstructured matrix of simplicity and emptiness. This matrix is a vast ocean of my autonomous manifestation and all individual mandalas are contained in it from the beginning. Everything is unified from the beginning in this hyper-seal (Mahamudra) matrix that has no specific identity.

O great being! My manifestation is invisible, interfusing and absorbing all visible form and audible sound. It is called 'the secret matrix' and it arises autonomously as the Body of Samantabhadra.

My manifestation, arising everywhere out of nothing, is called 'the integrated matrix of all-embracing essential natural purity' and it arises autonomously as the Speech of Samantabhadra.

My manifestation arising autonomously as the identity of every word and thought, is called 'the integrated matrix of naturally empty recollection and reflection' and it arises as the Mind of Samantabhadra.

O great being! The man or woman aware of the timeless sameness of all buddhas past, present and future is integrated into the matrix called, 'the unitary matrix of Samantabhadra'.

In that authentic reality, just as it is,
its timeless expression, its original radiance,
shines like the sun's rays

in a pellucid unclouded sky;
that unstained essential being,
the true unitary essence,
that is my mandala.

All consciousness integrated,
all separate realities consumed,
everything is the mind of Samantabhadra,
and this concept-free buddhahood,
by destroying the tyranny of subtle constructs,
allows the unveiled light to shine;
but since nothing can see itself,
just so I cannot be seen.

O great being! All apparent materiality is my display. Thus I, Samantabhadra, inseparable from all living beings, perform the specific ideal conduct in every variant prejudicial manner in the concentrated absorption known as 'the exhaustion of every possible expression of transmission', and in that I am indivisible from unmanifest space.

O great being! Such activity, the behavior of Samantabhadra, is called 'identity emergent in the three gnostic dimensions' and implies the view called 'the pristine awareness of natural perfection', wherein the immaculate cause is the fruition of buddhahood. In that moment, self-sprung, uncreated, the pristine awareness of my buddha-body, the display of my buddha-speech, and the activity of my buddha-mind are appearing in a unified hyper-expanse. This manifestation of immutable awareness appears of its own accord; in the process of imploding experience, all temporal elaboration dissolves by itself; consciousness emerges naturally like the sky: attaining mastery of the heart-essence in its concrete appearances, I am Samantabhadra, 'the master of all mandalas'.[55]

In the momentary process of assimilation of each experience to absence, the focuses upon aspects of mind are spontaneously assimilated to emptiness. Emptiness may be seen as the emptiness of free will, which in its pure empty nature, is the dynamic that binds all experience to absence. This is the ineluctable bind that grants us the opportunity of immediate recognition of the nature of mind. The dynamic of self-sprung awareness is the ineluctable bind of emptiness connecting the subjective and objective poles of all experience, and this bind implies an inevitable dissolution of appearances at the very moment of their inception.

The mandalas of natural perfection and non-specific, unaffected, ideal conduct having been revealed as the bind of absence, as the universal bind of utter emptiness (see also canto 28), the various techniques and all striving on a causal progressive path are shown to be effete:

30. The Bind of ` Absence Supersedes Rational Endeavor

Samsara merely a label, goal-oriented endeavor is undermined;
and in the emptiness that cannot be improved or impaired,
freedom is just another word, and there is no nirvana:
striving in the ten techniques accomplishes nothing.

Natural gnosis is innocent of moral conditioning, untouched by virtue and vice. Thoroughly mired as they are in confusion, those who teach and believe in the provisional transmission that relies on the principle of causality can never attain release. Surely natural perfection is realized in the absence of moral conditioning!

In the nature of mind uncreated from the first,
the ultimate nature of thought and intellect is revealed.
Insight verbalized, cloaking its own truth,
wordsmanship and rational thought promoted on high—
surely that is one of the lower hells.
Belief in labeled physical and verbal structures
built by the intellect, obscures the true reality—
is there any better antidote than the nature of mind?
Free of all compulsion, samsara and nirvana deconstructed,
can that be anything other than natural perfection itself?[56]

The ten techniques are view, samaya-commitment, empowerment, mandala, levels of attainment, paths, ideal conduct, pristine awareness, the goal and reality: these ten techniques realized as absence is the view of natural perfection:

Pure mind is like space,
and in reality, in the nature of mind that is like space,
there is no view to cultivate, no commitment to observe,
no ideal conduct to strive for, no pristine awareness to unveil,
no spiritual levels, no path to tread,
no subtle experience, no duality and no union,
and thus there is no transmission regarding mind,
and, in the absence of evaluation, no resolution of precepts:
that is the view of the pure mind of natural perfection.[57]

O great courageous being!
'There is no view to cultivate':
since the root of experience is oneself
and one cannot see oneself,
I teach there is nothing upon which to meditate
and therefore no view to cultivate.

'There is no samaya commitment to observe':
our uncontrollable, irrepressible mind
is self-sprung awareness,
a samaya that requires no observance.

'There is no ideal conduct to strive for':
natural perfection timelessly supersedes causality,
and since ideal conduct is an effect predicated upon a cause,
and natural perfection produces no effect
there can never be any ideal conduct to strive for;
and so I teach 'there is no striving for ideal conduct'.

'There is no path to tread':
all buddha past, present and future
and all sentient beings of the triple world
tread the same path, the path of pure mind,
buddha and sentient beings are one in pure mind,
and mind has no path to tread in mind.

'There are no spiritual levels to purify':
to those who aspire to release contingent upon purification
on this level of the spacious reality of pure mind,
on this level of the spacious reality of pure mind
I could never teach techniques of purification.

'Pristine awareness cannot be conceived as an object':
the objective field has always been self-sprung awareness,
and awareness cannot take awareness as an object.[58]

Yoked to the universal bind of absence, samsara and nirvana are just names. Specifically, the bind of absence refers to the absence of the ten techniques (see canto 11).

Mundane ambition in general, and meditation practice in the lower approaches in particular, is unavailing. The universal bind of absence obliges us to do nothing at all:

31. Nonaction as the Actual Bind

Exhausting exercises exacting struggle and strain,
with short-lived product, like a child's sand castle,
and, moreover, all moral endeavor,
all experience is caught from the beginning in the bind of absence.

Tantric meditation practice involving a gradual progression from the creative phase to emptiness (the goal of the fulfilment phase) may prove to be valid on a delusive conventional level, but ultimately, through the apprehension of absence, all such endeavor in the media of body, speech and mind is like building doomed sand-castles in the playground. The yogin or yogini binds all moral endeavor and conditioning in the hyper-nonaction that supersedes all hypocritical exertion:

Pure mind is inscrutable; who knows its purpose?
And what is stainless virtue?[59]
Nonaction is the precept,
so try effortlessness![60]

Furthermore:

O Great being!
We strive in meditation because we desire excellence,
but any striving precludes attainment;
excellent from the beginning, excellence is self-sprung,
and meditation distorts the buddha-dynamic;
if we try to devise enlightenment,
we will not encounter our true nature for an aeon.

O Great being!
Do not strive to concentrate!
Do not try to demonstrate primal awareness!
It is pointless to recite mantra or seed syllables,
superfluous to form ritual gestures with your hands,
or to visualize the radiation and absorption of light.

Just resting here, there is constant spontaneity,
just resting naturally, no one contrives anything;
unseeking, staying just as we are,
nonaction is revealed as supreme activity;
and realizing that, we abandon deliberate acts,
doing nothing, we stay with the zing of reality!
Whoever rests in things just as they are
attains infallible uncontrived perfection.
What is real is our unerring, uncontrived nature

and reality is its infallible essence:
there is no 'buddhahood', only reality just as it is.[61]

Moreover:

After failing to realize the uncontrived natural state,
consecrating the inner and outer, matter and energy,
and through ritual enactment in derivative total presence,
evoking the awareness buddha-deity in meditation,
making momentary offering, inviting union,
and then absorption and dissolution—
such repeated visualization and dissolution,
a childish game like building sand castles,
works against my simple, uncontrived reality.[62]

To build sand-castles is a metaphor for ordinary goal-oriented activity, consisting of physical, verbal and mental behavior (see canto 20), but here the image refers specifically to the meditation process of visualization in the creative stage. We are not told categorically to abandon tantric practice, but here mahayoga (the first of the inner tantric approaches) is stated as counter productive in the Great Perfection. The hyper-yogin or yogini, on the other hand, stays effortlessly in the space of reality. Atiyoga is the bind of natural contemplation (the buddha-dynamic) in the space of absence where no imperative to do anything on a causal path can arise. Causality and striving, however, are of course also bound in absence:

32. Bound in Freedom from Goal-oriented Endeavor

Now, the ati-yogin, the yogin of the essence,
forsakes all provisional techniques
designed for straight cause and effect babes
on the lesser, laddered, path,
and binds the gnostic dynamic
that supersedes all clever technique
to the yoke of the nonactive sky.

While we are young we play games; when we grow old, games are tiresome. Similarly, while we are psychologically immature, the eight lower approaches seem to provide valid experience (*dharma*), but when we grow up, the only reality (*dharma*) that matters is the consummation of Ati, living in the here-and-now, where all impulses and intentions, indeed, all experiences whatsoever, are spontaneously consumed, and where pure being is spontaneously accomplished.

The yogin or yogini realizes the intrinsic gnosis and spontaneous perfection of pure being and stays in the natural flow without striving in the ten techniques:

O great being!
Pure mind is the king of kings!
Everything made is made by pure mind
and nothing is made other than as pure mind.
Pure mind is flawless from the first
always existing, forever infallible,
and what is infallible cannot be adduced as true or false,
and all rational processes are superseded.
We may be ignorant of its timeless perfection,
but if we try to attain it through deliberate meditative effort,
there is no greater obstacle to pure and total presence.

With homeless mind, unreflecting, without any compulsion,
naturally abiding in the nonconceptual field of sameness,
complete and perfect from the first, without the slightest aspiration
whoever lives in such pure pleasure
he literally becomes the essence of all experience.

Without distinguishing between the purpose of self and others,
that one single essence integrating all and everything,
imperceptible, shines as the timeless buddha-mind,
and unveiled, it images the minds of all sentient beings.

O great being, listen!
I, the supreme source, fulfill all beings' needs
and what I do, need not be imitated.
I do not give contingent instruction,
for everything finite is perfect in me.
Complete and perfect from the beginning,
cultivation of view and meditation is futile;
immaculate from the first,
striving to keep samaya vows is useless.

All and everything abides in timeless total presence,
so no need to sustain the gnostic masters' level,
or to climb the ten bodhisattva stages.
In the light of unsought, timeless spontaneity,
striving for ideal conduct is utterly superfluous.
Self-sprung awareness takes no object
so it is futile to look for gnostic awareness.

Due to oneness, the unity of pure pleasure and pure being with mind,
in the absence of past, present and future, in the absence of time,
the teacher, the teaching, the assembly, the time and the place,
all particularities, all times and places, are one,
and since all is one, everything is perfect and complete in me,
and since natural perfection is perfect and complete in me,
as explained above, it is unavailing to strive to accomplish
the view, conduct, ideal conduct, commitment, levels and paths.

In ignorance of that, if we try to force it,
we violate the reality beyond causality,
we fail to encounter the pure pleasure of nonaction,
and we are rendered stupid by the disease of exertion.

Furthermore, since the natural perfection superseding causality
is not an arena for the disconnected and luckless,
the latter must practice on the graduated, causal path.[63]

Less favored yogins, unable to realize natural perfection,
cling to the provisional teaching of the causal paths.
If I revealed the perfection of our timeless sphere of activity
to those unfortunate believers in the laws of causality,
underestimating the capacity of their own minds
they would tend to inflate it or to denigrate it,
and born into the six realms, they would remain forever in samsara.[64]

The gnostic dynamic lies beyond all intention and motivation; it cannot be formulated in language; it is beyond dualistic experience (see canto 18). 'Doing nothing' is the praxis, implying the spontaneous dissolution of impulse and drive, compulsion and habit. 'Doing nothing' is the best way of accomplishing this imperative—although we will not admit any causal relationship. 'Doing nothing' does not imply a life of passivity or inaction, because the gnostic dynamic is a continuum of spontaneous creativity and synchronicity (see also cantos 74 and 75). Monastic or tantric practices and lifestyles need not be abandoned. The precept is to abandon all the stress and striving of ambition, and deliberate, committed, effort. Elements of the ten techniques may remain the husk or outer form of action, but the attitude is now informed by nonaction, the nonreactive propensity of the sky (see canto 40).

Rational thought to attain our ambitions and conditioned moral conduct lead us into the ways of samsara:

33. The Promise of Goal-Directed Activity is Fraudulent

Deliberate action deceives—look at treacherous samsara!
Diligence corrupts—consider the vicious cycle of suffering!
Neither virtue nor vice can stop the turning of the wheel,
and accumulated karmic propensity may lead up or down
but it gives no chance of release from existence.

Whatever physical, verbal and mental agenda we follow, we are cheated of gnosis by the ignorance evinced by the multifarious delusive appearances of the moment that are the product of past lives. Whatever effort we make obscures the essence of gnosis, and reborn as a denizen of hell, a hungry ghost, an animal or such, through the karma of goal-directed striving—behold the changes of samsara! Even engagement in a virtuous program can only lead to a divine or human body with their attendant pleasures, with subsequent changes. Vice matures into the woes of the three lower types of existence, where we must return again and again without chance of release.

Too clever by half, hoist by our own petard,
we cannot go beyond the triple world.[65]

Craving pure pleasure is an attachment sickness;
if it is not cured by the panacea of imperturbable sameness,
even the causal bases of higher states are infected by passion,
and the vicious circle perpetuated, no peace can be found.[66]

If we possess the intellectual ability to effectuate any desired result in samsara, then we are proud enough to believe in the efficacy of some clever technique to attain what is outside the field of reference of samsaric delusion and its dynamic (see canto 17), and this may lead us to create an agenda of deliberate spiritual praxis. The increasing oblivion created by the effort that agenda requires reinforces belief in the principles of causality and the promise of our vaunted technique turns to ashes and we are left hanging, disappointed in the vault of samsara. Constant and diligent in practice of morality, still the virtuous suffer and the vicious prosper and the wheel continues to turn. Even when the promise of rational goal-directed activity is fulfilled, satisfaction is only momentary. Any system in which we place our trust to release us from the trap merely pushes us more deeply into the mire.

In the absence of moral discrimination automatically we surrender to reality itself:

34. Nonaction is Integral to the Dynamic of Pure Being

For the yogin in whom the flow of good and bad ceases
there is no duality of union with and separation from reality,
and that hyper-yogin, certain in the great mystery,

*effortlessly reaches the natural state of original perfection
and abides forever in the royal citadel of pure being.*

Free of moral consciousness, the yogin or yogini unstirring from
the brilliant emptiness of gnosis, which is clear as the sky, 'holds
the royal citadel of pure being', and there he remains constantly
in the original disposition of nonactive natural purity.

*This baseless, rootless reality
just let be—how amazing!*[67]

*All that appears is uniquely one
and let no one try to change it!
In the majesty of uncontrived equality
lies the dynamic of unthinking pure being.*[68]

Stated in brief, insight into the emptiness of thought binds all experience to
absence:

35. The Epitome of the Bind of Absence

*In the very moment, therefore, of an event occurring,
whoever recognizes the language of biased projection
and morally discriminating goal-directed endeavor
as unreal, and like the nonactive sky,
he catches all experience in the snare of absence.*

All the actual and possible worlds of samsara and nirvana—at its
starting point, in process or at fruition—and every image, sound
and thought projection, is gnostic envisionment, and at the
moment of appearance it is caught in equivocal evanescent illusion
just as the image of the moon in water at the very moment of its
reflection is caught in nonexistence. Since gnosis is bound by sky-
like brilliant emptiness, an all-embracing utter emptiness, it is
cognized as the uncontrived space and unadulterated luminosity
of the natural clarity of nonmeditation.

O great being! The aspiration to realize pure mind
can only be fulfilled through an absence of craving,
so do not try at all to rest in unthinking sameness;
but relaxing easily in a nondiscriminatory field,
stay spontaneously in that unstirring space!

Mind is the essence of the natural state,
where all experience is known by its zing.
Let no one try to correct its natural perfection!
Let no one try to realize anything but its natural face!

Buddha sought but only ever found spaciousness:
this was done in the past; it is unnecessary to repeat it now;
what was established then need not be re-established;
so, unthinking, without purpose, remain in sameness.

O great being, listen!
Buddhas of ancient time
sought nothing but mind itself,
changing nothing from just how it is;
without cultivating any structured state
mind was realized without concept:
buddhas of the present and of the future
will also realize it through unthinking sameness.[69]

If all manner of experience is the evidence of a dualizing, biased, rational mind seeking to express itself, as such it is the outer reflection of inner linguistic structure. In so far as language by its nature is discriminatory, it provides evidence of the basic split of the mind that expresses itself in terms of good and bad, right and wrong and so on. It is also the tool whereby the tendencies of mind to conceive of reality as substantial are concretized. Qualitative, or moral, discrimination is the causal basis of all intention to change ourselves and to modify experience of ourselves as it arises in reality. Sky-like reality, however, cannot be modified—nothing can be done with it.

Resolution, as the final section in the description of absence as a theme of natural perfection, implies irreversible (see canto 41) recognition of the nondual nature of mind. Here the apparent process of dualistic perception is resolved in absence; all concepts are perceived as absence; conflicting emotion is utterly resolved in the absence of likes and dislikes and effort and striving. As resolution is attained in the nonconceptual view of sameness, without the movement of projected entities, the notion of linear time is superseded. This resolution is a culmination in every moment, a never-ending consummation. In this way, experientially, resolution, in a manner of speaking, is 'leaping through' or 'jumping through' the apparent concrete, dualistic, conflicting appearances of the moment:

I.4   Resolution in Absence

Resolution in absence is to establish both experientially and intellectually, once and for all, that all experience is insubstantial.

36. Extreme Beliefs are Resolved in Their Intrinsic Absence

Resolution in absence is the heart of the matter:
all the various events of samsara and nirvana
in their inherent absence belie their existence,
in their unceasing appearance belie their nonexistence,
neither existent nor nonexistent, being both is belied,
and since both are absent, being neither is also denied.
In the intrinsic absence of assertion and negation
reality, indefinable, cannot be indicated as any one thing.

Since gnosis and all experience arising in its scope lack any intrinsic nature or self or *ens*, it transcends existence. But since it appears without ceasing, it goes beyond nonexistence. Since it is neither existent nor nonexistent, it cannot be both, and likewise it cannot be neither either—it belies all expression.

In the very moment of appearance whatever arises is the buddha-dynamic in which the four modes of extreme belief simply melt away:

105

The filth of the four extreme beliefs is naturally pristine.[70]

Like a shimmering reflection in water,
appearance is not simply nonexistent,
and yet it is not existent—
beyond both existence and nonexistence,
the yogin or yogini has no chatter in the mind.
Gnosis in itself is unoriginated
and appearances never crystallize;
the attributes of gnosis are intangible
and the fruition of gnosis is uncontrived.[71]

Extreme views are reflected as either positive or negative assertions about the nature of an event and may develop into extreme attitudes to objects and people. Assertion or denial that an event happened at such and such a time and place, in such a way, that it had or did not have this or that quality, that it was good or bad, are extreme views. Philosophically we may say that reality is not existent, nonexistent, both nor neither, and the refutation of extreme views by the assertion of their intrinsic absence leaves, in Aristotelian terms, 'the excluded middle' as the sole reality. Superseding the dualistic categories of logic, nondual reality is the excluded middle because here no reflexive judgment of appearance in any dialectic terms can be made.[72]

Resolution cannot be reached by suppressing our habitual tendency to grasp at whatever appears to be concrete and secure; but attachment to conceptual thought simply vanishes when we regard fixed mental states—our own and others—as pitiful and worthy of kindness. Intolerance vanishes when idealism is naturally resolved in basic compassion:

37. Beyond Grasping: Resolution of Fixation Through Kindness

So reality is primordial purity,
yet the babes who are careless of that
stay attached to their various ideas and opinions.
What mania to believe in concrete ideas!
How sad to believe in an 'I' that is actually absent!

How disheartening to make an argument out of nothing!
How we love those fervent believers, eternal migrants in samsara!

Their inner eye blinded by varieties of conventional and religious opinions, the babes fail to see the reality of nonaction that lacks any discriminatory activity. Fixated upon one of the eight lower approaches, they are afflicted by belief in a notion of self that is colored by their respective ideology. Deluded by their cherished dogma, they exhaust themselves by compulsively taking sides in defense of their biased opinions. We bear love to those migrants on the wheel of cyclical existence who are caught on the horns of dualism.

By practicing meditation to attain awakening
we miss the involuntary awareness within;
by cultivating conventional virtue
we miss our intrinsic thoughtless presence;
by belief in words and letters
we miss the unspoken sovereign secret spell;
by belief in birth and death—a crucial point—
we miss our unborn and undying nature.

By the flickering of all kinds of wishes and intentions
we miss the thoughtless dimension of pure being;
by believing in our own samsaric stupidity
we miss the total clarity of the dimension of perfect enjoyment;
by attachment to beings' corporeal form
we miss their buddha-identity in the magical dimension.

By perceiving these three dimensions as plurality
we miss their ineluctable nature;
by differentiating view and meditation
we miss their indivisible unitary nature;
by regarding all phenomenal experience as mind
we miss the universal gnostic actuality.

But in essential total presence we can miss nothing,
so how can we conceive of error or obscuration?
There never has been any glitch or veil
and pure being has never been enshrouded,
so what affliction to dualize so insidiously!

Pure being is uncreated, spontaneity,
so what confusion to seek it as something specific!
Gnosis is uncreated and unmotivated,
so how tiresome it is to describe it!
Devoid of spontaneous insight into emptiness,
how pathetic our deluded intellect![73]

The four extreme beliefs are at the essence of all argumentative propositions. All views about the nature of existence may be subjected to the same dialectic however, and it appears that all beings of the six realms are caught on the wheel of life due to their opinions. From the standpoint of the yogin or yogini bound by absence, preconceptions about his or her own and others' faults and inadequacies are easily dissolved by the compassion that arises through recognition of suffering. Similarly, potential attachment to a person or thing to whom the yogin or yogini is attracted due to the tendency to project concrete attributes compounding another self or object 'out there' is dissolved through spontaneous love. Or negative attachment may be overcome by the perception of others engaged in conflict or dispute as objects of compassion due to their ignorance of the nature of mind. Like Nagarjuna, the yogin or yogini has no position to defend, so our attachment withers on the vine. Samantabhadra's compassionate warning is addressed to Buddhists who strive for enlightenment as a goal to be attained in the future (see canto 17).

The emotional torment involved in the desperate effort of people to attain existential freedom based on moral discrimination is likened to a summer storm that nurtures the seeds of samsara that grow into organic systems of mental complexes, eventually yielding the crops of the six samsaric realms. Moral duality must be resolved:

38. Resolution Beyond Moral Conditioning

White or black, virtuous or vicious,
all clouds equally obscure the sun of intrinsic gnosis.
Stressed by the lightening of frustrated discriminating endeavor
an incessant downpour of delusive satisfaction and grief
waters the seeds of samsara, ripening the harvest of the six realms,
and we love all the tormented beings!

The lightning of tense struggle for principled action demanding rejection of the bad and cultivation of the good strikes through the clouds, and a downpour of the gamut of pleasure and pain is the consequence. The hyper-yogin or yogini intuiting the pure reality of the moment feels compassion for the innumerable wanderers in endless samsara.

Lacking an unfabricated, non-supportive ground
corporeality traps radiant tonic appearance;
lacking an unbiased, impartial mind
self-assertive opinion bars the natural state;
lacking confidence in the ultimate freedom of nonaction
moody expectation precludes realization;
lacking crucial unsought natural relaxation
to depend upon the causal route obscures gnosis.[74]

The great Chinese master Hashang also taught the truth that black and white clouds equally obscure the sun, although at that time the small-minded could not contain it. It is kept hidden from adherents of the lower, progressive, approaches, because they cannot comprehend it, and they would denigrate it and fall into a lower rebirth through that karma.

'Do not utter even a word of this in the company of Disciples and Hermits. If you want to know the reason why, it is because they would be frightened and abhorrent and faint away when hearing it.

109

They would distrust the secret tantras and lose interest in them, and as for the karmic retribution they would necessarily plunge into the great hell. So we should not speak even upwind of them, not to mention our teaching them and their listening.' Speech Vajra asked, 'O Bhagavan, why is that so?' And Bhagavan replied, 'Disciples and Hermits are small-minded and cannot become suitable recipients of the tantras for innumerable aeons. It is as easy for them to comprehend natural perfection as it as for a camel to pass through the eye of a needle.'[75]

Do not talk about unconditional self-sprung awareness to those who believe in cause and effect—keep it hidden from them![76]

Conditioned to moral dualism we are doomed to frustration. Clinging to the illusion of our personal version of the world (views and opinions), we make distinctions between right and wrong that are emotionally motivated, and we act out of fear, hatred, desire and attachment, pride and prejudice. Pleasure and pain, conditioned by success or failure, reinforces our tendency to grasp and cling. The self-referential dynamic of action and reaction, generates feedback-loops of genetic and karmic conditioning, evolving into complex structures of environments and sentient organisms. Thus, the psychological environments of gods, titans, humans, animals, hungry ghosts and hell-beings are created. It is not 'evil' that obscures reality but the regular functions of the dualized intellect.

Hashang Mahayana (or Hwa-shang Mo-ho-yen), a Chan (Zen) master, advocating the doctrine of 'sudden enlightenment' at the great Samye debate in the 8th century famously employed the image of the sun equally obscured by black or white clouds. In the eyes of gradualists, who have formed the pragmatic Tibetan mainstream, this has remained a paradigm of heretical thought, which is one reason why it should be hidden from their contemporary brethren (see also canto 116).

What we Dzogchen candidates really need is a precept to resolve the duality of causal conditioning in the indeterminate immediacy of the moment:

39. Advice on Resolving Moral Duality

In the ultimate definitive analysis
just as golden chains and hempen ropes are equally binding,
so the sacred and the profane do both enslave us;
and just as white and black clouds are equally enshrouding,
so virtue and vice alike veil gnosis:
the yogin or yogini who understands that
fosters release from moral conditioning.

Pristine gnosis is as pure and simple as naked pure being and like the core of the sun it is untouched by anything whatsoever, utterly signless and transcendent. Yet all dogma, attachment and striving, without any exception, equally enshrouds it and binds it, just as white and black clouds are equally veiling, and golden chain and hempen rope are equally binding.

Golden chains and hempen ropes are equally binding.[77]

Understand that gnostic experience cannot be defined by the intellect. Accordingly, treat everything as inalienable from gnostic awareness and nowhere fixed and nowhere locatable! Treat everything whatsoever as open-ended! Treat every appearance whatsoever as unoriginated! Treat all and everything as unborn and unmoving! Experience all coming and going as nondual! Perceive nondual experience (gnosis) as final total freedom! Know all experience concept-free and thoughtless! Realize all experience unwavering from natural clarity.[78]

'The sacred' may be interpreted as religion, doctrine, dogma, 'spirituality', virtue, truth or 'The Good', whereas 'the profane' can be secularism, materialism, nihilism or evil. Attachment to the moral duality of right and wrong, good and bad, is the crux of the web of cause and effect that binds us in the trap of futile goal-directed activity. Repetitive moral decision-making conditions us to conceptual tyranny. Prejudice thwarts clear vision. Belief in moral dualism and causality and moral conditioning is dissolved in one single moment of penetrating awareness into the basic absence of the here-and-now.

Moral duality is resolved by pristine awareness alone arising by itself in the timeless moment of synchronicity:

40. The Essential Resolution

As self-sprung awareness arises from within
and the dark night of causality fades,
the clouds of moral duality melt away
and the sun of nondual truth dawns in the field of reality.
This is final, ultimate resolution,
induced by the absence of the ten methods,
exalted above all progressive approaches.

When the conditioned mind dissolves by itself into self-sprung pure being structured as space like the darkness of night vanishing at dawn, and all concepts of good and bad naturally melt away like a mass of clouds evaporating, then the clear-light mind-essence dawns in the field of reality like the sun in the sky. The clear revelation of the nature of the ten techniques as absence is likened to the sun arising in the pellucid, ordinary sky.

This pure mind, the ubiquitous essence—
its nature is spontaneously, originally, perfect;
so strenuously engaging with the ten techniques
is unnecessary, superfluous.

My nature is like elemental space
(that all-applicable simile):
existing in pure space, we need not strive for it;
existing in pure space, space is our striving;
all-creating space transcends all exertion.
Pure mind, the ubiquitous essence, is like that,
so transcending all cognitive activity

I am inscrutable and cannot be cultivated.
All the ten techniques are likewise transcended,
so nothing can be done to affect me.
Those who try to approach me on a causal path,
desirous of catching a glimpse of my face,
seeking me through the ten techniques,
fall straight to earth like a tenderfoot sky-walker,
tumbling down due to deliberate effort.[79]

In the tantric context where the aspirant strives for 'enlightenment' through the ten techniques (and also in the psychological context where the patient strives for release in therapy and so on), when the absence inherent in the form of his striving becomes evident an ultimate revelation of the nature of mind can occur (see also cantos 11 and 30). But seeking and striving preclude accomplishment.

In the moment of spontaneous intuition of absence, the nature of thought is resolved as pure vision, the dualizing function of the conceptual mind is suspended and all experience is consumed by the zero dimension of pure being:

41. Thought is Resolved in Pure Vision

The intangible samadhi that lacks any field of meditation,
pristine, simple, intrinsic gnosis,
consumes all events in consummate resolution,
and all experience spent, itself is consumed.
Since the consuming or non-consuming is resolved in absence,
its existence as ineffable is never in question.
What is, is a vast nonreferential panorama,
all experience consummate, 'no mind!'
and that is the yogin's delight!

A single field of dynamic space
integrating past, present and future,
an unbroken holistic field of reality,
this is the arena shared by buddhas and masters of gnosis.

113

Gnosis, all-consuming in its bare simplicity, itself is the dynamic of pure being in its own disposition, consuming all experience in unconditional, alpha-purity. All motivation and consequently all phenomena are ultimately consumed by it. It is called 'experience' or 'phenomena' or '*dharma*', but even its name is consumed in the conviction of its ineffability. The hyper-yogin or yogini realizing this gnosis in nonreferential freedom share a common arena with all buddha of past, present and future and all the great yogins. Buddhas and yogins and yoginis, all sharing the same field of thought, thoughts dawn freely and unrestrictedly without any bias, 'a carefree mind unfolding pure joy'.

Regarding the intuition of nonmeditative, natural samadhi:

Reality is blocked by concentration-meditation,
while in self-manifest samadhi, free of motivation,
reality, unstructured, is coterminous with the sky,
and no beliefs can be cherished about that field of pure vision.
Free of the four extreme beliefs, buddha is intrinsic gnosis:
beyond existence and nonexistence is pure being,
and the sole buddhahood that is beyond reckoning,
and pure being that holds assertion and negation as one,
and naturally blissful intrinsic gnosis beyond belief![80]

Then, intuiting reality, the joy springs easily:

What pleasure intuiting natural perfection,
this vast nonreferential, unmotivated mandala![81]

Superseding objectifying thought processes, the ultimate experience surpasses the intellect. The referential nature of thought definitively resolved, the notion of linear time is superseded and so joy arises (see cantos 18, 23 and 56). Freed of the parameters of temporality, thinking unfolds as the pure vision or creative imagination of Samantabhadra or 'buddha past, present and future'. It is revealed by unintentional absorption in the nature of mind, the spaciousness of the excluded middle.

With the resolution of all experience in inexpressible emptiness, the conventional idea of 'language' is also superseded. There is no duality in natural perfection:

42. Resolution in Nameless Super-Emptiness

The unchanging and indivisible, non-composite matrix,
the matrix of self-sprung awareness beyond endeavor,
the ineffable matrix where labels are a joke,
this is the nonactive space of Samantabhadra,
where everything is the spaciousness of Samantabhadra,
where empty appearances are neither good nor bad.

Absence reified as some 'thing' is delusive projection;
but in the very moment of projection,
there is neither delusion nor non-delusion,
and everything is resolved in hyper-namelessness:
that is the way of natural perfection.

The unchanging face of gnosis, free of all endeavor, beyond thought and expression, lacking intention and goal-directed activity, all-inclusive and indivisible, this is the -nature of Samantabhadra. Whatever good or bad experience of samsara or nirvana appearing in his space is actually absent from the start, so its existence is purely nominal, merely label. Then nominal existence, subjected to intense investigation, is resolved in pure nameless reality—inconceivable and ineffable.

Brilliant, without a shadow,
in the all-embracing awakened matrix of mind
veils are not imaged, obstruction is not reified
and so there is no awakening, and not even the notion of buddha;
there is no attachment, so no notion of sentient beings;
there is no thought, so no notion of delusion;
there is no fixation, so no notion of discursive thought;

there is no desire, so no notion of propensity;
there is no past, so no notion of 'future';
there is no present, so no notion of 'passion';
there is no absolute truth, so no notion of 'conventional truth';
there is no knowledge, so no notion of 'ignorance';
there is no buddha, so no notion of 'sentient beings';
there is no teaching, so no notion of 'the teacher'.[82]

Samantabhadra's matrix is 'nonactive' space in the sense that pure being and the field of reality offer no reaction to the activity of body, speech and mind; devoid of habit-traces, predisposition and instinctive reaction patterns, it remains, therefore, forever nonactive. The resolution of all experience in 'namelessness' is the resolution of linguistically conceived duality (such as true or false, black and white, sacred and profane) in the absence of any point of reference.

Finally, all dualities are resolved in the space of absence:

43. Absence: a Final Synopsis

In all experience of samsara and nirvana, inner and outer,
convinced of the absence of both delusion and freedom from delusion,
we do not seek to abandon samsara to attain nirvana;
with conviction in the absence of birth and birthlessness
belief in life and death, existence and nonexistence, is suspended;
with conviction in the absence of right and wrong,
there is equanimity in the absence of value judgement,
and all experience is resolved in Samantabhadra's matrix.

When nothing whatsoever is perceived as real in essence, the duality of delusion and freedom from delusion is resolved, and thereupon we lose any preference for samsara or nirvana. The concepts of birth and birthlessness transcended, we no longer believe in life and death. Transcending the notions of pure and impure, all discrimination and value judgement ends. All experience ends in the all-consuming ground, in the dynamic mind of Samantabhadra which is the actuality of absence; all virtue and vice, every cause and effect, all moral conditioning, positive and negative attitudes, both sacred and profane, unfold into timeless sameness, resolved in gnosis, empty and insubstantial.

From the perspective of pristine awareness there is no objective field to investigate. Nothing has ever happened, nothing will ever happen and nothing is happening just now. There is no karma and no latent tendencies (no susceptibility or proclivity) and no ignorance. There is no mind, no intellect, and no insight. There is no samsara, no nirvana, nor even gnosis. Nothing at all appears in pristine awareness. Beware! Self-sprung awareness has no life-force, so morality is superseded. Be careful! Beware! No one is doing anything, so there is no outer field of activity and no inner mind![83]

*****

Inscrutable gnostic space, where everything happens,
immaculate in the absence of moral conditioning,
a sky-like reality without striving and effort,
is revealed here in this bejewelled commentary to the first theme.

You brightest, most intelligent people,
scholars with vast learning and experience,
gods, demigods, and masters of gnosis,
and you innumerable oath-bound protectors—rejoice!

The first vajra-theme of *The Treasury of Natural Perfection*, teaching the utter ineffability of all experience, is completed.

The Second Vajra Theme: Openness
'All Experience Is the Unrestricted Freedom of Openness'

II.1 The Disclosure of Openness

44. Openness Revealed In Brief

*Now that you have sussed absence as the natural mode of being
I shall show you the nature of openness.*

*The transmission of atiyoga, the apex approach,
like space, is without center or boundary;
higher than the highest, it is Samantabhadra's vast mind,
an immense seamless super-sameness.*

The brilliant emptiness of gnosis with boundless extension is the
seamlessly open dimension of pure being; the transmission of
atiyoga, the vast mental space of Samantabhadra, free and
unrestricted as the sky, is the inexpressible 'zero dimension of no-
mind'.

*In the inexpressible nature of mind,
words have no association or context:
I, Samantabhadra, reveal
the inconceivable and unutterable.*[84]

*The transmission of atiyoga, the apex approach,
the highest peak of all, like Sumeru, the king of mountains,
higher than the highest, the vast mind of Samantabhadra
transfigures the minor approaches by its natural power.*

119

Likewise gnosis is autonomous in its matrix of sameness;
in the unitary super-matrix realization and non-realization,
release and non-release, are hyper-sameness.[85]

Openness is the totality of Samantabhadra expressed in terms of the unconditional freedom of all and everything, without bias or exclusivity in the all-inclusive spaciousness of experience of samsara and nirvana. Openness as the absolutely indeterminate nature of pure mind is boundless extension; a total perspective that admits neither center nor boundary, neither spatial nor temporal distinction, no limitation, fragmentation or partiality, no gaps, lacunae, fissures or interruptions or intervals in its seamless, momentary expression. 'Openness' however does not convey the dynamic of this hyperspatial extension. Never existing in any final mode, openness is a nonspatial, atemporal experience of spontaneity and that is the moment by moment transmission of Samantabhadra.

'Words without association' are words without history, without spatial or temporal reference, or secret words that cannot be thought or spoken— words to which there can be no attachment, the spontaneous expression of pristine, ever-fresh, pure mind.

Every moment of experience, without beginning middle or end, is the transmission of Samantabhadra:

45. Everything is Always Open

All inner and outer experience manifest
and unmanifest pure mind,
unstirring from unstructured reality,
ineffable, zero-dimensional,
remains open, constantly, without interval.

Since all experience is gnostic projection, its nature unrestricted and open-ended, unconditional and indeterminate, the starting point is openness; since all experience is gnostic projection, by the intellect inconceivable and imperceptible, the path is openness; since all experience is gnostic projection, free of expectation and fear, without potential for change, fruition is openness. Since appearances cannot move out of gnosis, the spacious field of reality is also openness; and gnosis being the nature of pure mind the field of release is also seamless, timeless openness: openness is 'unstirring reality'.

Governing all the ways of samsara and nirvana
nonaction alone dominates all and everything;
there is no limitation or reification anywhere;
nothing moves out of the matrix of nonaction,
the nonaction which is Samantabhadra's matrix.[86]

All experience is the projection of gnosis—an auto-generated gestalt of pure mind appearing right in the here-and-now without any precedence or consequence, simply as momentary spontaneous emanation of the totality. There is no linear process in the timeless space of pure mind. Nothing ever begins, happens or ends. Hopes of goal-attainment and fear of failure are both precluded as the notion of temporal sequence is superseded. Abandon the intellect and with it the idea of progression and there is unbiased no-mind—open mind.

There is nothing to do in order to receive Samantabhadra's transmission but relax into the boundlessly open center of all experience, the excluded middle of time and space:

46 The Sky-like Openness of Undivided Perception

In the moment, all things in the objective field,
in the absence of any substantial aspect, are open to infinity,
and intrinsic gnosis, wherein past and future are indivisible,
likewise, is open wide to sky-like infinity;
the past closed, the future unbegun,
the present is indeterminate pure mind,
and signless, rootless, without foundation or substance,
it is an untrammeled openness at the boundless center.

The objective field, the perceiving mind, and the gnosis that is the common ground of object and subject are all unbounded

121

openness. All objectified appearances as forms of emptiness lack any nuclear component or substantial element, and immaculate in the emptiness of past, present and future, they are essentially open-ended. The objective field is infinitely open, therefore, due to the inconceivable immensity of unfixed, uncrystallizing appearances (1); whatever happens in mind is open-ended due to the emptiness of partless moments, open due to its manifold appearance as indeterminate uncrystallizing display, and open due to the brilliant emptiness of gnosis that has no definite extension (2); and the singular space of reality is infinitely open, because it is the indivisible, ubiquitous, source of both subject and object (3).

In timeless buddhahood, in the nature of mind unadulterated by dualistic perception, both objective and subjective components of experience appear in their own shine and luster. All experience of (or in) the objective field is a form of emptiness and every moment of mind occurs autonomously, never moving out of the self-sprung awareness of empty gnosis.

Now I shall speak of the utterly inscrutable view,
the view that, without reference, has no focus:
it is insubstantial, omnipresent pristine awareness,
spontaneously perfect, intrinsic gnostic awareness.
Since everything whatsoever is included therein,
each instant of that intrinsic gnostic awareness
appears as an expression of all-inclusive awareness,
the timeless gnosis of Glorious Lord Vajradhara,
total awakening in the existential ground,
objectless, immaculate, nondual perception
and intrinsic gnosis abiding in its own expression.

Pure elemental space is pervaded by the actual space of reality,
so the pristine awareness of intrinsic gnosis
arises like the sun in the actual sky of reality,
shining throughout without bias or distinction.[87]

Scrutiny of the external-spatial-physical and of the internal-temporal-mental phenomena as they open up to infinity brings us to the infinite (excluded) middle which is the unlocalized source of all experience in the zero dimension (see canto 13).

The meditation techniques of tantrayoga are pointless—except that they open up into reality like everything else:

47. Goal-oriented Endeavor is Nondual Openness

In essential reality, which lacks all bias and partiality,
view, empowerment, mandala and mantra-recitation, are absent
and levels, paths, commitment, training and progress are unimaged;
all are wide open, unfounded, boundless vastness,
everything embraced by pure-mind reality.

There is no view, empowerment, mandala, mantra, levels, paths or samaya-commitment whatsoever in gnosis, so instruction in them and conscientious practice of them is meaningless and pointless. The gnostic dynamic of pure nonactive unengaged openness supersedes any process of improvement or impairment.

O great being, my nature is difficult to fathom!
Access, view and samaya-commitment,
ideal conduct, paths to tread and stages of practice,
pristine awareness and ultimate reality—these eight
are the vehicles of my three dimensions and my five aspects.
My theory and practice is out of sync with other systems:
access to me is involuntary;
the view cannot be cultivated;
the commitment cannot be observed;
ideal conduct cannot be attained;
the path cannot be trodden;
the stages cannot be purified;
awareness is unthought and unchangeable;
and my reality, the here-and-now, cannot be contrived.[88]

In perceptual openness, all experience appears as intangible light-form, filled to the brim with timeless sanctity:

48. Naturally Pure Spontaneous Openness

All experience, however it may appear,
is hallowed in its unoriginated nature;
arising spontaneously, never fixed or crystallized,
immaculate in its ontological indeterminacy,
it opens infinitely into the reality of natural perfection.

Ultimately unborn yet visible, like the reflection of the moon in water, whatever appears in empty gnosis is saturated by timeless brilliance, like water by wetness. Despite the ceaseless manifestation of images that never crystallize, the nature of mind remains immaculate, an infinite opening-up as the reality of natural hyper-perfection.

Empty appearances arise spontaneously perfect everywhere in the scope of pure mind:

All is one—all is unitary spaciousness;
unity cannot be contrived—spaciousness is unborn:
the illusions created within this unborn spaciousness,
utterly equivocal, are nowhere confined.[89]

In perceptual openness, everything appears fully saturated by pure-light energy. Everything is made of light. The sanctity implicit in timeless splendor is displayed in space-shifting holistic patterns of sublime inspiration, a constant stream of holographic information emanating from the motionless center of the natural perfection opening up to infinity like a fractal. But is this verse talking about patterns, patternlessness or momentary patterns of patternlessness?

The intrinsic clarity of Samantabhadra, openness offers a total gnostic perspective:

124

49. Intrinsic Clarity As Super-Openness

Gnosis, the essential reality of total presence,
with a 360 degree perspective, free of quantitative bias,
unsubstantiated by language or logic,
unsigned, neither eternal nor temporal,
subject to neither increase nor decrease,
without directional movement or pulsation,
immaculate in the immensity of immanent hyper-sameness,
it is seamless openness unconfined by space and time.

Gnosis as the nature of mind lacks any substance or attribute, so
it has neither spatial nor temporal extension. Lying beyond
conceptual and verbal categories, it cannot be understood through
speech or reasoning. Its essence cannot be apprehended, so it
cannot be described as either eternal or temporal, increasing or
decreasing, coming or going. On the contrary, in the absence of all
dualities it is an infinite opening up. Gnostic expression arising as
the unlimited display of Samantabhadra, whatever appearing
never leaving the scope of gnosis, all inner and outer, actual and
potential experience of samsara and nirvana converge in the *bhaga*
of Samantabhadri, opening up infinitely in the singularity of the
holistic seed.

In all-embracing, insubstantial, intrinsic gnosis,
seemingly concrete attributes are primordially immaculate:
Samantabhadra faces all ten directions
his gaze converging in the blissful unitary matrix of his consort's bhaga,
where the triple world melts into the sole holistic seed.[90]

The omniscient eye of pristine awareness is an eyeball looking in all
directions simultaneously, in the total 360 degree vision of the holistic seed,
the source of space-time in the zero dimension. In gnosis, no temporal
processes take place, there is no motion. Light has no speed. Nowhere
located, the zero dimension is omnipresent, a universal constant and the

'background' and context of all experience. It is Samantabhadra, the silent witness of all. In his all-round perspective, there is no historical judgment, no bias or partiality.

In the language of anuyoga, the clarity of whatever samsaric or nirvanic imagery appears is represented by Samantabhadra's vajra (dorje, thunderbolt, phallus) which resides eternally in the spacious bhaga (padma, lotus, vagina) of Samantabhadri, all-receptive to the power of imagination. This union of the adibuddha Samantabhadra and his consort describes the union of brilliance and emptiness in the field of spaciousness, of the field of radiance, a blissful unity in the sole holistic seed in which all things are united (see cantos 15 and 111). This is the zero dimension described above.

Openness is the natural atemporal, nonspatial continuum of the atiyoga of release at inception:

50. Spontaneously Arising Integral Openness

The gnostic dynamic lacks any intrusive hope or fear,
so nothing can happen to rupture seamless openness;
in such autonomous, genuine, unrestricted freedom,
we can never be caught in a cage of belief.

Whatever arises in the scope of gnosis is a display of gnostic potency, just as waves are a display of water, or like a fish in water swimming in its own pellucid medium. Its emergence without focus on any particularity, is 'the seamless openness of simultaneous arising and release'.

In an ocean of self-sprung awareness,
every flickering thought—
a golden fish darting in a pond![91]

Every thought and intention is entertained only as its own spaciousness;
and every intuition is realized only as its own spaciousness:
nothing at all is thought or intuited in pure mind,
in the mind of buddhas past, present and future.[92]

Ambition and frustration in symbiosis with hope and fear generate planning mind which subsumes the large part of thought dealing with 'the future'. Confidence in the simultaneity of the inception and release of thought, or 'release at inception' (see canto 26 and the Garab Dorje quote in canto 10), induces a constant opening up that turns into seamless thought-free openness. Thereafter the subjective knower can never be likened to a bird trapped in the cage of attachment to seemingly concrete objects and to ego-alienation.

At the moment of 'release at inception', samsara in its entirety is consumed in openness (see canto 41):

51. All-consuming Openness

All and everything reverted to openness,
its nature is beyond denial or assertion;
just as all worlds and life-forms open into space,
so emotion and evaluating thought
melt into hyperspaciousness.

Now here, now gone in a flash—thoughts leave no trace,
and opened up wide to seamless gnosis
hopes and fears are no longer credible,
the stake that tethers the mind in its field is extracted,
and Samsara, the city of delusion, is evacuated.

Like clouds emerging in the sky and then dissolving therein, all events originate in spaciousness and are finally released into the same space. Upon such intuition, assertion and denial and all emotion, all mental states and functions, return to the empty holistic seed, original hyperspaciousness, and thus the entire mentality of samsaric delusion dissolves into timeless purity. This secret transmission implies living in the undivided openness of intrinsic emptiness.

The sequence of causality reversed into the one holistic seed,
expectation and apprehension fade into the sky,

the sky of buddha-mind—so vast and exalted!—
the matrix of the one holistic seed, never lost nor gained,
neither realized nor unrealized, but liberated here and now![93]

Thought is either self-assertive or self-denying, inflating or deflating oneself or others, and it is attended by positive or negative attachment. When the subjective thinker is released from the hobble that keeps him wandering helplessly in his field of knowledge (when he is released from his cage) and the rigidity of dualistic perception dissolves, thoughts are liberated into limitless open space. That incurs a loss of reference, release of emotional and conceptual support, and the resolution of all conflicting tendencies—including expectation and apprehension—involved in discriminatory mental processes. The scattering diffusion of thinking—whatever the train of thought—is reversed and reverts to the all-consuming seed-potential of buddha-mind (also see canto 107).

Finally, all external and internal phenomena are disclosed as a focus of openness:

52. Openness Divulged: The Trailer

Whosoever recognizes the events appearing in the external field
and the internal mental emanation, all that play of energy,
all alike, as utterly empty openness,
to him is disclosed everything as this key—this crucial openness.

All experience is either gnosis or gnostic potency. Gnosis itself, the ineffable, unstructured nature of mind that is the source of each and every experience, is infinitely open without any spatial or temporal restriction. As for gnostic potency, externally, all objective appearances arise through belief that the luminosity of gnostic self-expression has specific identity, like a woman in a dream mistakenly identified as a former lover, while internally, the eight fields of consciousness, the relative mind and mental events, arise due to belief that the indeterminate, inalienable, medium of compassion has specific identity. Thus, all dualistic experience, objective and subjective, arises in the potency of the gnostic gestalt

128

as natural display and ornamentation. Moreover, all this dualistic perception is mere empty form, vividly appearing but actually absent, indeterminable as either external or internal, and thus in experience of its absence opening into infinity. Directly upon this realization, nothing rejected, naturally abiding, all experience is released as dream or magical illusion.

The mind can never be concretized,
so no matter how substantial the miserable states of samsara appear,
illusory like dream, enchantment, or the city of the lotus eaters,
they are fiction, lies, incredible lies.[94]

Gnostic potency is the expression of the fivefold spectrum of light in pure-mind spaciousness (see canto 69). Reification of gnostic expression occurs as the spectrum of light is projected outwards and solidified into the five perceptible elements (see canto 77). Dualistic consciousness and its mental functions also arise due to concretization of gnostic expression as an internal agent of thought and emotion—'I think (or feel); therefore I am'. Thus both external and internal phenomena are instances of 'misplaced concreteness', reification of gnostic potency (see also canto 8). Recognizing both external and internal appearance as equally empty, all experience is released into infinite openness.

In the following section, after openness itself is shown naturally assimilated to Samantabhadra's integral dynamic, sensory experience is revealed assimilated to openness:

II.2 Assimilation to Openness

53. First, Openness is Samantabhadra's Nondual Perception

The endless facets of reality are now assimilated
to the brilliant emptiness of intrinsic gnosis
which is the pristine awareness of openness;
'the perceiver' unloosed, the field of perception dissolved,
with nothing to hold on to, in wide open sudden wakefulness,

this unreflecting, undistracted, contemplation,
neither meditation nor nonmeditation, open-ended like the sky,
this is the super-matrix of Samantabhadra's contemplation.

Whatever may come to mind while cognizing appearances, without following or prolonging any train of association, simply letting go in a fully receptive, free and easy state of mind, Samantabhadra's dynamic is assimilated to seamless integral openness.

Directly released, pure in nature, unrestricted, totally complete,
free from any restriction, polarity collapsed into its own radiance,
the forever unsought super-matrix of nonaction is discovered
at the coincidence of appearance and emptiness,
without engagement of body or speech.[95]

To assume the gnostic dynamic, on the subjective side of experience, fixation dissolves in detachment from thoughts and the outer field losing its thought-governed determination dissolves into seamless openness. This happens by itself in the undistracted wide-open alertness that consumes memory traces (all and any thought can be defined as 'memory') without any recourse to any contrived meditation technique (see canto 11, 24, etc.). All reference excluded, the buddha-dynamic opening into infinity naturally consumes all time and space.

Openness is associated with the key of non-focus. Relax into an unfocussed state of nonmeditation, and thought and memory melt like snow under a warming sun. Perception of specific attributes of objects in a field reverts to a field-consciousness thereby, and therein the dynamic of nonaction engages.

Sense impressions are assimilated to nondual perceptual openness in detached relaxation (de-focusing) of the senses:

54. Assimilating the Unconfined Six Sensory Fields Left Loosely

In the vast gnostic super-matrix of brilliant emptiness,
no matter what evanescent particularity shows itself,

the direct sensory perception of gnosis illuminates its reality
and the image unconfined, cognition is pure pleasure;
the six sensory fields relaxed in the pristine-awareness matrix,
clear light, unobstructed, without outside or inside,
in artless super-relaxation—spontaneity!

Within the brilliant emptiness of gnosis, as we rest openly in supremely uninvolved natural clarity, the inherent brilliance of external appearances is unconfined and the senses hanging loose and free, since there is nothing to hang on to, the objects in the field of appearances are not fixated. In the vast existential silence of unmade seamless clear light, uninterrupted radiance in the matrix that allows no beginnings, appearances are like reflections in a pellucid lake.

Freely resting oceanic contemplation
has neither appearance nor projector;
it is neither emptiness nor anything that is empty;
it is not radiance, yet a field of supernal light!

It is not lethargic nor excitable;
it is unstirring, unstirred and unstirrable;
unmoving, unmoved and immovable:
look at nonaction, the ultimate method!

Without complication or simplification
this carefree contemplation
is neither immanent nor transcendent;
rest in the secret ocean of pristine awareness
in all-suffusing unoriginated spaciousness!

In the unfathomable profundity of that vast ocean,
behold the pinnacle of the forever-unfurled victory banner!
In the uncontrived zero dimension of no-mind,
doing nothing, attain the victory over all!

131

This pre-existent, uncontrived freely-resting contemplation,
unchanged by experience, untouched by the intellect,
abiding in the sky of reality, reveals the buddha-dynamic.[96]

The six fields of perception thoroughly loosened and hanging freely, external appearances are a limitless expanse of clear light opening into infinity (see canto 48). The indeterminate radiance is neither external nor internal and shines forth naturally in a state of supreme, uncontrived relaxation, all appearance shining in it like the moon on the lustrous surface of a lake (also see canto 36).

This 'freely resting oceanic contemplation', one of four 'freely resting' states of contemplation in the precepts of Cutting Through, is the inevitable, irrevocable natural state of mind. It is a non-method since there is nothing at all to do to attain it (see canto 23). The six sensory fields, left alone, are assimilated as vast openness. Any attachment is precluded in that openness (see canto 16). Pristine awareness is like an ocean without a shore.

In freely resting contemplation, which is effortless no-action, all experience is spontaneously assimilated to openness:

55. Adventitious Sensory Experience is Assimilated to Super-Openness

With the carefree mind of an idler,
neither tight nor slack, we rest easy;
here gnosis is infinitely open, like a crystal-clear sky,
and we linger gratefully in spaciousness without anticipation.

Deeply satisfied, like an old man, his work done, physically relaxed and energetically unwound, we leave things just as they are. In that way the duality of knower and known is resolved and we abide naturally in the brilliant emptiness of gnosis, the openness of pure being.

In pure mind, the existential ground of all and everything,
no matter what evanescent particularities ferment,

with direct perception it all shines forth as reality
and the image unconfined, gnosis itself is pleasure.

The six indeterminate, uncrystallizing, sensory fields
are now the matrix of self-arising pristine awareness,
and through the forever unveiled clear light uniting inside and outside
the self-imaged shapes in the mirror of intrinsic gnostic mind
admit neither focus nor non-focus in the space of their envisionment.

In a state of authentic simplicity, the organism relaxed,
with the carefree mind of an idler,
neither tight nor slack, we just rest easy.[97]

What role model actually possesses the mind that can be compared with the carefree mind of the Dzogchen yogi or yogini with the sensory fields left freely hanging in 'inconceivable nonaction' (see canto 20), in the nondual light of perception (see canto 77)? An idler, a retiree, a circus clown, an opium eater, an itinerant sadhu, an old man basking in the sun? 'Without anticipation' indicates a state of total equanimity free of both hope of success in uniting with, or avoiding separation from, the spaciousness of reality, and fear of failure to unite with, or be separated from, that spaciousness.

With recognition of pre-existent nonaction, the yogin or yogini attains full confidence in the dynamic of natural gnosis and captures the 'citadel of pure being' (see canto 34) in total perceptual openness:

56. Realization of Full Confidence in the Natural Dynamic

With spacious intuition of the brilliant emptiness of reality,
unconfined gnosis is a seamless infinite openness,
and free of belief, all ideation dissolving,
all things converge in the matrix of the gnostic dynamic.
The blissful ground and a happy mind blended,
inside and outside the one taste of pure mind,
this is the vision of reality as the consummate way of abiding.

Although appearances seem to be external objects, under scrutiny they cannot be apprehended or appropriated, so in that sense what is perceived is pure; and although appearances may arise internally in the mind, the mind cannot be measured, so in that sense the perceiver is pure. There is nothing solid in subject or object, just seamless openness and boundless clarity. The pure pleasure of the existential ground that is the natural disposition of reality and the pure pleasure of the mind that is natural gnosis unite as one and the yogin and yogini arrive at the all-consuming reality of natural perfection in the here-and-now. Reaching the land of never-ending bliss, and attaining confidence in the dynamic of natural gnosis, direct intuition of reality arises within.

In self-sprung pure pleasure, free of grasping thought,
the bodhisattva sees the truth of pure mind;
flooded by that realization—eternal bliss!
the elements in harmony—pure vision![98]

Bliss is the ubiquitous taste in the direct perception of reality as a boundless super-matrix of self-manifest nuclear light-seed with all things coiling together or converging and entwining (see cantos 25 and 49 and the quote from The Six Matrixes in canto 29 for the matrix of Samantabhadra). The matrix is an unbroken holistic expanse consuming all temporal experience in timeless purity (see canto 41).

Openness is assimilated as the nondual light of the mind:

57. The Epitome of Assimilation to Openness

At the moment of engaging with a sensory object,
the mind is opened to infinite, blissful vision,
and free of belief, as its luminous expression, its natural clarity,
it is assimilated to super seamless openness.

In brief, upon the appearance of a sensory object and perception of it, the tendency to fixate upon it is replaced by unwavering appreciation of it as blissful radiance and luminous self-expression. That is what is called the 'assimilation of sensory perception to openness'; it implies release from the confining parameters of fixation.

The display in the field of the threefold junction
is assimilated at the coincidence of mind and object,
nothing repressed, nothing excluded.[99]

'Fixation' denotes the automatic tendency of the intellect to focus upon the form of a thing and to remain attentive to it, clinging to it, coming to believe in its substantial reality in time and through space—in short to become attached to it—rather than to be aware of and appreciate its intrinsic nature as light.

With the assimilation of all experience to openness, gnosis is bound by openness because openness is the nature of the spaciousness of reality: pure mind binds all experience whatsoever and openness is the nature of pure mind; super-openness, the matrix of openness, embraces the intrinsic gnosis of pure mind and with it ignorance or the absence of gnosis:

II.3 The Bind of Openness

58. The Timeless Seal of Vajra-Space Affixed to Openness

In the clear sky wherein dualistic fixation has dissolved,
free of the turmoil of compulsive thought,
gnosis is bound in naturally luminous openness:
the vajra-dance of seamless unconfined reality,
pristine awareness of the hyper-sameness of the here-and-now,
holds the natural seal of Samantabhadra's timeless dynamic.

In gnostic space, seamless as the sky, every integral vision of dualistic appearances whatsoever is sealed with a timeless vajra-bind. Each perception, recognized as gnostic potency and display, is bound to nondiscriminatory hyperspace by giving it room and simply letting it be. With this vajra-bind of gnosis, whatever occurs can be nothing but gnosis arising in gnostic space. Gnosis therefore, is called 'the sun of immutable awareness, the pinnacle of the forever-unfurled victory banner'.

Ho! The vajra of intrinsic awareness of the cosmic inferno,
the vajra of formless vision of universal conflagration,
the vajra of super-emptiness untouched by fear of fire,
the stainless vajra-symbol, ruthlessly blazing,
the vajra-diadem of all-pervasive emptiness—
this is the infinite vajra of our inalienable natural perfection!
this is the infinite vajra of our unobservable commitment![100]

Gnostic luminosity is the seal of motionless vajra-space, and that is the buddha-dynamic (see cantos 53 and 63), Samantabhadra's contemplation. The ubiquitous matrix of pure mind is the gnostic vajra-bind (see canto 7):

59. The All-Inclusive Bind of Pure Mind

Sleep entraps our dreams
as unreal and empty images;
experience of samsara and nirvana is caught in mind,
evanescent in the pure-mind super-matrix.

All kinds of dream are enfolded by sleep as unreal and empty images. In the same way, all experience of matter and energy, samsara and nirvana, is embraced by pure gnostic mind, and as integral vision, insubstantial brilliant imagery, it should be known as gnostic display.

The imperative root teaching shows
that everything is pure mind;
that there is nothing now but pure mind
and there has never been anything other;

that all worlds, animate and inanimate, matter and energy,
all experience of buddha and sentient beings,
are all made by me, pure mind, the supreme source.[101]

Compare canto 7. All dualistic appearance whatsoever is empty gnostic image all bound by inherent openness:

60. The Inherent Bind of Openness

Just as all worlds and life-forms in the matrix of elemental space
are a seamless openness without center or circumference,
so all dualistic appearances within the gnostic matrix
are bound as empty images, open inside and outside.
This is the bind of pure mind that embraces all things
revealed as undiscriminating openness free of perceptual duality.

All the vast perishable environments together with the innumerable sentient beings of the six types that inhabit them are embraced by the one vast matrix of space. Likewise, the inconceivably numerous and diverse, actual and possible, experiences of samsara and nirvana are primordially embraced by the vast alpha-purity of gnosis. Thereby we realize that appearances are all we have, albeit empty images of absence in the nature of mind.

Every experience, whatever its shape or form,
and the nature of mind have ever been one,
so foregoing the constructs of the goal-oriented schools,
in simply focusing upon the mind just as it is
our own total presence is revealed as the nature of appearances.[102]

There is not a single thing that is not contained
in this tremendous super-matrix, the vast field of the mind.[103]

The essential emptiness of all imaged experience and the emptiness of the mind itself are one and the same, so, in a manner of speaking, they are 'bound' or 'constrained' in the same singular space by a greater field of emptiness.

Empty images in the matrix of space are the intrinsic self-imaging of gnosis, gnostic reflection in pure mind. Insubstantial yet vividly appearing, like the reflection of the moon in a lake, all inner and outer experience is bound by its own openness, like a knot tied in the void (see cantos 5 and 6, 44 and 46).

The bind of ineffable total gnosis opens up all our projections to original vast openness:

61. How Gnosis Is Bound by Ineffable Openness

The pure mind that binds all things is also bound,
bound by nonspatial, atemporal, super-openness;
like the vast space that binds all matter and energy,
it is without extension, utterly ineffable.

All experience is bound by gnosis, and gnosis, without any temporal or spatial restriction, is bound by an inconceivable and unutterable seamless openness that is as clear as the sky.

All things have the quality of space,
and the quality of space is its zing;
this zing *is also the quality of the three gnostic dimensions;*
all and everything has its zing:
however things appear,
they cannot be changed from their natural state. [104]

'Openness' evokes unrestricted space, space without center or circumference; but it can also be understood as spatial and temporal indeterminacy, or the lack of any spatial extension whatsoever. As all experience is gnostic envisionment, open inside and outside, gnosis is not bound by appearances but by openness only. All-penetrating openness is divulged here as the ineffability of gnosis (see cantos 9, 42 and 100), not through the effectuation of any change in appearance but by intuiting the zing of the here-and-now. The zing is the 'suchness' of every experience, its emptiness, 'just as it is'.

Nothing that we can experience in our agonies or ecstasies lies outside gnosis, the origin of everything:

62. The Bind of Gnosis as the Source

In gnosis, inclusive nonspatial sameness,
experience of samsara and nirvana never concretizes;
in the very moment no mind nor event can be specified:
everything is bound by wide open reality.

Since all actual and potential experience of samsara and nirvana arises in gnosis, appears in gnosis and is released in gnosis, it is bound by gnosis. Experience and gnosis are in turn bound by the openness that is the indeterminacy of things in themselves, the reality that cannot be defined or identified, and in this way all things are inherently immaculate.

Just as all worlds, inner and outer,
all forms of matter and energy,
the animate and inanimate world,
all contained in space, are absent,
so is the vast field, the matrix of pure mind,
with its buddhas and sentient beings,
its crucible and contents, environments and life-forms:
in immaculate reality everything is nondual
free of inflating or deflating conceptual projection.[105]

Gnosis is here defined as the origin of all things, which is the womb (Skt. bhaga or samodaya) that gives birth to the misery of samsara and the freedom of nirvana. The 'inclusive sameness' of all experience in gnosis thus implies the pure, immaculate indeterminacy of samsara and nirvana (see also cantos 20, 44, 59 and 66 and 67).

The bind of openness conceived as a seal of Samantabhadra's dynamic (gnostic expression of clear light, see canto 58) is Samantabhadra's vajra-bind of secrecy, accessible by gnostic self-recognition only, ignited by the Guru's grace:

63. The Epitome of Samantabhadra's Vajra-Bind

Out of time, the unbreakable pure-mind seal
is affixed for all in Samantabhadra's hyper-expanse;
reinforced by the dynamic of the lama, master of beings and truth,
it is naturally confirmed in the timelessly purified vajra-heart.
Accessible only to the most fortunate, not for all,
the sublime mystery of definitive truth,
the bind of the vajra-point beyond transition or change,
the dynamic super-matrix of gnostic clear light,
though innate, is difficult to keep in mind:
recognized by the grace of the lama, master of beings and truth,
it is known as 'the all-inclusive bind of seamless openness'.

No experience occurs outside the gnosis of pure mind, so this mind-bind is intractable, irrevocable:

There is no experience apart from pure mind.[106]

No experience of samsara or nirvana ever stirs from the nature of mind, the matrix of Samantabhadra:

Within Samantabhadra's nonactive space
samsara is all-good, and nirvana is also good.[107]

The actualization of atiyoga (Dzogchen Ati) is sealed by the lama's fearless intent and depends upon his grace:

To lay open the hidden meaning from within,
the teacher lives in the vajra-heart.[108]

This reality, the vajra-point dynamic, is the prerogative of only the broadest and keenest of minds:

Innumerable aeons ago
some ati-yogins with the good fortune and the karma,

140

with faith in me, the supreme source, and in my total presence,
perceived that there was no view to cultivate or commitment to keep,
no ideal conduct to strive in and no path to tread,
no climbing spiritual levels, no cause and effect,
no duality of ultimate and relative truth,
and nothing to cultivate in meditation,
and seeing that there was no mind to develop and no remedy
they saw the nature of mind:
this revelation is necessary for those like them![109]

The actual ineffable clear light dynamic recognized by the grace of the lama is way beyond rigid, conditioned, intellectual attitudes—it is openness itself:

Awareness with the speed of light, free of any intention,
that is the master's fountain of jewels.[110]

The intractable seal of openness, affixed at the beginning of time by Samantabhadra, is brought into awareness by the lamas' contemplation—it is not transferred from lama to disciple. The direct introduction into the nature of mind can only take place in the vajra-space of reality where we all share an intrinsic existential stance or mudra (cantos 60 and 61).

In the moment of gnostic self-recognition every dichotomy resolves itself like a snake untying its own knot, and we are awakened to our true identity:

II.4   Resolution in Openness

64. Resolution in Free-form Openness

Here is the essential meaning of resolution in openness:
coming from nowhere, abiding nowhere and going nowhere,
external events, unoriginated visions in empty space, are ineffable;
internal events, arising and releasing simultaneously,
like a bird's flight-path in the sky, are inscrutable.

All external events, appearances in the face of gnosis, are empty like apparitions that are vivid images of absence. Internal events, like the path of a bird in the sky, seem to develop but vanish in the act without trace. Neither external nor internal, events are nowhere attested, and cognition arising ceaselessly in the unoriginated gnostic foundation, its gestalt imagery is inconceivable from the first.

Imaged in the existential ground, without substance,
our experience cannot be articulated;
it all occurs autonomously, timelessly,
without linear sequence.[111]

All phenomena, outer and inner, are nondual imaging from the first, inexpressible in dualistic thought-form or language. The image of a bird's imprint in the sky indicates the trail of empty thought and emotion that appears to move in linear progression (a continuum) or to flicker on and off in momentary events (a plenum) but is better described as ineffable emanation of the buddha-archetype (yidam). Whatever is imaged in the existential ground, the pure basis of being, is divine archetypal experience.

Finally, all experience is resolved in the unconditional openness of nondual gnosis in the here-and-now:

65. Resolution in Unconditional Empty Gnosis

Mind in its field, just as it is, is surely self-sprung gnosis,
beyond any identity in its ineffable simplicity;
like the sky lacking any dynamic, it is an empty scope;
in the absence of deliberate action, it is beyond moral distinction;
and in the absence of causality, it is unattainable by the ten methods.
This ineffable matrix of vast untrammeled openness,
neither something nor nothing, utterly empty,
an inconceivable and ineffable reality,
this is resolved in no-mind natural perfection.

In the absence of mind in its field, light-form is the face of gnosis, like the sky, where phenomena are consumed, the intellect redundant; and in the absence of moral causality, the ten techniques superseded, all experience is resolved in the nondiscriminatory sameness of ineffable openness.

Since I am the heart of total pure presence,
there is no other source of secret precepts;
since I supersede all value judgement,
I resolve every event whatsoever;
since I am the one field of absence
the view is resolved in nonmeditation;
since nothing is to be cherished but me,
samaya commitment is resolved in nonobservance;
since nothing is to be sought but me,
ideal conduct is resolved in nonaction;
since there is nowhere to be other than in me,
spiritual levels are resolved in non-purification;
since I have never been, can never be, veiled,
self-sprung awareness is resolved in me;
since I am unborn reality,
mystical experience is resolved in me;
since I am the only destination,
the path is resolved in staying still;
since buddhas and sentient beings,
the environment and matter and energy,
all derive from essential total presence,
they are resolved in timeless nonduality;
in order to establish self-sprung awareness
it is resolved coincident upon this super-transmission;
since no experience is other than me,
I, the supreme source, resolve all.[112]

* * * * *

The pure mind that is the nature of all events
and the empty images of samsara and nirvana,
all is the inconceivable seamless openness
revealed in this bejewelled commentary to the second theme.

Buddhas of all time, gnostic masters and protectors,
you innumerable yogins, siddhas and oath-bound guardians,
you highest, you most fortunate faithful people,
and you hosts of sky-dancers, may you all be well pleased!

The second vajra-theme of *The Treasury of Natural Perfection*, wherein everything is established as seamless openness, is completed.

The Third Vajra Theme: Spontaneity

'All experience is timeless spontaneity'

III.1 The Disclosure of Spontaneity

66. The Simile of the Wish-fulfilling Gem

Timeless spontaneity,
forever present, is created by no one;
it is the pure mind that like a wish-fulfilling gem
is the origin of all our samsara and nirvana.

Just as a precious stone has an indefinable timelessly perfect quality within it, so the pure mind of gnosis has an indeterminate inherent quality or potency that may give rise to anything whatsoever, and this quality is 'spontaneity', which is the existential ground, the timeless spaciousness of all experience.

As nonspatial spontaneity, without inside or outside,
gnosis, without experiential limitation, is boundless as the sky;
it is unconstricted reality, the all-encompassing matrix,
without any spatial dimension, all-embracing,
integrating everything in an unoriginated, boundless, seminal seed;
fulfilling all wishes out of unity, it is inexhaustible,
and without increase or decrease, it is a treasury of precious gems.[113]

In the matrix of spontaneity, the source of everything,
ornamental circles of buddha-body, speech and mind,
quality and activity, occur without pattern or structure;

145

the spaciousness of reality is a wish-fulfilling gem,
presenting all and everything naturally and effortlessly.[114]

This pure mind, the ubiquitous essence—
its nature is spontaneously, originally, perfect;
so strenuously engaging in the ten techniques
is unnecessary, superfluous.[115]

'Spontaneity' has no object—it is the totality of the here-and-now. Its nature is without attribute yet it contains potency and in certain contexts implies spontaneous creativity (see canto 67). In reference to forms of emptiness it may be used adjectivally or adverbially as 'spontaneously arisen, accomplished, perfect, or present' (see canto 82). In the context of the four samayas, spontaneity never implies an impulsive or instinctual act of a samsaric body or mind. Creative potency is the natural function of nonspatial openness conceived as the all-embracing nuclear essence (see canto 49).

The 'ornamental circles' of buddha-body, speech and mind, manifesting as the physical/material, the energetic/vibratory, and mental, are called 'circles' or 'rings' because they are unpatterned, or perfectly random, and therein lies their beauty (see canto 72). Total randomness cannot be conceived by the intellect.

Pure mind is like the universal projector. All the confined, repressed, imagery of samsara arises in and as unconfined gnostic imagination:

67. The Cosmic Gestalt as Super-Spontaneity

Just as all environments and beings occur in space,
so samsara and nirvana never crystallize in pure mind;
just as a variety of dreams occur in sleep,
so the six realms and the triple world manifest in mind:
all events, at their arising, within the scope of gnosis,
are the cosmic gestalt of empty spontaneity.

Just as matter and mind appear in elemental space, so samsara and nirvana arise in the scope of gnosis as indeterminate

146

uncrystallizing potency. All potency manifests like dream arising from the potency of sleep; but in oblivion to gnosis, visions of beings in the triple world of matter and energy arise out of the potency of the ordinary mind with its eight-fold consciousness. Just as hallucination may arise from the potency of a heavy fever, so samsaric images arise as a matter of fact from the potency of a confused mind. Yet from their inception those images are just figments of imagination, immaculate and empty.

In the matrix of spontaneity, the source of everything,
all appearances in finite, kinetic form arise
as a circle of ornamentation in the unpatterned physical dimension;
all low, moderate and high frequencies of sound
as a circle of ornamentation in the unpatterned energetic dimension;
and the ultimate essential unity, all and everything indistinguishable,
as a circle of ornamentation in the unpatterned mental dimension.[116]

Gnostic amnesia, or a lack of gnostic presence, allows the potentiation of samsara/nirvana out of data accumulated by the eight consciousnesses (five external, three internal). Due to unawareness of the nature of mind as the creator, seemingly discrete moments of consciousness appear as the mere perceiver of seemingly objective images. Sentient beings' physical, energetic and noetic dimensions arise as mere reflected images of unrestricted buddha-body, speech and mind (see also canto 72).

The term 'gestalt' (gzhi snang) is employed particularly in this section on spontaneity and should be understood as the insubstantial configuration, pattern (circle of ornamentation) arising from gnostic potency as a samsaric or nirvanic vision of matter and energy integrated holistically so that the sum of its parts are realized as the spontaneity of gnosis. Every perception is the gestalt of spontaneity. The 'cosmic gestalt' (cosmogenesis) is the totality of potential experience embracing the macrocosmic and microcosmic universe to be realized as super-spontaneity.

Pure mind itself, the source of both samsara and nirvana, is nondual:

68. Nonduality as Spontaneity

The gnostic ground and its gestalt emanation,
neither identical nor different from each other,
occur in the medium of timeless gnostic spontaneity;
as the potency of the display samsara and nirvana
appear as impure or pure, respectively,
but in the moment—nondiscriminatory spaciousness!

The fundamental gnosis of pure mind (the existential ground) that is super-spontaneity as brilliant emptiness, and also the display of the existential ground that is all the actual and potential experience of samsara and nirvana that appears in its scope, all of that arises as spontaneity (or with spontaneity as the medium) and although there may appear to be discrimination in it, because unitary spaciousness is nondiscriminatory it is called 'the space of self-sprung awareness that supersedes unity and differentiation'.

All is one—all is unitary spaciousness;
unity cannot be contrived—spaciousness is uncreated:
the illusions created within this unborn spaciousness,
utterly equivocal, are nowhere confined.[117]

Buddha-being and knowing, and its qualities,
sentient beings' bodies and proclivities,
all actual and potential environments and organisms,
this is all the nature of pure mind from the first.[118]

Although 'spontaneity' may be defined as the spontaneous arising of gnostic experience, or the display of samsara and nirvana in the existential ground, pure or impure, good or bad, it actually refers to the nondual, hyperspaciousness of pristine awareness which cannot be differentiated. The moment of full awareness and gnosis may be indicated as the clear emptiness of pure mind or as a display of ordinary good or bad experience, but what actually happens is a moment of nondual awareness of suffering and release. This is experience of the nonduality of samsara and nirvana.

148

All images, whether pure or impure, are magical creations displayed in the ground, their identity utterly equivocal. Nonduality is ambiguity.

The ambivalent spontaneity of pure mind displayed in the three dimensions of the gnostic ground is likened to a crystal prism diffracting pure (colorless) light as the five rainbow colors of the spectrum:

69. The Three Gnostic Dimensions as Super-Spontaneity

In the unimpeded diffraction of a crystal's spectrum
the five colored lights are separately distinguished,
yet the potency of the one crystal prism is undiscriminating:
basic intrinsic gnosis diffracts like the crystal.
Its emptiness is the dimension of pure being,
its radiance, intrinsic luminosity, is the dimension of perfect enjoyment,
and as the indeterminate medium of its emanation
it is the magical dimension of gnosis:
these are the gnostic dimensions of spontaneity
within the spacious ground.

Since the crystal prism and the fivefold spectrum of light within it share a common field, there can be no qualitative distinction made between them. Just so, there is no qualitative distinction between the emptiness of gnosis (the dimension of pure being) which is like the crystal, its brilliance (the dimension of perfect enjoyment) which is like the spectrum of light within the crystal, and its unlimited potential for projection (the magical dimension) which is like the propensity of the light to emanate out of the crystal (as an external projection) because these three gnostic dimensions are one in essence. Furthermore, for the same reason, the imagery of the form-dimensions that is transfigured and the imagery of the potency of pure mind that is the nondiscriminatory dimension of pure being is all the apparitional display of the one gnosis.

I, the supreme source,
I am the essence of the three gnostic dimensions

that abide in nonconceptual sameness:
I am the unstructured dimension of pure being;
as naturally produced magical apparition
I am the dimension of perfect enjoyment, satisfying desire;
demonstrating exemplary compassionate activity,
I am the essence of the magical dimension.[119]

Like a flawless crystal statue, our immaculate nature,
stainless, translucent, is pure being;
it may appear as earth, water, fire, air and space,
and to the unrealized intellect it may seem concrete,
but nothing substantial is there, only the light of awareness.
Like a rainbow shining in the sky
having no existence separate from the sky,
located in space and thus indivisible from space,
in actuality, pure being is indivisible from reality,
the light of awareness arising, appearing and shining by itself,
appearing distinctly and inexorably brilliant:
unthinking awareness of light is pure being;
its intrinsic self-display is the enjoyment of timeless awakening;
and polarity resolved, compassion is magical emanation.[120]

Any attempt to revert to the source is redundant because there is no distinction to be made between the source and its manifestation. Likewise there is no qualitative distinction to be made between any variety of display—it is all unified in the one gnosis. The three gnostic dimensions may appear to be separate but are one in reality. The three are indistinguishable due to their common nature. The image is total reality, the brilliance is total reality and the essence is total reality. The magical illusion of the common light of day cannot be distinguished from the emptiness of reality.

The three gnostic dimensions may also be conceived as 'the three modes of being' or as 'three buddha-bodies', but they are still all one in reality, distinguished in order to be reunited.

As external projection, the diffracted lights of pure mind are gnostic potency for appearance in the form of the five elements: white earth, yellow water, red fire, green air and blue space (see canto 77 note 133).

All imagery of samsara and nirvana arises spontaneously in the gnostic ground through the creative dynamic of pure mind and as the three gnostic dimensions:

70. All Things Are the Perfect Spontaneity of Pure Mind

Even while the gestalt imagery arises in that ground—
whether as the masters' pure three dimensional display,
or as impure experience of samsaric worlds and life-forms—
as empty essence, clarity and unimaginable diversity,
it is the play of pure being, enjoyment and magical being:
all display is the gestalt imagery of the potency of the three dimensions
which is nothing but spontaneous envisionment.

With a clear understanding of these fine distinctions,
all experience of samsara and nirvana is realized
as the three dimensions of spontaneity in pure mind.

All experience as the spontaneity of the three gnostic dimensions and spontaneity in the ground as the one nature of those three dimensions is explained in the cantos above. Now, all the matter and energy appearing in images of samsara and nirvana within that spontaneity occurs as display of three dimensional envisionment in the existential ground. Thus the unitary source and manifest multiplicity combined are to be understood as the one 'spontaneity of the three gnostic dimensions'. Pure or impure display (pure display as buddha pure-being in which arise the five families as perfect enjoyment and disparate emanation as magical appearance, or impure display as physical, energetic and mental samsara as pure being, perfect enjoyment and magical emanation), everything takes place in the same unified empty field of perfectly creative spontaneity. In total absence of discrimination, everything is 'the spontaneous play and ornamentation of spaciousness' or 'the field of perfect creativity'.

Phenomena, whether pure or impure, are all spontaneous creations of pure mind, the gestalt of pure mind in the existential ground. Pure mind is nowhere located; samsara and nirvana are visions in timeless gnostic space.

The nature of mind, changeless spontaneity, a matrix of space,
the matrix of compassionate magical emanation, gossamer display—
here everything is the adornment of spaciousness,
and there is no other field of suffering's cessation.[121]

The previous canto shows the identity of the existential ground with the spontaneity that is the unity of the three gnostic dimensions in the simile of the crystal. This canto shows the instantaneous unfoldment of the buddha-archetypes in the ground of being like visions of light within the crystal. The 'fine distinction' that is to be understood is the distinction between two different aspects of spontaneity: the spontaneity of the existential ground itself viewed from the side of emptiness (pure mind or gnosis as the existential ground), and the spontaneous emanation of formful imagery from the side of brilliance, the archetypal images of the six realms displayed in the ground. This topic is treated clearly by Shabkar Lama in *The Flight of the Garuda* (Dowman 2003, p.85-6).

The gnostic ground appears as either the pure experience of nirvana or as the impure experience of samsara. Both, however, consist of the three gnostic dimensions arising from the same holistic field of empty creativity. Since neither manner of display is preferable to the other, all experience is the field of perfect creativity. The mahayoga tantras represent these three dimensions as Guru, Devata and Dakini and hence all is 'archetypal' experience.

All and everything is the spaciousness of pure mind, so 'why strive for buddhahood?':

71. Every Experience is Pure mind

The pure being and pristine awareness of all buddhas,
the creatures of the three realms' physical, energetic and mental complexes
and the karmic-emotional tangle of inner and outer worlds—
there is nothing but pure mind!

Consider the nature of gold: a fine statue made from pure gold, a necklace, a beautiful bracelet fashioned from gold, and a filthy bedpan made of gold, all are gold, and just as pure gold is incapable of discrimination so pure mind makes no distinction between pure buddha and impure sentient beings, between different action patterns and varying propensities. Because pure mind and its potency are identical spaciousness, these distinctions, finally, are mere labels of temporal mind states.

Buddhas and sentient beings, conduct and propensities,
all experience, nothing excepted, is just pure mind![122]

Thus, spontaneity is the storehouse of everything in samsara and nirvana:

72. Spontaneity is the Universal Treasury

The matrix of spontaneity is the source of all and everything:
insofar as all external and internal, animate and inanimate forms
occur as unpatterned buddha-body, a circle of ornamentation,
insofar as all frequencies and volumes and qualities of sound
occur as unpatterned buddha-speech, a circle of ornamentation,
insofar as all mind and awareness, realized or unrealized,
occur as unpatterned buddha-mind, a circle of ornamentation,
and insofar as buddha-quality and ideal conduct are also unpatterned,
spaciousness is the precious wish-fulfilling gem,
and because it is unsought, everything arising by itself,
it is called 'the spontaneous creativity of self-sprung awareness'.

Gnosis itself and all the actual and possible experiences of samsara and nirvana that are its envisionment arise involuntarily from the first: the functions of sentient beings' physical, energetic and mental complexes arise spontaneously as circles of ornamentation from buddha-body, speech, mind, quality and activity. Therefore, pure mind is called 'spontaneity, the unitary fountain of jewels'.

The display and the qualities and functions of samsara and nirvana, all the archetypal envisionment of living beings in an environment of matter and energy, appear within the immaculate super-ground by virtue of the six modes and two media of emanation:

Spontaneity, equivocal in nature,
arises in eight modes of emanation:
indeterminate in its presentation,
it emanates as compassion,
providing a sanctuary for all sentient beings (1);
within the intrinsic clarity of its appearances
it manifests as five-colored-light illumination (2);
through its ceaseless emanation of knowledge
it is the medium of pure pristine awareness
wherein indeterminate images arise as the path (3);
through perfected envisionment of the finite body
it is the pure dimension of all experience (4);
through the unitary essence of cognition
it is nonduality (5);
through the absence of any place of its own
it is ultimate unbounded release—
spontaneity as indeterminate basic spontaneity (6).
Through the unitary perfection of gnosis
its purity is the medium of pristine awareness itself,
spontaneity being of the essence (7);
and because emanation is indeterminate,
as the aspect of all-pervasive light
spontaneity is also the medium of impure samsara
and the origin of living beings.(8)

These are the eight modes of emanation
and because its inception is involuntary,
it is called 'spontaneous manifestation',
precious miraculous appearance.[123]

'Circles or rings of ornamentation' evoke the rings around the moon and the planet Saturn, like levels of vibration appearing as matter, sound and thought. Likewise, the external sensory organs seem to be at the center of their external sources of light and sound, and the internal sense organ may be conceived to lie at the center of a globe, as in dream. But these 'circles' are the unpatterned ornamentation of the moment and as such are utterly random; therefore they are 'circles', and to that extent they are the unsolicited gift of spaciousness. (See the quotes from The Junction of the Three Gnostic Dimensions in cantos 66 and 67 and see also 'ornamentation' in canto 8.)

Since the three gnostic dimensions are primordially perfect in the matrix of spontaneity, calculated action in order to actuate them is not only futile, it is actually harmful to our mental health. Spontaneity renders all spiritual endeavor redundant:

73. Involuntary Spontaneity

Multifarious events in their ground of spontaneity
are pure mind, perpetual spontaneity,
so the three gnostic dimensions, unsought, are naturally present;
since moral discipline is thus redundant,
relax into the authentic yoga of nonaction.
The matrix of spontaneity requires no discipline,
so do not try to gild the lily.

Buddha-qualities are achieved from the beginning in the essence of gnosis, so it is unnecessary to strive to attain them now, and since there is no effective moral conditioning there is no need for strenuous discipline. If effort is applied, achievement is precluded and we will be deprived of self-sprung awareness. Simply relax into the natural state and watch the exhaustion of all aspiration and motivation.

Free of old habits and ambitions,
impelled by no cause and allured by no goal,
through the desirelessness of the gnostic dynamic

155

natural spontaneity resumes its dominion.
Do not try to effectuate what already exists;
nothing has ever left the natural state,
so force is futile:
all experience arises spontaneously in perfection.
No realized buddha past, present or future
ever recommended that we rely on calculated effort.
If we search for realization in meditative absorption
not only will we fail to find it, we will be harmed by it.[124]

I, the supreme source, already complete and perfect,
I could never teach the necessity of therapeutic action to anyone,
lest my retinue be struck by the disease of striving,
lest they deprive themselves of self-sprung awareness,
lest they err in attempting to contrive authentic reality;
if such falsehood is allowed to compromise the truth,
hypocritical endeavor precludes attainment of the truth of nonaction.[125]

Thus spontaneity is realized without action (see cantos 32 and 34). There is nothing to do in order to realize what is already present as perfection:

74. Nonaction Is Spontaneity

The total presence of buddha past, presence and future
is achieved spontaneously in natural pure pleasure;
so eschewing low level, graduated, causal techniques,
watch the nonactive sky-like nature of mind!

Gnosis is actual buddha, magnificent super-spontaneity itself, and that is realized only in our own natural disposition without any modification or distortion and never by seeking and striving.

O great being, listen!
Buddhas of ancient time
sought nothing but mind itself,

changing nothing from just how it is;
without cultivating any structured state
mind was realized without concept:
buddhas of the present and the future
will also realize it through unthinking sameness.[126]

All teaching on cause and effect is directed at the less fortunate neophyte as a provisional instruction for a narrow mind susceptible to wrong views. It is irrelevant for ati-yogins and yoginis of high capacity. Just as a piece of wood cannot become a jewel by polishing it, we cannot become buddha by discriminating between positive and negative causes and effects.

Furthermore, since the natural perfection superseding causality
is not an arena for the disconnected and luckless,
the latter must practice on the graduated, causal path.[127]

Unlucky people, without the karmic connection,
cannot understand natural perfection
even when it is openly revealed to them.
Infected by the poison of goal-oriented ambition,
like someone hankering after the wish-fulfilling gem
and trying to make it by polishing wood, they fail.

The connected ati-yogin with good fortune
has no view, no commitment, no ideal conduct,
no path or spiritual level,
no progressive awakening of the enlightened mind,
no meditation agenda, and no remedy.
To see the nonduality of 'absolute' and 'relative'
by perceiving the reality of things just as they are—
that is the great imperative![128]

Buddhahood is the spontaneity of pure mind achieved without doing anything, and that includes any contrived meditation upon the nature of

157

mind—any such meditation arrives spontaneously and that is the spontaneous gnosis of nonaction. The point of nonaction has already been introduced (see cantos 19, 23, 34 and 47).

The 'unlucky', in psychological jargon, includes the neurotic and psychotic; but the 'neophytes' or 'children' referred to here are those caught in the trap of logical and rational thought that does not allow any escape from the linear progression from birth to death. These are the luckless and disconnected.

Perceiving the unity of the ultimate and the relative, the Dzogchen yogi or yogini has understood the nature of the mind:

75. 'Do Not Strive for the Spontaneity That Is Already Here'

Uncontrived, timeless, magical super-spontaneity,
just as it is in the here-and-now, cannot be contrived;
jumping through all the hopes and fears of the strobe-like mind,
recognize unsought super-spontaneity in spaciousness!

When the sun is shining there is no need to turn on the light. Likewise, since gnosis is realized, pure being has been achieved and it is futile to try to accomplish it again with conscious effort.

With homeless mind, unreflecting, without any compulsion,
naturally abiding in the nonconceptual field of sameness,
complete and perfect from the first, without the slightest aspiration,
whoever lives in such pure pleasure
becomes literally the nature of all experience.[129]

The sun of nondual pure mind (see cantos 40 and 46) shining spontaneously from the first, all emotional conflict is resolved in a single, unsupported moment of pure pleasure.

To sum up, the phenomenology of our mental life, all touched by hope and fear, is always the three gnostic dimensions' spontaneity:

76. The Spontaneity That Dissolves Hope and Fear as the Essence of the Three Gnostic Dimensions: A Summary.

Every experience, whatever it may be,
is the uncontrived triad of essence, nature and compassion,
the display of pure being, enjoyment and magical emanation;
since samsara and nirvana are the three-dimensional matrix of pure mind,
spontaneously perfect in uncontrived hyper-sameness,
samsara is not to be rejected here, nor nirvana attained.
All evaluation silenced, we abide at the heart of reality
where every experience is pure mind,
and timeless spontaneity is disclosed as the key.

All experience of samsara and nirvana, inner and outer, arising as empty essence, radiant nature and diverse compassionate emanation, is an expression of the three gnostic dimensions and exists in and as magnificent super-spontaneity. Since the essence, nature and compassion of gnosis is spontaneously perfect in and as the three gnostic dimensions of the existential ground, there is no independent samsara to be rejected and no separate nirvana to be attained. No experience is to be avoided, because samsara and nirvana are identical in and as the nature of mind; the essence of all experience is thus disclosed in and as the actual dynamic of spontaneity.

We are *the three aspects of gnosis—*
the original essence, nature and compassion.[130]

I am pure mind, the supreme source,
my pre-existent nature is spontaneity,
while the essence of all buddha is threefold
its nature the uncontrived dimension of pure being,
its essence the uncontrived dimension of pure enjoyment,

its manifest compassion the dimension of magical emanation;
and these three gnostic dimensions cannot be willfully effectuated.[131]

Regarding 'empty nature' and 'radiant essence', these terms are employed here to distinguish between the natural state as emptiness and the holistic nucleus or source as radiance, while conventional usage of 'empty essence' and 'radiant nature' differentiates the spaciousness that is emptiness from the nature of the spaciousness that is brilliant clarity. But in fact the emptiness that is the dimension of pure being, the radiance that is the dimension of perfect enjoyment and the emanation that is the magical dimension are one and the same.

Spontaneity is the nature of reality and with the recognition of the nature of mind all phenomena, inside and outside, are understood as spontaneity through the timeless process of assimilation. The first to be assimilated is the mind that reveals the five elements in images of samsara and nirvana and simultaneously teaches the elements as the potency of the nature of mind, its radiance and its ornamentation:

III.2 Assimilation to Spontaneity

77. Assimilating the Phenomena of One's Own Mind as the Teacher

All experience is assimilated to spontaneity:
the five elements, matter and energy, all appearance,
arise to demonstrate timeless, unthought, spontaneity;
self and other deconstructed, as pure intrinsic radiance
the elements are assimilated autonomously as ordinary mind.
Let the six senses relax in the amorphous perceptual field!

In the scope of its original hyper-purity, empty and clear, self-sprung gnostic awareness, like a crystal prism, contains the fivefold spectrum of the natural light of spontaneity that is the internal radiant aspect of the five elements. Momentarily projected externally, just as the crystal's internal light is projected outside as its colorful expression, the spectrum of light is still the internal radiance of form. In their momentary appearance the 'sediments' of the five elements may be misidentified as the universe of matter and energy; but when the imagery of the delusory process of misidentification is recognized as the pure 'tone' of the five elements' source that is intrinsic gnostic potency, then upon the emergence of the five elements—earth, water, fire, air and space—having lost the construct of self and other (inside and outside) we abide in the elements' intrinsic radiance. That illustrates vibrant yet illusive intrinsic gnosis as we are absorbed into the natural clarity of appearances without any attachment to delusory display and without any interpretive projection. Accordingly, even as apparitional light and light-seed appear in our direct perception and we settle in that vibrant yet elusive state of thoughtless natural clarity, it is said that the yogin and yogini are composed in the contemplation of the five aspects of nonconceptual sameness revealed in the five elements that arise in the face of appearances and which are therefore, 'the teacher'.

Within pure mind, the universal source,
the five elements arise as mind—
as the five pure-mind teachers:
they arise in the dimension of perfect enjoyment;
their teaching is an exposition of their very being;
their revelation is their nature—intrinsic gnosis.
As teachers in the dimension of perfect-enjoyment,
themselves the dynamic, they know it not,
and nor do they construct objective teaching;
these five pure-mind teachers
reveal the totality, the zing *of reality.*

Pure-mind pristine awareness,
self-sprung as the buddha-teacher of earth,

does not teach with words and letters
but reveals the nature of gnosis,
and free of concepts of self and other
he reveals the mind of thoughtless sameness.
All beings of the triple world,
realizing this, are one with buddha—
the reality they seek is attained unsought.[132]

Then the same is stated with regard to the pure-mind teachers, sources of revelation, of water, fire, air and space.

The five 'primary' elements are the intrinsic radiance of the spectrum of light spontaneously emanating from the crystal prism of pristine awareness. Projected externally, these lights are reflected in the five lights of external objects (sights, sounds, smells, tastes and tactile sensations), and thus are like external reflections of the lights projected by the intrinsic glow of the crystal. When these external reflections are concretized in the process of perception, different configurations of the five elements—mere 'sediments' of the lights—come to be misconstrued as matter and energy, worlds and life-forms, habitats and inhabitants. Yet throughout this confusion, they have intrinsically remained pure-light potency, though fractured as impure vibrations of the five elements.[133]

'Light-seed' composes the apparitional forms that are the projected five elements in the sambhogakaya. The light-seeds become apparent as the yogin becomes familiar with intrinsic radiance in Cutting Through, whereas they become a focus for contemplation in the Jumping Through phase (see canto 122ii).

In atiyoga the five pure-mind teachers appear as the lights of the five elements in the dimension of perfect enjoyment. They reveal their nature as gnosis and that is their teaching insomuch as the natural brilliance of the elements provides a conduit into the nature of mind as its dimension of perfect enjoyment. Thus the teachers of the radiant nature of the elements belong to the sambhogakaya.

As all thoughts of concreteness dissolve into light, perception of appearance is assimilated in the sambhogakaya dimension:

78. Assimilating Sensory Perception as Thought-dissolving Emptiness

Gnosis, the universal source, is luminous spontaneity,
and unmodified by the five senses, by projection or concentration,
the empty gnosis of pure being is spontaneously perfect contemplation.
With incisive recognition, just leave things alone in simplicity!

To relax into pellucid gnostic clarity without losing immediate sensory perception of the five external objects as they appear, that is the key to bathing in the brilliant emptiness of sensory perception.

The forever unsought super-matrix of nonaction is discovered
at the coincidence of appearance and emptiness,
without engagement of body or speech.[134]

In the nonreactive nature of mind,
artless perception is heightened:
I, Samantabhadra, reveal
'the contemplation that consumes all movement'.[135]

To leave sensory perception unstructured means to leave it in 'simplicity' without withdrawing attention from it or projecting a screen upon it. This implies the absence of any belief about the ontological status of an object or event (see canto 36), which in turn implies a nonconceptual or thoughtless state. This defines direct sensory perception. The simple mind of child or saint is close to the mind of natural perfection.

All experience is assimilated to spontaneity in intrinsic concentration (see canto 23):

79. Assimilation in Intrinsic Concentrated Absorption

In the fertile unconfined super-matrix of intrinsic gnosis
whatever appears in the field of mind through sensory perception

as a crucial locus of seamless sameness is assimilated
in spontaneity's natural concentrated absorption.
Always, incessantly, like a great river's flow,
uncultivated spontaneously-arising awareness uninterrupted,
all things, in essence self-sprung in the primordial matrix,
reach fulfillment in Samantabhadra's contemplation.

People talk about their twenty-four-hour-a-day meditation and the impossibility of distraction, but it is just compulsive idle talk; here uncultivated meditation is defined as 'a strong current of concentrated absorption'. Every event occurs in gnostic freedom and at the moment of inevitable recognition, in total release, seamless liberating openness is an uninterrupted flow of self-purified, brilliant emptiness. Arising ceaselessly without beginning and released in the unborn matrix, that self-purifying flow is a powerful current of concentrated absorption.

People pay lip-service to the unborn nature of mind,
and even play-act as if nothing has any substance;
but who realizes the unborn actuality?
With an understanding of the supreme source,
however, surely we live it without distraction.
Evading stress, eschewing self-improvement,
moving past fascination, treating memory lightly,
every event is actually myself,
Samantabhadra—so we jump into it![136]

In the nature of mind beyond cultivation
light-form is nonspatial, reflexively released:
I, Samantabhadra, reveal
'the all-inclusive contemplation of integral openness'.[137]

Letting everything come and go naturally within the scope of self-recognition, the process of auto-purification in the empty luminosity of the seamless openness of subject and object is an unbroken continuity.

All experience is assimilated to spontaneity in carefree detachment (see canto 16):

80. Assimilation to Spontaneity in Zero-attachment

All experience is grounded in pure mind,
and pure mind is like space, that universal simile.
Just as everything is contained in the matrix of space,
through the very lack of exertion, naturally pure,
so all inner and outer experience is spontaneously assimilated
in the crucial nonaction that supersedes all intention and ideation,
and with the vital zero-attachment to whatever appears.

As elemental space contains all matter and energy, so gnosis includes all samsara and nirvana. Cognition coincident with whatever arises, resting freely in its own natural state, habitual thought processes cease.

In the reality of every act and event,
unthinking, I reveal freedom by letting go.[138]

This impurity—it is samsaric delusion:
to leave the doors of the senses wide open,
the crux is freely resting contemplation
and the precept is 'change nothing!'
With a mind that does not cling
to appearances that cannot be grasped,
looking with eyes that are uninvolved,
we are drawn along the reality-path of absence.
Conveyed to the source of no-view and no-meditation,
we are one with the ideal of effortless nonaction,
where there is no end to the light.[139]

In the nature of mind free from anxiety,
light-form is without hope and fear:
I, Samantabhadra, reveal
'the contemplation of confident ease'.[140]

Freely resting contemplation, like the super-flow of concentrated absorption, is an aspect of ineluctable spontaneity. It is no meditation yet it may be called total detachment and it is the natural state of being (see cantos 16, 22, 26 and 54).

In order to assimilate all experience to spontaneity, we must do nothing at all but give up all effort and 'stretch out' like an old man basking in the sun (see canto 20). The gnostic dynamic is 'nonaction', 'spontaneity', 'samadhi' and 'contemplation':

81. Effortless Assimilation to Spontaneity

Timeless—unborn and unceasing,
motionless—without coming or going,
the masters' contemplation is all-inclusive,
so spontaneity is a pure unwavering samadhi
and all events are assimilated to nonaction.

Unless we consciously and willfully try to do something, we do not stir from the basic natural state, and through the spontaneity of the buddha-dynamic the body does not stir, speech does not resound, and the mind is silent—we are relaxed in the perfect equilibrium of spontaneity, fully alert, as if hovering in the boundless center of the vault of space.

Abiding in nondiscriminatory pure and total presence
like the sky, the body-mind is not contrived,
and lacking compulsive ideation, there is no meditation;
tranquil like the sky, free of any trouble,
eschewing the objective field, contemplation has no reference.[141]

In the thoughtless nature of mind
unceasing light-form is uncrystallizing:
I, Samantabhadra, reveal
'the recognition of intrinsic gnostic light'.

In the unmotivated nature of mind
self-existing holistic imagery shines:
I, Samantabhadra, reveal
'the contemplation reverting the four vibrations'.

In the unreflective nature of mind
any movement is intrinsically pure light-form:
I, Samantabhadra, reveal
'the absorption that naturally frees attachment'.

In the nonactive nature of mind
artless perception is heightened:
I, Samantabhadra, reveal
'the contemplation that consumes all movement'.[142]

Without moving an inch, saying a word or entertaining any idea, we simply 'stretch out' in the brilliant space of emptiness which is like the vast vault of the sky, leaving everything as it is (also see canto 46 for the boundless middle or epicenter of all experience).

We rest assured that every moment is assimilated to spontaneity. There is no need to dwell upon uncertainty since every event is inescapably bound to spontaneity. Thus every moment is naturally perfect:

III.3 The Bind of Spontaneity

82. First, All Experience is Bound in Pure Spontaneity

All and everything is caught in the bind of spontaneity:
all inner and outer worlds are spontaneously imaged,
the whole of samsara and nirvana is a spontaneous display,
and pure mind is primordial spontaneity—
there is nothing other than spontaneous perfection.

All actual and possible environments and sentient organisms, all matter and energy, arise spontaneously as images of pure mind,

167

just as dream images arise spontaneously and perfectly. All experience of samsara and nirvana arises spontaneously and perfectly as a display of gnostic potency, like the fivefold spectrum of light appearing in a crystal prism. Pure gnostic mind in its brilliant emptiness and original hyper-purity is spontaneously present from the beginning like the sky.

The ground of samsara and nirvana is pure mind,
the ground of pure mind is spontaneity,
and the face of spontaneity is indeterminate:
since spontaneity is not something we can produce,
this unborn spontaneity is outside time.

The face of samsara and nirvana is pure mind,
the face of pure mind is variable,
and the variable ground is spontaneity:
since this variability is not something we can contrive,
unborn, it is outside time.

The actuality of samsara and nirvana is pure mind,
pure mind is actually unoriginated,
the nature of the unborn is spontaneity
and the face of the unborn is indeterminate:
since this unborn reality never comes into existence,
it is atemporal, outside time.
The identity of samsara and nirvana is pure mind,
and the identity of pure mind has neither beginning nor end;
this beginningless and endless ground is spontaneity,
its beginningless and endless face is ambiguity:
since this beginningless and endless actuality is unborn,
its seat is unlocated, outside time and space.

This timeless natural state cannot be contrived:
its timeless emanation is uncrystallizing,
its timeless condition is unnameable,

its timeless liberation is unceasing,
its incessant reality is the matrix of sameness,
and everything resides in this matrix of sameness.[143]

Gnostic spontaneity is revealed here as its threefold spontaneity of envisionment under three aspects of identity—its ground, original face and its actuality.

The three gnostic dimensions are unconditionally—spontaneously— present as spontaneity and to that extent their gnosis is perfect and complete. Insofar as all experience is thus spontaneously present there is only all-inclusive singular spontaneity. The magical dimension is like dream; the internal instructive dimension is like the diffracted spectrum of a crystal; and the dimension of pure being is like space.

The bind of spontaneity implies an absence of any effort:

83. The Bind of Involuntary Spontaneity

Since the nature of mind is timeless spontaneity,
pure mind contains the ground, the source and the essence:
because spontaneity is unattainable through the ten techniques,
forced concentration upon view and meditation is redundant,
extraneous support, such as goal-oriented application, is superfluous,
and egoistic ambition and apprehension is dispensable:
spontaneity is alpha-pure being here and now!

Pure being has always been present in the face of gnosis, so that all egoism, all the vicissitudes of ambition to attain the view, meditation, conduct and fruition, and all practices and procedures involving generation and completion meditation, are superfluous. Anyhow, pure being is unattainable through the ten techniques.

The supreme source, the teacher of teachers,
popped the following instruction to his fully receptive audience:
The yogin and yogini who realize the unborn nature of all things
do not strive in the ten techniques;

169

once they know the nature of pure mind, the supreme source,
they lose their dualistic vision, so they are left with nothing to reject;
gaining mastery by realization they stay right here,
in the spontaneous dynamic of the supreme source![144]

This revelation does not resemble in any way the teaching that seeks to attain a positive result:

The view and conduct of natural perfection
are inimical to goal-oriented endeavor;
both are pure mind itself, which is like space,
and space is beyond analysis.
Analyzing pure mind scientifically,
will not facilitate sky-like total presence.[145]

Spontaneity is the immutable dynamic of vajra-space (see canto 58). We cannot escape the spontaneous perfection of the moment:

84. The Epitome: Changeless Spontaneous Perfection

In the unchanging sky of the matrix of mind's nature,
in the matrix of the three gnostic dimensions,
samsara and nirvana indeed occur adventitiously,
yet they never move from this threefold matrix—
equivocal display is a treasury of compassionate magic.
Since all and everything at once is all-good spontaneity,
samsara and nirvana are overwhelmed by their own spaciousness;
since everything is good, including the bad,
all is spontaneous perfection, the spaciousness of the vajra-essence
and all experience is held in its ineluctable bind.

No actual or possible experience of samsara and nirvana can ever move out of the super-spontaneity of the three gnostic dimensions. That field of spaciousness is called 'Samantabhadra's nonactive spontaneity'.

Pure mind's potency pulsating,
outside contracting, inside expanding,
nothing in itself, appearing as anything,
invisible yet evident everywhere,
this is the wonderful paradoxical non action at work;
by undermining every approach to samsara and nirvana,
this one holistic nonaction suffuses all and everything.
There is no destination other than non action
and nowhere to go out of this single, motionless matrix.

Within Samantabhadra's space of nonaction,
samsara is all-good and nirvana is also good;
in this all-good matrix there can be no samsara or nirvana.
Appearance is all-good and emptiness is everywhere good;
in this all-good matrix there can be no appearance or emptiness.
Birth and dying are all-good and pleasure and pain are both good;
in this all-good matrix there is no birth or dying.
Self and other are all-good, and eternity and annihilation all-good;
in the all-good matrix, there is no self or other, eternity or annihilation.
All these are labels mistaken due to perception of absence as existence.

All arising at one in Samantabhadra's spontaneity,
all dualities, without exception are completely resolved,
all and everything unified within:
this holism, incommensurable, is greater than the great.
Higher than the high, Samantabhadra's spaciousness
governs everything, like an emperor,
ruling samsara and nirvana, but falling into neither.
Everything is all-good, good even when seemingly bad;
there is no good or bad, only Samantabhadra.[146]

The all-good matrix of Samantabhadra is the brilliant emptiness of self-sprung gnostic awareness, pure from the beginning. Therein, life and death, happiness and sadness, and so on, at their appearance in the moment, having not an iota of substance, are unitary gnosis and gnostic display. Since there is no life and death, happiness and sadness, in gnosis, whatever appears does not exist as such but rather as an image of the ever same nonactive reality, pure from the first. Thus, since samsara does not exist as it appears it is not to be rejected and since nirvana does not exist as it appears it is not be cultivated. The natural state, like space, need not be worked for or striven for, but phenomena and the intellect are mutually consumed in a timeless process of integration wherein the crux is to do nothing at all.

Here the gnostic actuality, free of karma, has superseded morality. If there is karma (effective moral conduct and consequent conditioning), then a lack of self-sprung awareness is the problem.

We tend to interpret congruous distinctions
as 'karmic' relationship;
inasmuch as 'karma' holds sway
pristine awareness is lacking.[147]

If we say 'I *know* that suffering exists!' then that illusion at its inception in the uncreated potency of pure mind is lacking in self-sprung awareness. Belief in the substantiality of suffering is due to the lack of ever-fresh awareness which is like the belief that the sky's gathering clouds are the sky itself rather than a display of the sky's potency:

The suffering of beings is pure mind,
and with consummate mastery, it is song and dance;
insofar as there is no refuge from suffering,
we live in sky-like equanimity.[148]

Samantabhadra's reality as spontaneity is defined here as nonaction, but nonaction as the paradoxical product of pure mind's potency wherein simultaneous outward contraction and inward expansion are a nonactive function. The matrix is not apparent anywhere, or in anything, because it is everything. A magical, mysterious, inactive reality, rules samsara and nirvana, just as this atiyoga rules all dualistic approaches. This holistic, free-form reality embraces everything in light. The spaciousness of the here-and-now could thus be called 'the spontaneous free-form field of Samantabhadra' or 'my self-accomplished motionless field of reality'.

There is no objective reality 'out there' that could be reached as a final destination; there is no stirring from this single free-form matrix; nobody has ever left it and no one ever will. Samsara and nirvana are all-good within this space. Since it has never really existed the world is all right, but emptiness is also good. Since the world and its emptiness have never been apart, life and death are also all right, and happiness and suffering are both good. These things have never existed in the matrix of Samantabhadra, so oneself and others are all-good; eternalism and nihilism (Christianity and Atheism) are also good. These things have never existed in the matrix; they are all confused projections of the mind.

The whole world appears all at once as a unitary, spontaneous 'all-good' reality, 'a holistic creation of Samantabhadra', which resolves every duality, without exception. Dualities are all one within the field, so this holistic singularity, without any rival, is 'the greatest of the great'.

Where 'karma' is defined as action that motivates a similar action, or reinforces the propensity to cause a similar action, when we engage in self-conscious virtuous conduct to produce a positive result, pristine awareness suffers. Karmic concatenation is defined as mentally contrived causal connection between affinities (typological similarities or 'congruous distinctions'). And insofar as there is an inverse relationship between karma and pristine awareness, directed action and karmic thought-projection may be called 'sin' (see the heading of canto 17).

This next section shows how when surrendering to spontaneity we attain gnostic reality, dissolution or a body of light:

III.4 Resolution in Spontaneity

85. First, Resolution in Ineffable Spontaneity

Resolution is spontaneously accomplished:
within nonspatial spontaneity, lacking inside or outside,
all experience is indisputable, motionless, auto-envisionment;
an all-embracing matrix, without top or bottom,

it is utterly ambiguous, nowhere restricted,
beyond indication, inconceivable and ineffable.

Pure gnostic mind can be neither consumed nor eliminated and it cannot be transformed; without inside or outside, top or bottom, whatever occurs in it, however it is imaged, is the same ineffable spaciousness.

Integrating everything, pure mind is the root;
inalienable and unattainable, pure mind is nondual;
devoid of self and other, it is identical spaciousness;
all-equalizing, pure mind is compassion;
the ultimate benefactor of beings, pure mind is ideal conduct;
and immutable pure mind is the uncreated field of reality.

Hierarchy may arise in the field of reality,
but pure mind has no top or bottom;
inner and outer may arise in the field of reality,
but the nonactive instant allows no inside and outside;
the reality-instant is holistic transparence
and every event is an occasion for gnosis in this indivisible space.[149]

This insubstantial reality, never crystalizing,
cannot be seen by looking nor found by searching;
both inner and outer are the outside itself—
there are no conceivable hidden depths.[150]

The first line of the root verse, 'Resolution is spontaneously accomplished', introduces the entire section. Spontaneity is synonymous with pure gnostic mind. It is beyond the possibility of proof or refutation, because there is nothing to think and talk about as such. Since it is timeless, it is beyond change and transition. Spatially indeterminate, it has no outside or inside, no cardinal directions, no right or left, nor top nor bottom. Whatever arises in it is an utterly indeterminate, spontaneous display of the inconceivable and inexpressible spaciousness of reality.

Every ineffable apparition in the field of reality is a spontaneous junction of the three gnostic dimensions.

All experience is resolved in the spontaneous creativity of nondual pure mind:

86. Resolution is the Essence of Spontaneity

Since experience is alpha-pure in essence,
and spontaneity is its very nature,
free from the four extremes—
existence, nonexistence, eternity and annihilation—
it is nondual pure mind.

All experience is gnostic awareness, and pure gnostic mind, empty in essence, belies the extreme of eternalism, and due to its clear and radiant nature it belies the extreme of nihilism. Belying the four extreme beliefs regarding the status of our being—existence and nonexistence, both and neither—all events are timeless spontaneity, 'indisputable, immutable, alpha-purity'.

Since everything is reality,
there is nothing at all to promote
and there is not the slightest thing to retain;
reality is total absence.[151]

Free of the four extreme beliefs, buddha is intrinsic gnosis
and beyond existence and nonexistence,
eternalism and nihilism, it is pure being.[152]

Alpha-pure in its essence,
it is spontaneity in its nature.[153]

Pure gnostic mind is the heart of the matter and 'alpha-purity' and 'spontaneity' are the keys to the two aspects of Dzogchen praxis, Cutting Through and Jumping Through. It is also the excluded middle (see canto 36).

The 'heart of reality' is the atemporal source of samsara and nirvana—even ignorance and delusion emanate out of it:

87. An Elaboration of 'Resolution in the Essence of Spontaneity'

Alpha-purity, in essence, is nowhere attainable,
its sky-like nature primordially pure;
spontaneity, in essence, can be contrived by no one,
its emanation never crystalizing, it can appear as anything;
the source of all samsara and nirvana,
it is without past or future, beginning or end.

The alpha-pure face of gnosis, the nature of mind, belies the polarity of existence and nonexistence—it is inexpressible.

Simplicity, the primordial purity of reality,
the immaculate face of the existential ground,
pre-verbal, beyond language,
does not articulate,
does not make conventional evaluation,
does not conceive of subject and object;
it contains no buddha or sentient beings,
no dogma nor concept of dharma;
it has neither something nor nothing.[154]

The nature of gnosis is the timeless spontaneity that is the gnostic ground where all manifestation of samsara and nirvana arises; but while its potency and display may appear as either, the nature of mind is neither samsara nor nirvana.

Beware! There is no delusion in me—delusion is a product of my potency. Emanating from the unchanging ground, my indeterminate nature beyond reification, ignorance arises from my indeterminable compassion. Just as the clouds in the sky have no concrete existence, evanescent, arisen adventitiously, so while the gnostic ground remains free of ignorance, ignorance emerges by itself within compassionate emanation. This is 'the natural mode of basic spontaneity'. It is ambiguous, indeterminate, envisionment. Its eightfold emanation is called 'the natural mode of the precious charm box' and 'the open door to sensory enjoyment'.[155]

All the imagery of samsara and nirvana arises thereby, samsara in the impure medium and nirvana in the pure medium, and although it appears as such in the face of gnosis, it cannot move out of gnosis:

Samsara and nirvana arise naturally in the three-dimensional matrix, but nothing ever stirs in three-dimensional spaciousness.[156]

Cantos 85, 86 and 87 reiterate the impossibility of escape from the natural nondual spaciousness of spontaneity, even when ignorance dominates and we think that there is only karma and suffering. Thus the basic fact of ineluctable release and resolution is established. The root verse of canto 88 restates this principle of spontaneous resolution in the here-and-now, the commentary defines it as integration with the holistic seed of pure being in every moment of cognition, while the commentary to the Garab Dorje quote applies it specifically to the dissolution characteristic of the illusion of dying, which may also be regarded as a metaphor for the moment by moment dissolution of materiality. Canto 89 describes the super-resolution wherein the vestiges of ineffable reality are dissolved and there is no longer the possibility of samsaric and nirvanic emanation in the spaciousness of spontaneity. Canto 90 makes a clear distinction between these two modes of resolution.

There is no life or death in gnosis, and the body and environment as a bunch of archetypal projections may be abandoned here and now. Death is no different from any other moment in that appearances are released as spontaneity; but death has ceased to be an issue with the realization of the absence of birth and birthlessness (canto 43). Canto 90 has, 'Whether or not there is freedom from the shell of corporeality, there are no distinctions in gnosis':

88. Materiality Resolved in Spontaneity

Unborn spontaneity is the indeterminate ground:
its timeless emanation is inexorable,
its empty empirical mode is nonreferential,
its intangible mode of release is uninterrupted;
in the place of its arising, its resolution is inevitable,
and that is dissolution into pure being,
the all-consuming spaciousness of the ground.

All experience first arises as indeterminate emanation in an instant of gnostic spontaneity, in the present moment it appears in the face of gnosis, and finally it is released into the instant of changeless spontaneity that is pure gnostic mind. The yogin or yogini who lives therein has 'captured the fortress of time', integrated into the zero-dimensional, holistic seed of pure being:

The beginningless and endless ground is spontaneity,
its beginningless and endless inception irrepressible,
its beginningless and endless existence nonreferential,
its beginningless and endless release uninterrupted,
without interruption reality is the same breath,
everything inhering in the matrix of sameness,
and in that singular dimension of reality
there is neither sameness nor difference.
Because sameness itself is uninterrupted
it is the 'sky-fortress', an unpatterned ring of reality;
since the four extreme beliefs revert to singular spontaneity,
it is the 'earth-fortress', unpatterned, all-embracing;
top, bottom, middle and interstices all connected,
that is what the masters call the 'integrated celestial fortress'.

This fortress is unpatterned, all-inclusive vision;
this citadel is the castle of pure gnostic mind;
this land is the matrix of unborn spaciousness;

its name is Jumping Through in Self-sprung Awareness
and its secret weapon, The Blade of Natural Ambiguity;
the protective razor-wheel is unpatterned spontaneity
that severs attachment to concretizing determinacy:
the zero-dimensional seed containing everything,
we are released in the unsought, undifferentiated matrix.[157]

Further in this regard, having cherished the unpatterned spontaneity that arises in every moment as timeless visionary dream, with freedom from mortality the entire deluded external-internal play melts into the womb of reality, and when archetypal visions arise as spontaneity, through the precept of recognition of vision as the nature of mind, the images revert to their own source in reflexive release. The razor-like precept of 'reflexive cognition of the nature of mind' is the razor wheel that dissolves spontaneous envisionment and provides release into hyperspaciousness and that is called 'integration in the sole holistic seed of pure being'.

Each moment is a process of 'jumping through', whether the spontaneous visions that arise are samsaric play or the archetypal visions of dissolution, including the basic illusion of corporeality in a material environment. 'Whatever arises is the nature of mind!' is the precept given in the Tibetan rites of dying, but this precept is meant for the living—too late for the dead! In death as in life we rest in the matrix of indeterminate spontaneity. There are no intermediate bardo states in this resolution. The illusion of materiality may have dissolved but in the integrated celestial fortress, the zero-dimensional seed, there is a body of light. The equivocal ground of being allows the resolution of corporeality at any or every moment in either a rainbow body or a body of light (see canto 122ii).

While atiyoga assumes full recognition of the nature of mind in this lifetime, if that does not occur then eventually, in super-resolution, the entire complex of samsara-nirvana, and the corporeal illusion fades, finally, into the spacious ground:

179

89. Final Dissolution as Resolution

Like clouds evaporating into the sky from which they emerged,
like colored light retracting into a crystal prism,
the archetypal imagery of samsara and nirvana
that arises in the ground of spontaneity
recoils into the alpha-purity of the essential ground.
This convergence in the spaciousness of spontaneity,
this is the ultimate super-resolution of all experience,
natural dissolution of all structure into the unthought matrix.

Confirmed in the view that the delusive samsaric appearances that appear now before the senses as a diversity of dualistically perceived environment and sentient life, matter and energy, are from the beginning inalienable uncrystallizing gnostic potency; meditation increasing familiarity with that view; unconstrained conduct bridging every abyss; and fruition dissolving egotism with all its expectations and apprehensions; when the yogin or yogini is freed from confining mortality, delusive dualistic appearances revert to their origin. Then during the five days that the visionary fields of nirvana arise (in the bardo of reality) as pure being and pristine awareness, through autonomous reflexive recognition of the nature of mind, those spontaneously perfected visions dissolve into the essence, and the yogin or yogini is ultimately released. Like clouds vanishing into the sky from which they emerged, all delusive samsaric appearances cease; like colored light retracted into the crystal, the visionary fields of nirvana dissolve; and like discursive thought bursting through into emptiness, the myriad mental projections and constructs, affectations and pretensions, vanish and there is buddhahood in the original ground of gnosis.

The implication here is that in the present moment, the essential gnostic dimension of pure being and the form-dimension that is its self-expression are present in spontaneity, but bound by corporeality they are unable to manifest. Upon release from corporeality they resume their natural state in alpha-purity:

In the body of each sentient being
lies the pure vision of pristine awareness,
but it is confined, unable to express itself fully.
What is contained and veiled, however,
as in a womb or an eggshell,
at its maturity will emerge:
as soon as the conceptual body is abandoned,
there is a coalescence with the imaged field
and the intrinsic gnosis of pristine awareness,
its own unthinking essence, is realized
and the pure vision of awareness is realized
and buddhahood is discovered.[158]

How is it that although they are the same in reality, samsara and nirvana appear separate in the face of gnosis? The difference lies in the manner of arising: the diversity of material and energetic appearances, environment and sentient life, in the present moment, are images of samsara, and the visions of pure being and awareness in the intermediate state (bardo) are images of nirvana. But, since they are both images of emptiness arising in spaciousness and released into spaciousness, samsara and nirvana must be understood as identical.

In this final dissolution, or disappearance, even the body of light dissolves, and even those who have not realized the celestial fortress in this lifetime, although knowing the reflexive release of positive and negative projection in the moment, are released into the ground of being. This is the moment of climax of the yoga of Cutting Through. The child clear light merges with the mother clear light. The samsaric illusion of corporeality dissolves and the buddha-fields of nirvana arisen in the bardo of reality (chonyi bardo) likewise revert to their source. There is no further emanation and of course, no rebirth. 'Death' is reversion to the gnostic source.

Although the distinction is not entirely evident in the root verses, resolution in spontaneity is twofold: first, resolution in the sensory fields here and now, like uniting internal and external spaciousness, and second, resolution in complete disappearance. The first is like finding a timeless body of light

181

through purification of materiality in this lifetime and the second is final dissolution of the elements (see canto 122ii). This may be restated as first (canto 88) finding death (release) in life and the second (canto 89) as finding life (release) in death:

90. The Two Modes of Resolution

In the here-and-now, whatever appears,
all objective appearances, melt into pure being,
into the natural disposition of the six sensory fields;
thereby outside and inside are instant by instant resolved
in the interfusing spaciousness of spontaneity.

Similar to resolution in manifest buddhahood
as total presence of the ambiguous gestalt of samsara and nirvana,
when the flicker of inner-outer imaging
naturally settles in the matrix of clarity
in an unthought, unstructured, natural state,
the immediate resolution in the crystal clarity of brilliant emptiness
is known as 'settling in the cavern of jewels'.

All and everything is resolved in precious spontaneity in two ways: in the present moment, as images arise in the six senses (the five outer senses together with the intellect), letting them alone without modification or adulteration through projection or deconstruction, with all-embracing pure clarity we enter with equanimity into the brilliant emptiness of zero-dimensional gnosis that is like the sky. No longer veiled by the concepts and constructs of corporeality, the internal luminosity of pure being coalesces with the sky of spontaneity; this dissolution into precious spontaneity is like the interior space of a house merging with exterior space as a door is opened. Leaving the eyes wide open, like an open door, empty and alert, gnosis is also pure and alert.

When we are entirely free of corporeality, the internal luminosity of the three factors (subjective, objective and unitary luminosity— pure being, exterior space and 'the eyes') melt into the one undifferentiated spontaneity, which is like the coalescence of interior, exterior and intermediary space as a house collapses.

Yogins and yoginis of the highest wit attain final release in this very lifetime. Through buddhahood in immanent transparence, without any transition, the ultimate manner of liberation is a spontaneous 'jumping through' or a quantum leap:

Those of highest acumen,
through holistic super-transparence,
without even a moment of transition,
live in the here-and-now.

In the space of intrinsic purity
lies the essence of clear reality;
translucent gnosis arises therein,
or, rather, it has always existed there.

When building a house, for example,
translucent space is divided;
by opening a door to the house
the space inside the house
and intrinsically pure space are united.
Unhindered gnosis arises like that.

When gnosis in the cavern of karmic potential
and gnosis resident in the sky
are conjoined by the open door of awareness,
physical proclivities are set free,
and we stay in nondual super-transparence.

If we possess such profound realization
then like a lion leaping long and high,

on super-transparent awareness,
without any transition of birth and death,
we jump through into the cavern of jewels,
abiding in timeless ultimate freedom.[159]

Basic gnosis, unoriginated brilliant emptiness, is the 'mother' clear light of spontaneity, while the emptiness of unoriginated luminous self-expression is the self-sprung 'son' clear light. This pair, luminous self-expression and natural clarity, though separate are blended or conjoined. With freedom from corporeality, they coalesce and the natural state in the 'mother' disposition is resumed; whether or not there is freedom from the shell of corporeality, there are no distinctions in gnosis. The medium of pristine awareness is a gnostic mixture of luminous self-expression and clarity, which is illustrated by the union of mother and son.

The first mode of resolution is like the opening of a door allowing the coalescence of external and internal space in the here-and-now (canto 89) where in 'the cavern of karmic potential' appearances are naturally recognized as gnosis. The second mode is likened to the complete collapse of the house in total corporeal dissolution (canto 89 and see also canto 122ii). Super-transparence is the medium of the quantum leap in the first mode.

Techniques of concentrated absorption in meditation do not facilitate these processes. Only nondual existential knowledge in the moment is valid. Without resolving all experience arising in the moment in 'child' clear light, there can be no 'jumping through' to the 'mother's lap' at the time of death:

91. Resolution: The Actual Precept

Resolution in natural spaciousness occurs in the moment—
there can be no subsequent liberation into the present ground;
obsessive concentrated absorption imprisoning basic space
provides no occasion for freedom from divine trance.
Cherish therefore, every instant of resolving intrinsic samadhi
in the interior spaciousness of the here-and-now!

If we cannot recognize natural concentration just as we are in the alpha-purity of the here-and-now, our 'stable meditation', similar to divine trance, unable to effectuate liberation, will give us only a higher rebirth in another state of bondage:

Able to meditate, yet unable to let go—
just another divine trance![160]

Therefore, with gnosis holding its natural primacy in the internal spaciousness of brilliant emptiness, as soon as the body is abandoned, precious pure being mixes inseparably with spontaneity and the two form-dimensions (perfect enjoyment and magical emanation) spontaneously serve sentient beings.

More specifically, regarding 'the contemplation of riding the breath', without making any deliberate effort, in the gap between the ending of exhalation and the beginning of the next inhalation when the breath is still, internal gnostic clarity is freed from subtle vital energy and in the consequent absence of mental propensity the inner clarity of pure being arises as sky-like contemplation. Through that recognition of the nature of mind, buddhahood is attained in the very moment in immanent transparence.

Consider the great garuda, king of the feathered race,
who yet unborn overpowers serpent-spirits,
and developing full-grown wings within the egg,
hatching from the shell, soars immediately into the sky:
what other birds need to learn through practice
the garuda performs with natural elegance;
and indifferent to enlightenment,
without concern for now or later,
he is unhindered in the open space of sameness.

And whoever aspires to freedom through the nine approaches,
through intense training, renunciation and self-development,
whatever is suitable, he is happy in the great approach,

for everything is easy in the pure-pleasure matrix of pure being
and there is no one who is not liberated there,
for reality is self-creating in the pure being of our vajra-heart,
and our conditioned body is perfectly potentiated essence.
Without the transition of birth and dying, the body abandoned,
unitary gnosis is inseparable from the totality,
and magical emanation pours forth incessantly
possessing everything and everyone unhindered:
that is the activity of the lazy yogin who 'rides the breath'.
Unknown and unbefitting on the gradual path,
the crucial fruition of Dzogchen Ati is gnosis.[161]

While still confined in an eggshell, the garuda is capable of over-awing certain serpent-spirits with his resplendence, and developing powerful wings within the shell he is able to soar into the sky immediately he hatches. Likewise, the yogin or yogini who enters the sovereign approach overarches the lesser gradualist approaches and by the realization that bridges the abyss of samsara he is able to pass into the space of reality. Hatching from the egg and flying away is like abandoning the corporeal shell in buddhahood.

For natural concentration or intrinsic absorption in the moment see cantos 23, 56 and 79. For the metaphor of the great garuda see cantos 122ii and 125.

In canto 29 Samantabhadra declaims: 'O great being! Such activity, the behavior of Samantabhadra, is called 'identity emergent in the three gnostic dimensions' and implies the view called 'the pristine awareness of natural perfection', wherein the immaculate cause is the fruition of buddhahood. In that moment, self-sprung, uncreated, the pristine awareness of my buddha-body, the display of my buddha-speech, and the activity of my buddha-mind are appearing in a unified hyper-expanse. This manifestation of immutable awareness, appears of its own accord; in the process of imploding experience, all temporal elaboration dissolves by itself; consciousness emerges naturally like the sky: attaining mastery of the heart-essence in its concrete appearances, I am Samantabhadra, 'the master of all mandalas'.'

To sum up, the ineffable nature of spontaneity is the ultimate way to go:

186

92. The Epitome of Spontaneity

Each and every experience resolved in the spontaneity of gnosis,
spontaneity resolved in the natural state of original hyper-
    purity,
and alpha-purity resolved in the inconceivable and ineffable
that is the ultimate resolution of spontaneous perfection.

Since every experience has its genesis in gnosis, every experience is finally resolved in gnostic spontaneity. Spontaneity is resolved in the natural disposition of pure being, the internal spaciousness of alpha-purity, and alpha-purity, free of extremes, inconceivable and ineffable, is resolved in final release.

The place of release is where it all begins.[162]

All-inclusive and indivisible! released into the matrix of spontaneity;
without union or separation! released in the nuclear matrix.[163]

*****

Everything resides in the spontaneity of pure mind,
from the first self-arisen, self-liberated, in hyperspaciousness,
the nature of the sole holistic seed, the heart meaning,
and this has been revealed in this jeweline commentary to the third theme.

Virtuous gods and oath-bound protectors,
vajra-heirs and inspired yogins,
hosts of sky-dancers and liberated deities,
great masters, glorious saviors—may you rejoice!

The third vajra-theme of *The Treasury of Natural Perfection,* establishing the ultimate spontaneous perfection of all experience, is completed.

The Fourth Vajra Theme: Unity
'All Experience is Solely Self-sprung Awareness'

IV.1 The Disclosure of the Unity of Self-sprung Awareness

93. First, The One Ground of all Experience

And now let me tell you about unity:
gnosis alone the experiential ground,
'appearing as multiplicity yet unmoving from unity',
self-sprung awareness is the unitary source.

In the one cat's eye gem, under different conditions,
distinct images of fire or water appear;
just so, in the one source, intrinsic gnosis,
illusions of both samsara and nirvana appear,
one of recognition, the other of ignorance,
both based in the single nondual pure mind.

Just as a single cat's eye gem appears in sunlight as fire and in moonlight as water, so the very same gnosis appears, through ignorance, as samsara, and, with recognition, as nirvana. Although these visions are quite distinct, as display or emanation of the same gnosis, they are undifferentiated in essence, not stirring from it.

All things are one in the pure mind base:
in the essential total presence where everything occurs,
all buddhas and sentient beings,

all environments and life-forms, matter and energy,
absent in unity are an inconceivable multiplicity.
Body and speech whether of buddhas or sentient beings
are pure mind, timelessly free of perceptual duality.
Wherever perceptual nonduality is achieved
the totality is realized and the root of all experience.[164]

The zero-dimensional seed encompasses everything in the moment:

94. Unitary Spaciousness is Self-sprung Awareness

Samsara and nirvana, all gnostic vision,
as it appears, is one in its empty face;
like dream, enchantment, reflection of the moon in water,
like the four visions and gossamer celestial space,
one in ultimate emptiness, total emptiness, it is simplicity itself.
Since everything is a single field, pure from the beginning
there is no 'duality', everything contained in a single seed,
that is zero-dimensional pure being! Ho!

All inner and outer experience is the same spaciousness in its empty, brilliant images of absence, and therein the nature of mind is a single matrix in and as the unstructured simplicity of its empty brilliance that is like the clear sky. The emptiness of gnosis and the emptiness of appearances in their common emptiness have one taste in the seamless nonduality of the one seminal seed. Thus 'the source is pure being in the zero-dimensional spaciousness of the sole holistic seed'.

The source of all experience is all-creating pure mind;
whatever appears, that is my essence;
whatever happens, that is my magical display.[165]

The four gnostic visions represent the stages of assimilation to gnosis evoked in the Jumping Through phase. The first vision is the intimation of reality in direct perception in initiatory experience. The second vision is increasing visionary experience by letting go into the moment and into the contemplation induced by the buddha-dynamic. The third vision is optimal gnosis, where each moment is a singular light show but wherein a residue of self-consciousness remains. The fourth vision is no-vision, for all traces of dualistic consciousness have vanished and there is no longer any sense of reality or unreality. (See the root verse in canto 56, and cantos 41, 65 and 77 and also canto 122ii in the final stanzas of the quote from Beyond the Sound.)

In and as self-sprung awareness, we are all buddha:

95. Pure Sameness as Self-sprung Awareness

The five elements manifested in pure mind,
unoriginated, cannot escape unitary sameness;
though appearing to exist, the six types of beings are empty form,
all gestalt imagery, unstirring from the gnostic scope;
though pleasure and pain are surely felt, they do not move
from essential total presence, sole self-sprung awareness:
know all experience as the one spaciousness, as emptiness,
the same unborn reality of pure mind!

Whatever manifests as the seeming material reality of the five elements arises in the gnostic scope, appears there and is released in the same gnostic scope. Whatever appears as sentient beings also arises there, manifests there and is released there. The environment and life-forms are forms of emptiness.

O great being!
Pure mind is the face of the here-and-now;
the nondual actuality of pure pleasure
takes a myriad forms that are utterly formless;
timelessly unstructured like the sky,
nonreferential, 'the one' is incalculable.

While pure mind itself cannot be measured or indicated,
what is made out of pure mind is an infinite variety.

191

What are the phenomena created by pure mind?
Inner and outer worlds, matter and energy,
buddhas and sentient beings,
all pure mind in nature, are created from that essence
and become manifest, fully revealed;
the five elements and the six types of beings are revealed
and the two gnostic form-dimensions of being that give them meaning:
this is the infinite variety emanated in purity by the pure nature of mind.[166]

Sky-like gnosis, empty and brilliant, is the super-emptiness of the myriad forms, the supreme clear light of all forms, the pure being immaculate from the first, in which arises impure samsaric projection and utterly pure nirvana. Whatever arises, no image stirs from the gnostic scope, and apparently concrete images are not taken as truly existing. Whatever appears is pure in the three gnostic dimensions of timeless buddhahood.

And yet no sentient being
attains gnostic awareness contingently.
Rather, all experience congruent
in self-sprung awareness
samsara is nonexistent
and for that reason only are we buddha.

Birth itself being realization,
our time in the womb is experience of spaciousness,
the unity of body and mind is gnostic space,
and life in the body has the three gnostic dimensions.
Old age exhausts motivation and delusory projection ceases,
through sickness we understand life,
death provides recognition of emptiness:
so sentient beings are all buddha![167]

The source is the formless dimension of pure being and the manifestation occurs in the two dimensions of form—perfect enjoyment and magical emanation.

The matrix of pure mind is the home of gnosis—the all-embracing seed:

96. The Seat of Gnosis is the Super-Matrix

Actual spaciousness is the super-matrix of intrinsic gnosis
wherein lies the sole dynamic of all buddha;
multiplicity unimaged, without fragmenting structure,
it is the unshakeable palace of total presence:
it is nothing but self-sprung awareness.

The reality-field of spaciousness, super-emptiness, the alpha-pure face of gnosis is simple, unstructured, pure being, and pure and total presence is spoken of as the sacred palace of self-sprung awareness.

My nature unstructured and undivided,
the entire field of reality is my creation—
it contains nothing but total presence itself.
My nature disclosed, all-pervading,
the clear sky is the palace of pristine awareness—
it is nothing but self-sprung awareness.[168]

Pure being (dharmakaya) may be otherwise stated as the field of spaciousness (dharmadhatu) that is the nature of gnosis (rigpa).

Every experience whatsoever is a pure-land:

97. Gnosis Yields the Three Dimensions of Samsara and Nirvana

A wish-fulfilling gem, a cornucopia of precious experience,
the three gnostic dimensions of spontaneity are the buddha-fields.

Gnosis is the pure-land of all buddha: both the pure visions of nirvana and the imagery of ignorance as the six realms of samsara are the envisionment of the three gnostic dimensions. Thus, nothing goes beyond and nothing is excluded from the nondual circle of the three gnostic dimensions.

The triple world and sentient beings,
are all contained in the media of body, speech and mind,
so do not look elsewhere for the three gnostic dimensions—
although to seek them is to lose them.
How amazing to see something that is not there!
This marvelous display
of buddhas and sentient beings, undifferentiated,
is like clouds billowing in the clear sky,
self-sprung and naturally perfect.[169]

Since I am at the heart of every experience,
the five elements, the triple world and the six realms,
there is nothing other than my body, speech and mind;
all is my nature and everything is my array.[170]

In changeless, objectless, all-suffusing pure being,
outer and inner, matter and energy, arise as perfect enjoyment,
and appearances, like reflections, are the magical dimension.
Everything perfect as the three dimensions' adornment,
it is all the emanation of buddha-body, speech and mind.
The innumerable pure lands of buddha
also emanate in the three-dimensional matrix of reality,
and the base of samsara, the six cities of ignorance,
also emanating there, the chasm of the body of instincts,
and the suffering that appears as dualistic birth and death,
is all liberated in the matrix of the psycho-organism
without transition or transformation.

The mind, birthless and deathless, like the sky,
the body ephemeral, like a bubble,
body and mind nondual, like a vajra,

194

all is gnostic awareness in the vajra-heart,
where no adversity can spoil it or destroy it:
this is unchangeable, invincible Vajradhara,
the master who no one knows.[171]

The nondual circle, like the sole holistic seed, is an image of non-duality.

Unity is inescapable in the one base:

98. The One Root

Within the sole holistic matrix, made by no one,
the entire gamut of multifarious experience is projected;
yet causality reverted, experience is one in its projective base
as the brilliant emptiness of the vastness of reality
shining in the timeless, nonspatial, pure sky.

However we treat samsara and nirvana, with affirmation or denial, simply by gazing at whatever occurs we reach the brilliant emptiness of gnosis, which is motivation-consuming bare immediacy, pure like the vast vault of the sky.

In the actual essence, gnosis itself,
there is nothing made, so no creator,
no creation—no lord of creation,
no view—no need to philosophize,
no vision—in the eye sheer clarity,
no projector—no biased projection,
no defilement—total connectivity
no quest—no endeavor,
no singularity—no multiplicity,
no beholder—no time![172]

Everything that we experience is pure mind:

99. Gnosis Alone is the Spaciousness of Reality

All of samsara and nirvana is created spontaneously,
but basic gnosis itself, uncreated by anyone,
like the sky, lies beyond endeavor;
in accord with that simile
unitary spaciousness, the vast super-matrix,
stills the inflating and deflating imputations of multiplicity.

Through lack of the intuition that gnosis is sky-like pure mind, samsara is created, appearing as matter and energy, the environment and sentient life. When we intuit that gnosis is pure mind, nirvana is created and appears as pure being and pristine awareness. Everything is created by gnosis, but gnosis is unique in that it is created by no one. It is timeless spontaneity, which is known by its simile of the sky, by its actuality as gnosis and by the evidence of indeterminate, uncrystallizing emanation in pure mind:

I am the teacher, the supreme source, pure mind,
and pure mind is the supreme source;
buddha throughout time is made by pure mind,
the triple world and sentient beings are created by pure mind,
the environment and sentient life are made by pure mind,
and matter and energy are made by pure mind.

Cause and effect, simile, actuality, and proof are all in accord:
as cause, I create the five elements
and as the result, I create the triple world and sentient beings;
as the simile, I am the universal metaphor of space;
as the actuality, I am unborn, universal truth;
as the evidence, I am all-creating pure mind;
as the proof, I reveal self-sprung awareness:
thus all five factors are in harmony.

196

Pure mind, uniquely uncreated, creates all;
everything made is the nature of pure mind,
and the unique uncreated cannot be created.

Those who fail to realize my nature as universal reality
objectify, conceptualize and label my creation,
and due to thirst and attachment, appearances concretizing,
they cling to fleeting illusions that inevitably perish,
like blind blundering fools.[173]

Nothing whatsoever in experience can be substantiated:

100. The Original Face of Mind is Ineffable

At the heart of the matter, beyond affirmation and negation,
the display of indeterminate events, whatever they may be,
is the matrix of the ineffable nature of mind
that lies beyond all conventional words and expression.

However samsara and nirvana arise in gnosis itself, in the essential universal gestalt, in the spaciousness of the alpha-pure natural disposition, in the spontaneity of self-sprung awareness, nothing whatsoever can be substantiated.

In primordial alpha-purity
there is no 'delusion',
so how can there be 'non-delusion'?—
delusion is pure from the first.
In the super cosmic gestalt itself
nothing can be called 'ignorance',
so nothing can be identified as 'error';
there is no 'intelligence' to label,
so 'stupid mistakes' can never occur;
there are no names or language,
so no misidentification;

OLD MAN BASKING IN THE SUN

the concept of 'knowledge' is unknown,
so no intellectual confusion is possible;
since no 'mind' or 'thinker' is attested,
there can be no confusing thought;
since the coarse and the subtle are one,
there can be no spurious reasoning;
'the doing' is one with 'the doer',
so where is the delusive attachment?
Since sense object is indivisible from the sense,
there is no delusory dualistic perception.[174]

The corollary to the assertion that nothing whatsoever can be substantiated is that no single experience or insight has any greater significance than any other. All experience whatsoever is equally the spontaneity of pristine awareness. No single image can be identified as the cosmic illusion, the universal gestalt, the archetypal meta-image, and therefore every image, every envisionment, has the same absolute value. By the same token no distinction can be made between delusion and clarity, between what is correct and what is error.

Nonduality is our inescapable reality:

101. Plurality in Unitary Gnosis

In total presence, the essence where everything happens,
there is no duality, yet an incalculable multiplicity;
buddhas and sentient beings, matter and energy, are resplendent,
all unmoving from the one immediate reality.

An inconceivable and incalculable multiplicity of samsara and nirvana, matter and energy, occurring in utterly ineffable unitary gnosis, in the moment nothing ever leaves the nonduality of dualistic perception.

In total presence, the essence where everything occurs,
in the absence of unity, there is an inconceivable multiplicity;

198

body and speech whether of buddha or sentient beings
are pure mind, timelessly free of perceptual duality.

To sum up, all is the one gnosis:[175]

102. The Singularity of Gnosis: The Trailer

Interconnected in unity, everything is perfect and complete
and that is the exalted quality of pure mind;
whatever manifests, in that very moment,
all conventional imputations are resolved.

As luminous expression of the empty nondual nature of mind,
both external phenomena—objects of knowledge,
and all internal phenomena—bare pristine gnosis,
in the reality that is neither one nor many,
are disclosed here as a single field of gnostic realization.

Recognizing all seemingly external objects as indeterminable, inalienable qualities of gnostic self-expression, like light diffracted in a prism, we no longer believe in their separate existence. Realizing that the internal experience of the unattested objective field laid bare as pristine gnosis is like a crystal prism, we know that there is no perceiving mind. In the absence of both an objective field of perception and a perceiving mind, there is no longer any dualistic perception, so 'all experience is consumed' in alpha-purity. With the field of nondual perception recognized as the spaciousness of pure-mind display, in the one reality of self-sprung awareness all experience has the same taste.

Pure being as emptiness,
self-sprung awareness as unthinking spaciousness,
is the heart of the brilliant emptiness of gnosis;
through empty, selfless, pristine awareness
all experience is the spontaneity of natural perfection.[176]
The spaciousness of reality is a wish-fulfilling gem,

presenting all and everything naturally and effortlessly—
it is the glory of self-sprung awareness to fulfill all desires,
the all-integrating base and the source, pure mind,
never lost, never regained, nondual pure mind,
neither self nor other, a spacious field of sameness.[177]

The notions of an outside and an inside of our skin, our 'self' and 'the other', are delusions of the dualizing mind: outside and inside are one in reality. When the fields of outside and inside are unified, the totality is luminous self-expression. For all-inclusive spaciousness as a unitary billowing ocean see canto 26.

IV.2 Assimilation of All Experience to the Singularity of Self-sprung Awareness

103. Assimilating Cognition to Self-sprung Awareness

The assimilation of all experience to the one taste:
in the imaged field of empty delusive appearances,
whatever appears, let it rest in its uncontrived singularity,
and in that moment it dawns as brilliant emptiness.

Whatever appears, in that moment, left alone as gnostic luminous expression in the zero-attachment of indeterminate clarity, the unstructured brilliant emptiness of reality emerges.

Immediate super self-sprung perception
unstructured, spontaneously arising,
is assimilated at the coincidence of cause and effect.[178]

Everything is experienced in unbegun immaculate samadhi:
irrespective of 'meditation' or 'nonmeditation',
all events whatsoever being the object of meditation,
since there is no technique of contemplation,
leaving things just as they are in the natural state,
unsought, assimilated, that is meditation.[179]

In the ungrasping nature of mind
pure light-form is indeterminate:
I, Samantabhadra, reveal
'the samadhi of the grand hyper-display'.[180]

Whatever the perception, leave it in its pristine condition, without any fascination for its radiance, and the brilliant empty light of its unstructured being will shine out.

In every movement in mind lies the stillness that releases attachment to the flow and thus all mental activity is assimilated to the dynamic of self-sprung awareness by the detached release of thought at inception:

104. Assimilating Release at Inception to Self-sprung Awareness

In the empty scope of myriad self-dissolving thoughts and visions,
whatever moves, relax and let it alone, just as it falls,
and contemplation of reality arises within the movement.

With the understanding that whatever moves is the play of self-sprung awareness, like water and its waves, free and easy relaxation brings release in the nonduality of stillness and movement.

The devious games of mind and intellect are assimilated
at the coincidence of truth and mental projection.[181]

In the pure and total presence of reality free of meditation,
since meditation and the field of meditation are one,
eschewing meditation, simply being is meditation.
Ultimate reality, ubiquitous meaning, is unoriginated
and when we know each concrete thought as that,
whatever idea, without exception, crosses the mind,
it remains unstirring in its unoriginated state;
recognizing all ideation whatsoever as meditation,
we rest undistracted in nonmeditation.[182]

201

In the unreflective nature of mind
any movement is intrinsically pure light-form:
I, Samantabhadra, reveal
the absorption that naturally frees attachment.[183]

This is the basis of the precept in Cutting Through on the unity of stillness and movement in gnosis. All movement is relative to a static point. If there is no static point of reference, as in pristine awareness and the reality-dynamic, movement is stillness itself. The mind can never wander since it is always at the point of stillness.

All images, whether still or proliferating, melt immediately into the nondual light of awareness:

105. Assimilating the Nonduality of Stillness and Movement

In the moment when mind and objective field are seamless sameness,
relax into its aimless, traceless, natural purity,
and internal luminosity shines as heightened pristine awareness.

To sustain the assimilation of sensory perception and release at inception to self-sprung awareness as described above, the mind and objective field seamlessly united, crystal clarity ensues, and by staring directly like a statue at that scintillating spectacle with eye and consciousness, it shines internally as traceless pristine awareness.

By gazing into the field of brilliant gnostic reality,
gnosis, devoid of multiplicity, is seen within;
gazing into the intrinsic gnosis of multiplicity,
super concept-free pure being is found within.[184]

On the mode of assimilation:

The forever unsought super-matrix of nonaction,
with body and speech inactive, is assimilated
at the coincidence of appearance and emptiness.[185]

There is nothing to be done, so make no effort!
There is no focus, so no notion of meditation!
There is no variation, so just be mindful![186]

In the nature of mind beyond cultivation,
light-form is nonspatial, reflexively released:
I, Samantabhadra, reveal
'the all-inclusive contemplation of integral openness'.[187]

Heightened perception (vipashyana) is insight into the intrinsic emptiness of every appearance. When inside and outside are a single field of purity, stasis and movement are equally light.

The foregoing three aspects of assimilation to unity reveal the nondual dynamic of pure being and the contemplation that is implied:

106. The Integration of Those Three Functions

When those three key functions are assimilated to a single essence,
realization and non-realization are always the same,
mind and its field are one in pure being,
glitches and veils are one in the dynamic of sameness,
and without intermission, we enter upon the natural state,
without tightness or looseness, we discover the definitive essence,
without a break, we abide in the reality-dynamic,
and willy-nilly there's no transition or change.

Within the nondual sameness of mind and its objective field that is freely resting appearances, the gnostic dynamic is discovered where there is neither hanging on nor letting go. Within the natural samadhi of flowing movement that is freely resting gnosis, there is no difference between realization and non-realization, and the unmoving dynamic of reality is discovered. Through the nondual sameness of glitches and veils that are the nonduality of stillness and movement the uninterrupted gnostic dynamic is discovered.

These three, assimilated without any distinction, unwavering from the natural luminous expression of reality, the six sensory fields are loose and relaxed and the doors of perception are wide open:

The warmth of the authentic relaxed natural state,
is assimilated at the coincidence of samsara and nirvana
as we escape into our own primal place.[188]

Listen! Just like that, involuntary pure pleasure!
body, speech and mind unstressed,
no fabrication, no fictive projection,
letting go the intellect's apparent concrete constructs,
just relax in the pleasure of self-sprung awareness!
The body unconstrained, the senses unsuppressed,
speech uninhibited, without any deliberate action,
the mind, settling nowhere, stays unmoving within.[189]

The nature of mind where the mood does not change
meditates in hyper-equanimity:
I, Samantabhadra, reveal
'the contemplation of relaxed sensory perception'.[190]

This threefold intuition is assimilated by the yogin or yogini who realizes the sameness of past, present and future:

For the person who does not retain and pursue traces of the past, who does not anticipate the future and who allows present perception to rest naturally in its own state, all cognition blends into one without past or future, which is called 'one aggregation, one essence'. In this the gnostic yoga of timelessness, by allowing reflective thought processes to run down naturally, samsara and nirvana are integrated in nonduality. Dwelling in past memories is thereby, eliminated, attention to the future is precluded and analysis of the present naturally fades away. That is 'the gnostic yoga of timelessness'.

Further, whoever puts no trust in the past, who has no faith in the future and who distrusts the intellect in the present is 'the gnostic yogin or yogini who understands timelessness'.

Whoever does not belittle past ignorance, who does not forestall future ignorance and who does not reject present ignorance is 'the gnostic yogin or yogini who dwells in timelessness'.

Whoever does not cling to past hatred, does not attract future hatred and does not revel in present hatred is called 'the gnostic yogin or yogini who understands timelessness'.

Whoever does not remain entangled in webs of past stupidity, does not pave the way for future stupidity and does not initiate a downpour of present stupidity is called 'the gnostic yogin or yogini who understands timelessness'.

Whoever does not respond to past awakening, does not waste energy on future awakening and does not celebrate present awakening is 'the timeless gnostic yogin or yogini'.

Whoever does not rue past desire, who is indifferent to future desire and who ignores the object of present desire is 'the timeless gnostic yogin or yogini'.

Whoever does not cling to past jealousy, who does not envision future jealousy and who does not admit present jealousy is 'the gnostic yogin or yogini who understands timelessness', 'the gnostic hyper-yogin who has realized the sameness of samsara and nirvana', whose buddhahood is self perpetuating.[191]

Through experiences of this timeless yoga in the unitary empty light of gnosis, fourfold view, meditation, conduct and fruition arise in singular spontaneity:

Pure mind is like the empty sky,
without memory, supreme meditation;
it is our own nature, unstirring, uncontrived,
and wherever that abides is the superior mind,
one in buddhahood without any sign,
one in view free of limiting elaboration,
one in meditation free of limiting ideation,
one in conduct free of limiting endeavor,
and one in fruition free of limiting attainment.[192]

At the time of going beyond, the concentrated absorption that brings neither union nor separation arises, and this is its essence:

Thoughtless pure being is naturally pristine meditation;
without any object of reference we realize our true reality
which is ineluctable hyper-absorption,
and that is natural fruition.[193]

In unbroken intrinsic concentration
there is no volatility—how wonderful![194]

By leaving appearances as they are (canto 103), the nonduality of objective and subjective aspects of experience is discovered, and we fall into the contemplation which requires neither the abandonment nor adoption of the content of any perception. By leaving gnosis just as it is, every movement and projection of the mind occurs in our natural absorption, and understanding and misunderstanding of reality equalized, constant contemplation is discovered (canto 104). In this realization of the nonduality of stillness and movement (canto 105), glitches and veils, implying the two mental processes of deviation and obscuration, are equalized, and infallible contemplation where there can be no error is discovered.

To sum up, the intrinsic dynamic of release gives us liberation just as we are:

107. Unitary Liberation—The Epitome

Vast! spacious! the mind of the masters is the same as the sky;
ineluctable! it is the matrix of the holistic seminal seed;

206

released as it stands! with neither realization nor non-realization;
experience consummate! no mind! it is open to infinity.
On the pinnacle of the forever-unfurled victory banner
the rising sun and moon illuminate the microcosmic realms.

As all-suffusing gnosis awakens to its nakedness in timeless freedom, we reach the all-consuming dynamic of pure being. On the pinnacle of the forever-unfurled victory banner of realization, the clear light of the sun and moon of self-sprung awareness shines forth. Arising in the vast, all-suffusing super-emptiness of gnosis, 'it illuminates the murk of the existential ground where samsara and nirvana are bound'. At that time, there is release into the origin.

All-inclusive and indivisible! free in the matrix of spontaneity;
without union or separation! free in the nuclear matrix;
arising in all possible ways! free in the matrix of ambiguity.[195]

The mode of release:

Moreover, freedom attends reality:
free at the core, any effort is wasted;
timelessly free, no release is needed;
free in itself, no corrective is possible;
directly free, released in the seeing;
completely free, pure in nature;
constantly free, familiarization is redundant;
and naturally free, freedom cannot be contrived.

Yet 'freedom' is just a verbal convention,
and who is 'realized' and who is not?
How could anyone be 'liberated'?
How could anyone be lost in samsara?
Reality is free of all delimitation![196]

Freedom is timeless, so constantly present;
freedom is natural, so unconditional;
freedom is direct, so pure vision obtains;
freedom is unbounded, so no identity possible;
freedom is unitary, so multiplicity is consumed.

Conditions are released as conditions,
and so I am free of all constructs;
objects are released as objects,
so I am free of dualistic perception;
a cause is liberated as the cause itself,
so I am free of the duality of samsara and nirvana;
all events are released as phenomena,
so I am free of all verbal convention;
mind itself is liberated as mind,
so I am free of signs, symbols and expression.

Like washing off dirt with dirt,
purity is released by purity,
every poison cured by poison.
Iron bars are cut by iron,
stones smashed by stone,
wood burned by wood—
each is its own nemesis,
or there could be no release in the moment.[197]

Then to apply the principle of immaculate timeless freedom:

There is no freedom through striving—
we are free from the start:
method and wisdom conjoining,
our father and mother are pure cause;
the paroxysm of karmic energy—
that is the pure pleasure of gnostic mind;
the seed composed of the five elements—

that is imagery arising within the field of emptiness;
the blissful equanimity of union—
that is perfect insight arising from method;
with entry into the mother's womb,
the peaceful imagery of intrinsic gnosis arises;
in the first seven weeks realization develops,
within ten lunar months the ten levels are traversed
and at parturition a tulku is born.
The developed body is a field of archetypal images;
physical being is the ground of being;
in old age, our delusion melts away,
in sickness realization is confirmed
and in death we dissolve into empty reality.
In that way, all embodied beings
are effortlessly, utterly free.

Ho! Conduct changes nothing—our lives are already free!
Meditation achieves nothing—our minds are already free!
The view realizes nothing—all dogma is freedom!
Fruition demands nothing—we are free as we are![198]

A victory banner (gyeltsen) consists of a pole holding aloft a tube of layered multi-colored cloth, carried in procession or used in the decoration of god-houses. Its 'pinnacle' on top of the pole is the symbol of unitary clear light and pristine awareness, the junction of sun and moon (see canto 58).

Freedom is spontaneous, automatic and an autonomous function of mind. Being free in themselves, just as pure mind is the nature of samsara and nirvana, all things release themselves. Thus the homeopathic principle of freedom—like cures like—makes Samantabhadra of us all. In fact we are all born as tulkus by virtue of natural perfection: the identity of particular individuals as 'tulkus' conflicts with the precept adjuring abandonment of all spiritual identity (canto 17), and thrusts us back into samsaric confusion.

The holistic interconnection of all experience:

IV.3 The Bind of Unity

108. Unitary Spaciousness Is Bound in Self-sprung Awareness

The one intrinsic gnosis binds all experience:
environments and life-forms, infinite and unconfined,
whether of samsara or nirvana, arise in spaciousness;
spaciousness, therefore, embraces all experience at its origin.

All experience occurs within gnosis; at its initial appearance it is already bound by integral gnosis.

The non-conditional heart-essence
governing everything, effectuates everything.[199]

Experience arising in the moment is a unitary field of awareness:

109. Appearances, Just as They Are, Are Bound in Gnosis

Whatever multifarious appearance arises in the moment,
inalienable, it is never anything other than gnosis,
bound in the matrix of self-sprung awareness.

Whatever appears in this very moment appears in the face of gnosis and is bound by the nature of mind.

Existing, I exist as pure mind;
abiding, I abide in the spaciousness of reality,
shining, I shine in the sky of gnosis.[200]

In its dissolution experience is still bound by unity:

110. Finally, the Bind of the One Gnosis

Even in simultaneous inception and release,
fading into spaciousness,
since gnosis does not become anything other than pure mind,
it is bound by the one all-consuming original reality.

Finally, every experience reverts, liberated, into gnosis, like clouds dissolving into the sky. Thus, consumed in the spacious field of pure being that is empty gnosis, it is bound by integral reality.

The deluded mind, distinguishing between sameness and difference,
is released in unity, released into the matrix of reality;
blocks to total presence, desire in the material world,
are instantaneously released, released in the matrix of awareness.[201]

To sum up, everything is always integrated in unity:

111. Everything is Bound in Self-sprung Awareness: The Epitome

Thus, all events are bound by unitary gnosis
and indeterminate gnosis, the essence of total presence,
is bound by the heart of reality without transition or change—
instantaneous unconditioned fulfilment!

Since all environments and living beings, samsara and nirvana, are integrated in the gnosis that is the reality of Samantabhadri, no experience is other than pure gnostic mind.

Samsara and nirvana, matter and energy, composed of the five elements,
are contained in the bhaga *matrix of Samantabhadri.*[202]

Just as all worlds, inner and outer,
all forms of matter and energy,

the animate and inanimate world,
all contained in space, are absent,
so is the vast field, the matrix of pure mind,
with its buddhas and sentient beings,
its crucible and contents, environments and life-forms.[203]

I, the supreme source, never proclaimed
to any past buddha emerging in me
that there was anything other than mind.
To those present now or arriving in the future,
the supreme source teaches only pure mind.[204]

The matrix is personified as Samantabhadri, the consort of Samantabhadra, while gnostic reality is Samantabhadra. (See also cantos 15 and 49.)

No transmission is necessary, since all is automatically fulfilled:

IV.4 Resolution of All Experience in Self-sprung Awareness

112. Resolution in the Heart-Essence Without Beginning or End

There is only one resolution—self-sprung awareness itself,
which is spaciousness without beginning or end;
there everything is complete, all structure dissolved,
all experience abiding in the heart of reality.

All experience at the very moment of its appearance is without beginning or end, all contained in self-sprung awareness, never moving from the actuality of brilliant emptiness.

Unmoving within, it is nothing that can be found within,
and turning outside, it cannot be imaged or isolated;
neither extruding nor intruding, this self-less compassion,
which no one can give or take, is present from the first.[205]

All experience is resolved in nondual perception—objectless self-sprung awareness:

113. Resolution in the Imageless Perception of Self-sprung Awareness

So experience of inner and outer, mind and its field, nirvana
*   and samsara,*
free of constructs differentiating the gross and the subtle,
is resolved in the sky-like utterly empty field of reality.

External and internal objects of perception, lacking discrete particles, are baseless images in the spaciousness of gnosis. The mind, lacking discrete moments, naturally melts away into emptiness without trace, purified in gnosis. The mind and its field are both pure like the sky, baseless and utterly empty.

Both inner and outer are the outer itself—
there are no conceivable hidden depths
and 'subtle existence' is a false concept.[206]

Everything is up-front and in our faces and there are no complex subtle hidden structures of mind except those of delusive concoction. By elevating the subtle and demeaning the gross, creating comparative constructs, structures of varying subtlety, reality is still zero-dimensional, incapable of fragmentation.

All experience is resolved in ineffability:

114. Resolution in Ineffable Gnosis

And if pure mind is scrutinized, it is nothing at all—
it never came into being, has no location,
and has no variation in space or time,
it is ineffable, even beyond symbolic indication—
and through resolution in the matrix of the gnostic dynamic,

which supersedes the intellect—no-mind!
nothing can be indicated as 'this' or 'that',
and language cannot embrace it.

No matter what dualistic perception or style of samsara or nirvana, whatever environment or life-form, arises in self-sprung gnostic awareness, it is contained in pure mind, and complete in pure mind it is contained in natural perfection. Although the reality of pure mind is all-embracing and everything rests in it, since its nature transcends the field of verbal elaboration, it remains as elusive as the sky.

O great being, listen to me!
My nature is like this:
I am just one unitary whole
and yet revealing, I reveal two aspects,
and emerging, I emerge as the nine lifestyles,
and integrating, I integrate into natural perfection,
and abiding, I abide in the spaciousness of reality,
and existing, I exist as pure mind,
and shining, I shine in the sky of gnosis,
and embracing, I embrace life-forms and environment,
and emerging, I emerge as matter and energy.

Yet revealed, I have no concrete attribute,
and I cannot be seen as an objective entity,
and I cannot be known in verbal expression,
and since my nature does not follow from a cause,
I am free of all verbal imputation.

To really understand my nature,
take the sky as the illustration,
'unoriginated reality' as the definition,
and the elusive nature of mind as the evidence.

214

As 'sky-like reality'
it is indicated by the simile *of sky or space;*
as 'nonreferential reality'
the impossibility of its objectification is indicated;
as 'inexpressible in words',
the expression 'inexpressible'
shows my nature to be without reference.

This concise teaching serves to clarify my actuality;
it should be enough for you to realize my reality.
If this does not suffice,
then no matter how I speak of it,
we shall not meet,
and straying from me, obfuscating my nature,
you will fail to realize the heart of reality.[207]

To sum up, everything is resolved in 'supreme namelessness' (see also canto 42):

115. Resolution in the Great Nameless Consummation: The Epitome

In the super-matrix—unstructured, nameless,
all experience of samsara and nirvana is resolved;
in the super-matrix of unborn empty gnosis
all distinct experiences of gnosis are resolved;
in the super-matrix beyond knowledge and ignorance
all experience of pure mind is resolved;
in the super-matrix where there is no transition or change
all experience, utterly empty, completely empty, is resolved.

Every experience of samsara and nirvana, arising in simple, unstructured gnostic space, is finally resolved in the same space.

The place of release is where it all begins.[208]

215

All gnostic experience is resolved in unborn, empty gnosis:

This amazing, miraculous display
is nonactive just like elemental space.[209]

All events of pure mind are resolved in nonduality:

The pure pleasure of spontaneity arises
from the intrinsic power of gnosis,
the gnosis of holistic pristine awareness,
that is nondual knowledge and ignorance,
and it can be found nowhere else.[210]

All empty experience is resolved without transformation:

Unchanging, it is simply being,
and like the never ending sky,
reality is contingent upon nothing.[211]

Thus, the reality of the three uncreated gnostic dimensions in self-sprung empty gnostic awareness, its nature pure from the beginning, is the super-spontaneity of brilliant emptiness:

As the nature of the vajra-body,
I am unchanging and indestructible;
as the nature of lotus-speech,
I am the indeterminate, ubiquitous essence;
as the nature of the circle of mind,
I am thoughtless hyper-absorption.[212]

The three gnostic dimensions are the clear light of emptiness:
nothing eternal, without substance,
nothing ephemeral, the buddha-body is clear light;
undifferentiated, without inside or outside
the buddha-body is translucent empty space;

216

indivisible emptiness and appearance, utterly intangible,
the buddha-body is birthless, deathless and immutable.

Buddha-speech is actually unoriginated,
unarticulated, free of meaning,
beyond all words and expression.

Buddha-mind is sky-like gnostic purity,
without mentality, mind and intelligence—
no feeling, so no sensation,
no ideation, so no sense of self,
no karmic impulse, so no incarnation,
no consciousness, so no delusion,
no five sensory fields, so no grasping,
no desire, so no attachment,
no virtue or vice, so no maturation,
and no self-identity, so no egoism.

With the five doors of pristine awareness wide open,
the nature of everything is the same buddhahood,
body, speech and mind without defilement,
and there is no view, no meditation, no conduct,
no paths to traverse no levels to climb.[213]

Unthinking awareness of light is pure being;
its intrinsic self-display is the enjoyment of timeless awakening;
and polarity resolved, compassion is magical emanation.

All levels of being and all manner of lives
are touched by pure total presence—
no process leads to that supremely total presence,
and trying to approach it, pristine awareness recedes.
Forever lazy and profligate, nothing accumulated,
yet the store of merit and wisdom is always full;

217

unpracticed, untrained, unpurified,
yet the veils of passion and knowledge are always transparent.[214]

* * * * *

Within the all-inclusive field of self-sprung awareness,
through the one immaculate taste of all and every experience,
nondual unity is established:
that is the revelation of this bejewelled commentary to the fourth theme.

Victorious buddhas abiding in all time and space,
sky-dancers, siddhas, gnostic masters and protectors,
all fortunate people worthy of the highest teaching,
may you be pleased by this profound and vast instruction!

The fourth vajra-theme of *The Treasury of Natural Perfection*, establishing the unity of all experience as the pristine awareness of basic gnosis, is completed.

The Fifth Vajra Theme
Advice to Recipients of the Transmission

This fifth theme consists of five parts treating 1. the recipients, 2. the teacher, 3. the essential precepts (i. the view; ii. surrender to the gnostic dynamic; iii. recipients: caste and color), 4. obligations of the recipients and 5. the benefits of the transmission.

Firstly, concerning who are suitable recipients for instruction, there are two kinds of candidates—the acceptable and the unacceptable:

116. Candidates Generally To Be Rejected

The elixir of this most profound approach
should be offered only to the most favored and brightest,
not to adherents of the lower approaches,
to those caught up in their moral conditioning
or to unfortunate narrow-minded people.

Even if untalented people with little karmic affinity were taught, they would not understand this profound teaching. Narrow-minded people unable to digest it would decline it. Adherents of the progressive approaches, attached to their own philosophical systems, would mistake the view. Then if this sky-like reality were revealed to those attached to their moral conditioning, those who weigh everything only in terms of karmic cause and effect would dispute it and criticize it. Such candidates are unsuitable and this unexcelled teaching should be kept hidden from them:

O great being! If I were to reveal natural perfection to adherents of the lower approaches they would say that according to the materialistic belief in causality everything has a cause and thus natural perfection is illogical.[215]

Do not give my transmission of the ubiquitous supreme source to those who believe in cause and effect! If you reveal this definitive transmission to them, they will assert that every good or bad action has a cause and an effect, and judging and criticizing my immaculate nature they will divorce themselves from it for ages.[216]

Do not utter even a word of this in the company of Disciples and Hermits! If you want to know the reason why, it is because they would be frightened and abhorrent and faint away when they hear it. They would distrust the secret tantras and lose interest in them, and as for karmic retribution, they would necessarily plunge into the great hell. So we should not speak even upwind of them, not to mention our teaching them and their listening.[217]

117. Particularly Unsuitable Recipients

It should be concealed from those who revile the teacher,
who are hostile to their brothers and sisters,
who violate secrecy in gossip,
who are faithless, avaricious and dishonest,
and who are preoccupied with mundane affairs.

It must not be taught to trespassers, those who cannot respect the teacher and have a negative idea about their dharma brothers and sisters, those who cannot keep a secret and disseminate it publicly, to the faithless, the very greedy and the dishonest—as well as to the ordinary person who believes that the delusory appearances of his present life are real. Such trespassers are particularly ill-suited, because they are hostile to the ethos of the teaching and to the teacher:

Unable to show respect and esteem,
misconstruing and perverting tantrayoga,
lacking spiritual breeding and character,
with little insight,
betraying others' kindness,
boasting about their family,
adorning themselves with fine ornaments,
addicted to meaningless lifestyles:
such people cannot be called students,
rather, they are enemies of the teacher,
and natural perfection should not be expounded
to people who will not embody it.[218]

Who are the unfit characters?
Those who delight in the social spotlight,
the arrogant, who cannot respect what is sacred,
those who are easily discouraged and rejected,
those who do not accept the tests that arise,
those who want power through rivalry in practice,
those who inhibit the spreading of the teaching,
those who nurse invidious comparison with others—
the Great Perfection is kept from such people.[219]

118. Acceptable Candidates

Only the brightest and best receive the Great Perfection:
those who respect the teacher and possess deep insight,
who are open-hearted, even-minded and most generous,
who have little critical thought and little concern for it,
who do not care about this life but aim for supreme awareness,
who have faith and perseverance, and can maintain secrecy.

The qualities required by the recipient to receive the Great Perfection include faith in the teacher, the teaching and his or her fellow students (dharma brothers and sisters), devotion and

221

magnanimity, a spacious mind and an open heart, a good nature,
strong conviction, a positive attitude, little concern about pure
living, great perseverance and trustworthiness:

The worthy disciple possesses
powerful faith and persistence,
deep insight and detachment,
a wide purview and tantric conduct,
ability to persist in thoughtless composure,
capacity to keep and sustain commitments,
a steady affectionate loving disposition,
clear and bright meditation,
obedience to the word of the master,
a clear and resolute sense of obligation,
the ability to conform to conventional behavior,
through humility and sincerity, a light mind,
the ability to follow by a single word of revelation,
and all such activity that brings benefit to oneself.

To maintain entrustment and secrecy
fulfilling the vajra-purpose;
associating with highly educated people
to benefit oneself;
gentle speech lacking conceit
to accommodate hostile minds;
and to treat the teacher and buddha alike:
these are the qualities of the good student
and whoever possesses these qualities
is said to be a vessel for the Great Perfection.[220]

The signs of faith and commitment
preparing us to receive the heart-essence
are faith, commitment and perseverance,
compassionate sorrow and a still intellect;
and with the detachment from the body,

from son, partner, servants and wealth,
*that allows giving them up in joy and faith.*221

119. The Conduct of the Student

The student pleases the master with gifts,
and having previously made his commitment
he requests the teaching with deference;
granted the transmission, he accomplishes it appropriately,
and finally surrenders to the natural state of being.

Before asking for the heart-essence of instruction, the receptive student pleases the teacher in many ways and makes a commitment to fulfillment. Once accepted by the master, he or she gives up all concern for the present life, practices conscientiously and resolves the duality of samsara and nirvana in this very life, arriving at consummation in the natural state:

'Once I have received this essential instruction,
what to me are all the vanities of the world!
I will suffer any difficulty!'
*Such is the committed attitude required.*222

The common behavior of the student without insight into the nature of mind is to venerate the lama, to aspire for nothing but realization of the teaching and to continually reflect on the qualities of the master and the teaching. The teacher welcomes and accepts us with compassion and cherishes and fosters us like children, giving us timely indications so that an unbreakable impetus is established together with a mutually affectionate relationship.

To the vajra-master who gives us precepts, let us offer
our brothers and parents, our very eyes,
our children and wives, our precious wealth,
*whatever we cherish and value!*223

Let us please the spiritual master
with our most precious belongings,
our bodies and dearest treasures![224]

In brief, we should offer body and life,
not to mention our property and livestock.
Even if the lama does not need them for himself,
he will accept them on behalf of the Three Jewels.[225]

Never cutting the cord of compassion,
nor breaking the two-way flow of affection,
master and student remain connected.[226]

120. The Qualities of the Teacher

The master is learned with high qualities.

In general, the regular vajra-master, at the apex of the vajra-tradition, is learned and compassionate. If he is completely empowered and committed, and if he has the general tantric background of fully developed generation and completion stages, then he has the capacity to liberate others. In particular, in addition to that, a master of the Great Perfection has received the definitive empowerment of the great mystery, to which he maintains total commitment, he is conversant with the tantras, commentaries and precepts and he has surrendered to the immaculate view and meditation that is like the sky. With these qualities he can lead others to happiness. In short, the fully qualified vajra-master holds in his hand a treasure that never diminishes in the same way that a victory banner is never furled:

The master of vajra-reality
is an honest person with high teaching skills.
Through empowerment he has absorbed the tantric ethos
and knows inner and outer tantric practices;
in inseparable union with the buddha-deity,
he remains always in undistracted samadhi.

He is wise in the secret tantras
containing the precepts of the Great Perfection,
and he knows both external and internal meditation liturgies;
never shrinking from the total vision of reality,
he has renounced all outer, inner and secret action
and the inexhaustible treasure he holds in his hand
is like a special precious jewel.[227]

The fully qualified master
is a source of all gnostic qualities,
firmly grounded in perfect total presence.[228]

Certain lamas are better avoided:

Unaware of his deep conceit,
stupidly preoccupied with sophistry,
unfamiliar with the meaning of tantra,
arrogantly mortifying the weak,
pursuing self-destructive lifestyles,
afraid to gaze into powerful mandalas,
violating the samaya commitment,
failing to respond to questions,
uneducated and conceited,
unfit to be called master,
he is the student's bane;
he cannot teach Dzogchen Ati
so do not associate with him![229]

121. The Method of Instruction

The teacher, knowing his students,
gives the keys appropriately;
to conceal them from the unsuited,
he should affix the seals of ban and entrustment.

A lama first examines the students' suitability and then bestows the essential instructions gradually, scheduling their practice for several months or years. He does not tell them everything at once, because some frivolous students could confuse the main points and lose inspiration. But even suitable characters, if they do not mature steadily, may become disillusioned with the process due to earlier experience:

Know your students and grant them instructions over time rather than all at once, keeping them hidden from those fixated on mundane concerns.[230]

Suitable disciples feel devoted to the dharma, so they request instruction with reverence and gifts which the teacher may not need, yet accepts as a token of the students' best intentions—it is a way of making auspicious connection. Ill-suited disciples, on the other hand, are not genuinely motivated and pay mere lip-service.

Candidates' faith should be put to the test:
respectful students approach the teacher with precious gifts,
while others may be arrogant and greedy.
Do not teach the supreme source to the latter![231]

Precepts should be granted to worthy recipients and concealed from the unworthy:

Do not pour the nectar of natural perfection
into ordinary, inferior vessels!
It is meant just for the faithful few.
If we teach it also to the unworthy,
the worthy may be infected like them.
So keep it from the small-minded![232]

To keep it hidden from small minds, we do not even think about sharing such profundity with them, nor verbalizing it, nor giving them a book to read. Even when we give it to worthy persons, we

226

bid them maintain secrecy. We affix 'the seal of the ban' to conceal it from the unworthy, and 'the seal of entrustment' to reveal it to the worthy.

122. The Essential Instruction

Entrust the essential teaching of definitive meaning
to talented and favored heart-sons.

In the following verses the main teaching is elucidated and then its recipients described. The central revelation is pure gnostic mind, which supersedes causal conditioning and deliberate effort. It is treated under two headings: the initiatory view and surrender to the buddha-dynamic.

i. The Initiatory View

Whatsoever appears in gnosis does not stir from the original face of gnosis and is non-affective, producing neither positive nor negative effect. Thereby, causality and moral conditioning are superseded in the natural perfection of a single all-encompassing instant of the transparent here-and-now:

I am the thoughtless sky that is pure being,
and unthinking, I take nothing and reject nothing;
nonjudgmental mind is like space,
and like nondiscriminatory space
Samantabhadra accepts nothing and rejects nothing:
I am nondiscrimination.[233]

In essence there is no cause or effect:

Total presence is like elemental space
and space has neither cause nor effect.[234]

Buddhahood is not realized through virtue—
if it could be realized by virtue,
natural, unconditional, perfection would be a lie.

Samsara is not precipitated by vice—
if evil doing could precipitate samsara,
self-sprung awareness would be a lie.[235]

To sail though these treacherous waters, consider that it is only in the gradualist approaches that people believe in virtue and vice, good and bad. Failing to recognize their naturally perfect condition and yearning for and insisting upon objectively positive experience, in their resulting bewilderment good and bad appearances are projectively affected. There is no good nor bad in pure mind, but such morally dualistic appearances arise in the same way that delirium is generated by high fever. Just as the principles of birth and death do not apply to what is uncreated— elemental space is not a seed wherein a seedling germinates—so the principle of delusory cause and effect is inapplicable to the nature of mind.

Since natural perfection is beyond causality from the first,
it is attained by nonaction, not by deliberate effort.
The transmission of a teacher with a causal view
defines a hierarchy of mundane temporal qualities,
and working from a cause affects a desired result—
pure mind has no cause and never any effect.
Since nothing originates in pure mind,
to take the life of an ordinary person for example,
any presumption of birth and death is misplaced;
unless and until non-contingent spontaneity is intuited,
a hierarchy of material, temporal qualities defined,
principles of causality asserting their relationship,
comprising the limited causal approach, is all we get.

O great being, listen!
When I talk about 'self-sprung awareness',
I mean unceasing awareness that encompasses everything,
unique awareness that has no cause
yet produces everything—there is no other source.
Defining a hierarchy of temporal, causal, relationships
and searching for pure mind, nothing will eventuate;
since pure mind cannot be produced by any cause,
do not place it in a temporal index;
since pure mind is not a product of any condition,
do not treat it as a component of the relative world.

O great being, listen!
We strive in meditation because we desire excellence,
but any striving precludes attainment;
excellence resides only in timeless self-sprung awareness.[236]

It is futile to try to realize buddhahood through ordinary causal development. What is never attainable through effort is unconditional pure being, the natural state to which we all aspire; if it can be reached through endeavor it is a conditioned thing that implies impermanence. Simply resting without artifice in natural gnosis, we are participating in the dynamic of all buddha past, present and future:

Being naturally present without any need to seek it,
buddhahood cannot be attained by endeavor;
it is perfected spontaneously, without effort—
rest in the thoughtless state of natural gnosis![237]

Buddhas past, present and future,
all buddha, are nothing but pure mind:
buddhas of the past gained realization
by seeing the uncontrived nature of mind;
buddhas of the present act for the sake of all beings

due to knowledge of uncontrived mind
as 'uncontrived', just as it is;
buddhas of the future have never been taught
to modify the self-sprung nature of mind
and presently without trying to correct the precious mind
buddhas appear traversing an uncontrived path.

We may not realize that all events are pure mind,
but no correctives will help.
Ignorant, but aspiring to realization with a contrived agenda,
we may invest many, many aeons in practice
but we will never discover adventitious happiness thereby.

The three gnostic dimensions are not mind-constructed,
so when in the sutra The Teacher of the Three Dimensions,
the notion of contriving the three dimensions occurs,
it is clear that the teacher, although possessing the three bodies,
is not the teacher who is the nature of mind.
When the teacher speaks of 'developing the three dimensions',
since the teacher always speaks the truth,
it is the provisional—not the definitive—teaching he reveals.[238]

ii. Surrender to the Buddha-Dynamic

Resting free and easy in the nature of mind, planning nothing, analyzing nothing, surrendering to pristine reality, no intellect remaining, bare gnostic pure being superseding causality and moral discrimination, here is pellucid natural clarity, brilliant shining emptiness, timeless uniform luminosity. This uncontrived, unadulterated space is uniform in its natural flow, immaculate in its natural transparence, at ease in its natural freedom, pellucid in its natural purity, relaxed in its natural disposition, and the doors of the senses are held wide open in a constant state of awe. In this vast matrix of open space, the mind's hold on linear progression,

230

the past, present and future, is irrevocably broken and in equilibrium we rest in naked, unthinking, indeterminate clarity.

Through unfathomable depths of clarity,
brilliant emptiness all-suffusing,
dancing in fields of pure pleasure,
one-pointed, this is ultimate spaciousness.[239]

Brilliant emptiness, an all-pervading field of light,
undefiled by ideation, memory purified,
free of any structure or elaboration,
all-inclusive and empty like the sky,
naturally pure, it is utterly beyond any indication.[240]

Intrinsic gnosis is congruous with emptiness,
and through providential familiarity with that
the thoughtless dimension is apprehended
along with the light of my compassion
and you are one with me and share my lot.[241]

In the indeterminate nature of appearances,
a dull mind's thoughts evaporate,
and in that intrinsically pure spaciousness of appearances,
in thoughtless gnosis,
knowing unmoving sameness,
in the field of identical sameness,
our thinking ultimately exhausted,
we abide in naturally pure spaciousness.

When appearance and verbal expression are one,
in undivided spaciousness
we rest in super-relaxation.

Through holistic transparence,
laid bare, unblemished,

we rest in timeless original super-purity
and that immaculate spaciousness,
forever, is our identity.[242]

Familiarizing ourselves
with natural perfection,
just waiting we hear the meanings;
without meditating, pure pleasure expands,
and we gain direct insight into the nature of things.

Even though guilty of heinous crimes
whoever discovers the nature of mind,
and familiarizes himself with it, is absolved,
and, without doubt, escapes hell.[243]

The indeterminate reality free of grasping attachment
is the supreme nondual dynamic of the gnostic masters;
the reality that entails no striving, pure as it stands,
this is the reality-field of consummate samadhi.[244]

Since sky-like identity is original timeless purity,
pure being is indeterminate, without any motivation;
a vast super-expanse without outside and inside,
the expanse of reality is boundless, without substance.[245]

These contemplations, the gnostic dynamic, the inherent clarity of
the nature of mind, are unobscured by lethargy or agitation and
their antidotes. In this even expanse, through the purity of the
seamless whole without outside and inside, we are released from
the aberrations of grasping particularities, and from glitches and
veils:

Ever-fresh uncultivated nonmeditation
clarifies the doors of perception;
with the conceptualizing mind in abeyance

it is attentive only to cognition itself,
disinterested in externals,
unmotivated to revert distraction,
unmoved by any decline or failure,
impervious to fluctuations of satisfaction,
free of lethargic equanimity,
clarified memory always restorative,
averse to any process of corrective training,
the perceiver fluid and easy within,
form perceived as radiance,
colored symbols ringing changes—
when there is no partiality,
meditation is without deviation.

The manifest visionary quality of this meditation
is the brilliant emptiness of gnosis,
untrammeled by any specific quality,
wherein dualistic perception has ceased
leaving only the pure face of reality.
This vision being nondelusive,
in the pure nature of all causes and conditions
the tangible and intangible naturally dissolve,
and attachment to the five sensory objects dissolves,
and the coarse elements of materiality dissolve,
and pure awareness expanding
we surrender to reality.[246]

Thus moving towards self-actuating purification in emptiness, initially we no longer identify coarse and subtle elements as such. The visionary experience of the brilliant emptiness of pristine awareness gradually increases, and finally all particles of matter, gross and subtle, break apart and, like mist evaporating, corporeality—the illusion of material reality—dissolves. Reaching the point of surrender to the alpha-purity of gnostic pure being, it

233

is said that we have 'consumed ourselves' reaching our natural state:

Now, undirected, remaining in the natural state,
all the articulation of pure mind
appears as manifest understanding in each intellect
even without that person having learnt it.
Through familiarity with this understanding
now unmanifest and nonconceptual,
all appearances dissolve by themselves,
and as holistic transparence,
are patterns of super empty brilliance.
The four elements—earth, water, fire and air,
the potentialities of each unmanifest,
dissolve like mist evaporating in the morning sky.
Our diverse delusory attachments,
our ideas about things, remain unborn,
dualization, as subject and object, is self-inhibited,
and nothing appears—self-consumed.
Illumination being our own experience,
all embodied beings are similar.[247]

In the finale of natural perfection,
all phenomena fall into their natural state,
and ordinary consciousness and reality coinciding,
we reach the carefree detachment of timeless release.

The gnostic dynamic supersedes reason,
all specifics dissolve into their own pure nature,
the polarity of emptiness and substance is resolved,
movement consummate in thoughtlessness,
and, with no-mind, the intellect is superseded.[248]

The culmination of Cutting Through to alpha-purity is a dissolution of the elements, whereas the culmination of Jumping

Through to spontaneity is purification of the elements. These two phases of realization are alike inasmuch as both external and internal corporeality dissolve. The two differ, however, according to whether the body of light manifests. As soon as the partless particles of the body dissolve there is immediate release into the ground of alpha-purity; but whereas in Cutting Through no body of light appears, in the Jumping Through phase, a body of light allows uninterrupted metamorphosis. There is no distinction however, in the manner of release into the natural state of alpha-purity.

This sovereign approach enables the yogin or yogini to overcome everything through all-suffusing radiance and to resolve causal conditioning in this lifetime. Finding confidence in realization consonant with the interior emptiness of reality, the delusion of causality is destroyed. Noncompliant with the lower, progressive, approaches, ignoring their many theories of causality, we have broken out of the eggshell of philosophical opinion. This is achieved by the realization of self-sprung awareness alone—adherents of the eight lower approaches are unable to speak about that.

Ho! This vast brilliance of manifest pristine awareness,
nonspatial, synchronicitous awareness,
the mysterious awareness of natural perfection,
this is the cosmic climax.

To take a simile for the view of natural perfection,
it is like a great garuda soaring in the empty sky.
The language of the lower approaches is rich and various
but the lion cannot bark like a fox—his belly is too big,
and the fox cannot roar like a lion—his throat is too narrow;
the Great Perfection expressly reveals intrinsic gnostic awareness
while the lower progressive approaches demean that view.[249]

Further, some say that just as the garuda must start from below to reach the high cliff from which he may take off on his first flight, so we must first climb the ladder of gradual development before we can achieve the effortlessness of the garuda gliding in the sky. This is not true. Indeed, some may need to refine their skills, but our original simile addresses the moment of gliding in the sky and indicates nothing else about the garuda. A simile never tells the whole story, or else it would be the story itself, not a simile. Anyway, given that beings both human and divine have different capacities, the Great Perfection is the prerogative of those with capacity for instantaneous realization; it is not for the narrow-minded:

Beings, human and divine, have different capacities:
some struggle to refine their sensibility
while others have timeless instantaneous insight,
and I teach according to need.[250]

Even in the common approach it is said:

Some are ready from the first
while others need training.[251]

I have appended this section (canto 122) as an epitome of the four previous samaya themes and as a key designed to unlock them. The four samaya-commitments of natural perfection are like a four-storied storehouse of jewels and the four themes are like keys to those four storeys, while this summary is like a master key that unlocks the treasury where those other keys are kept.

iii. Recipients: Caste and Color

Worthy recipients of the definitive essence are first described in general and then in more specific terms. In general:

It is meant for uncomplicated people with spacious minds;
idle and innocent, carefree and easy-going.[252]

And more specifically:

'*O Bhagavan Vajradhara! If the secret precepts of natural perfection*
cannot be freely revealed, please tell us to whom this sovereign
transmission, this supreme message, should be disclosed, their
social caste, their occupation and their complexion.'

Then Bhagavan Vajradhara emerged from his samadhi and
answered his retinue: 'Listen to me now, good people! Listen to my
teaching! I reveal the definitive reality of tantra to the warrior and
priestly castes, to the great merchant caste and also to the
proletarian caste. The outcastes, moreover, whatever their
complexion, both men and women, are suitable recipients of the
Great Perfection. Specifically, to those with strong limbs and dark
complexion, with spotless white teeth, with slightly bloodshot
eyes, with great locks of hair, dark brown, curling clockwise, to
those with little regard for the body, with common external
behavior and with forceful forthright speech, and to those able to
repeat word for word what was said by another person, to all such
people I reveal the Great Perfection precepts. If someone has all
these features complete—even if he or she is a butcher, a prostitute,
a rag-picker, or any underdog—he or she should be given the
teaching without reservation.

Upon passing into nirvana I have taught these secret thrice-distilled
precepts—considerations of caste and color—which as an elixir of
secret precepts are like an absolute monarch. Please teach the
foregoing precepts to people who possess such qualities!'[253]

123. Obligations of the Recipients

They, in return, should keep this eternal truth
in their hearts, without dissemination;

if secrecy is violated, retribution will follow,
and ensuing criticism will diminish the heart-teaching;
so cherish the mystery with a quiet and easy mind
and attain the kingdom of pure being in this very life.

The particularly worthy students to whom the teaching is entrusted, in general, should not pour the elixir into an unfit vessel, but share it only with suitable people. They should not even speak of it upwind of those particularly unsuitable. Even when they impart it to worthy disciples, they should do it slowly, examining the candidates' qualifications. Specifically, when transmission has been given in its entirety in a gradual way, holding nothing back from those who prove trustworthy, they affix the seals of ban and entrustment, bidding the recipients preserve the heart teaching and protect it against its demise. The teaching is spared criticism and the bad karma of repudiation is prevented if propagation to ill-suited characters is avoided. By teaching it only to the worthy, the heart teaching is caused to remain long in the world, making it possible for the most favored to attain liberation and enlightenment in one lifetime.

Teaching the Great Perfection to unworthy people causes harm to both ourselves and others:

If this discipline regarding the heart-essence is abused
certain obstacle-creating demons and spirits
and skilled dakinis can bring teacher and student
under a cloud of fear and to untimely death,
and through adverse criticism the way of the heart will decline;
for this reason abandon unresponsive people.[254]

The essential teaching should be taught only to the qualified:

To rid them of worldly attachment and as a character test
the master accepts their bodies and their possessions,

and having examined their capacity and found them qualified,
he reveals to them the essential meaning of the supreme source.[255]

In particular, the teaching is entrusted to supremely favored individuals:

As part of the this oral lineage revealing the ultimate message,
a constant essence, neither waxing nor waning, hidden in your heart,
the supreme source is hereby entrusted to you![256]

Finally, in praise of the benefits of instruction:

After receiving the actual transmission of the Natural Great Perfection the benefits of instruction should be sung. Those most favored disciples should delight the master with honor and reverence. After receiving the meaning of natural perfection they should actualize it so that present and future well-being is assured.

We serve both root and lineage masters
replete with their various qualities,
with all our power, our physical bodies,
our dependants and all our possessions.

Pleasing them in body, speech and mind,
we treat the masters as buddha;
we follow them with faith and intelligence
and with undeluded devotion,
and without misunderstanding their injunctions
we serve them with clear faculties.

The benefits of such comportment are immeasurable,
greater than from the wish-fulfilling tree,
the wish-fulfilling gem or the ever-provident cow.

Let us serve the masters with this thought in mind,
so that we may repel the armies of samsara![257]

*****

The great mystery of the vajra-pinnacle,
atiyoga, the spontaneity of spaciousness,
how it is taught, by whom and to whom,
has been revealed in my bejewelled commentary to the fifth theme.

You hosts of lamas, buddha-deities and dakinis,
with your billows of immemorial compassion,
and those taking immense overt joy in this teaching—
you oath-bound protectors—enjoy!

Through buddha-compassion, you men and gods,
endowed with perfect integrity and impeccable devotion,
regents of buddha, embodiments of the great approach,
whoever you may be, may you be happy hereafter!

The commentary on the fifth vajra-theme of *The Treasury of Natural Perfection*, describing the kind of people to whom the teaching is entrusted, is completed.

The Conclusion of the Treatise

The final section includes a dedication to the release of the triple world of samsara and to the universal spread of the Great Perfection (cantos 124-125), the colophon (canto 126) and inspiration for the fortunate (canto 127).

124. Dedication of Merit to the Total Liberation of the Triple World

The meaning of natural perfection, the ultimate secret,
is no longer hidden—its message here is fully revealed:
may all migrant beings of the triple world, without effort,
realize their intrinsic freedom in hyperspaciousness!

This illuminating composition unveils a shining lamp of the unsurpassable teaching that is like the heart of the sun: may all beings transmigrating in the triple world understand the nature of their minds as self-sprung awareness, and without any striving may they all find perfection in Dzogchen Ati, the wholly unconditional state of natural perfection, and may they all become perfect masters abiding in Samantabhadra!

When the inscrutable nature of mind
arises spontaneously as the holistic world illusion,
the triple world is released as it stands
and the super-simple being of Ati is perfected.[258]

125. Dedication of Merit to the Spread of the Great Perfection

Shattering the encasing shell of conventional views—gliding high,
in the apex approach—the field of the great garuda king,
may the message of atiyoga—exalted above all,
spread everywhere as an eternal victory banner!

In the manner of a great garuda broken out of its eggshell of limiting views, fully grown and immediately soaring into the sky, the yogin and yogini of the natural perfection of Dzogchen Ati leave behind both projection and resolution of their aspirations:

As with the soaring garuda in flight
no complication, no simplification![259]

This apex approach is like the peak of a mountain:

The transmission of atiyoga, the apex approach,
the highest peak of all, like Sumeru, the king of mountains,
higher than the highest, the vast mind of Samantabhadra,
transfigures the minor approaches by its natural power.[260]

May this revelation, never declining, remain forever like the crest-ornament of the precious victory banner, spreading and shining throughout the ten directions!

126. The Author and Structure of the Composition

The three series, and nine matrixes contained within the four themes,
its definitive meaning structured in sixteen sections,
this exegesis of The Precious Treasury of Natural Perfection,
was carefully composed by the good Longchen Rabjampa.

All the various topics and precepts of the Natural Great Perfection fall into one of the Three Series of Mind, Matrix and Secret Precept. They are also gathered into the nine matrixes: the matrix of alpha-purity (essence) (1); the matrix of spontaneity (nature) (2); the matrix of indeterminate emanation (compassion) (3); the matrix of freedom from causality and endeavor (4); the matrix of basic purity of glitches and veils (5); the matrix of the timeless purity of view and meditation (6); the matrix of uncontrived spontaneous nonaction (7); the matrix of the seamless gnostic dynamic (8); and the matrix of universal release (9). These three series and nine matrixes are encompassed here by the four themes of absence, openness, spontaneity and unity since they are bound by the unchanging reality of these four. Each of these four themes is elucidated according to the four key points of disclosure, assimilation, the bind and resolution, so that this exposition is sixteenfold. It is composed to fully reveal the definitive, direct meaning of the Great Perfection.

The Treasury of Natural Perfection is a metaphoric title given to the treatise because, like a storehouse of precious stones, it fulfills all desires. It was composed by Longchen Rabjampa, a yogin of the sovereign approach, whose name means All-embracing Super-Matrix, because he opened his mind to a boundless vision and meditation of sky-like reality. He composed it carefully in order to benefit people of future generations, inasmuch as the sovereign secret precepts would induce the highest degree of perfection in others, revealing precisely the dynamic of Dzogchen Ati, the nature of mind, and thereby vanquishing and dissolving the hardened attitudes of all lower progressive approaches. Thus the heart-essence is called the 'vajra-hammer':

The field of reality, without birth and cessation in time,
an uncompounded matrix, unchanging and undivided,
shattering all limitations, is called 'the vajra-sledge-hammer':
it is the sovereign secret precept that destroys all bias.[261]

127. Inspiring Joy in the Lucky Ones of the Future

May the definitive meaning of the five themes
in this treasure-house of natural perfection
finely adorned with its pearls of breadth and depth,
elegant in its structure of finely tuned meaning,
bring joy to hosts of the fortunate!

Like the treasury of a universal monarch triumphant to the four corners of the world, adorned with immeasurable wealth, ornamented with a splendid array of treasure, this treasure-house of spontaneity, the vajra-pinnacle, *The Treasury of Natural Perfection*, contains five themes of clearly defined structure like a five storey palace. Within, a wealth of marvelous meaning broad and deep ornaments it, and an array of unambiguous well structured definition decorates it. Composed as a precious and inexhaustible treasure for a multitude of highly favored individuals of future generations, as basic instruction for a complete spiritual praxis may it bring them complete satisfaction. May the samaya-commitments of those embarking upon the sovereign approach be miraculously fulfilled and may the teaching last for ever! This auspicious benedictory ornament marks the conclusion.

Benediction induces good luck and well-being:

Luckiest amongst the lucky,
be famous in luck and virtuous in renown![262]

May the auspicious sun's beneficial radiance
dispel the shadows of bad luck in the four continents;
may this marvelous, auspicious, profound truth
reveal the auspicious Dharma and bring happiness to all beings!

May the clouds of nectar gathered in the auspicious sky
unleash a wish-fulfilling storm of constant good fortune;
may the dance of the auspicious apex approach
precipitate an auspicious storm of total presence!

To that end, The Treasury of Natural Perfection
provides bountiful good fortune as boundless as space,
and the meaning of the supreme approach, broad and deep,
provides a veritable gold-mine for the fortunate.

With intelligence shining like the sun
in the vast space of knowledge,
distilling the essential elixir of tantra, transmission and precept,
I have composed this on White Skull Snow Mountain.

Through the compassionate light of the sages
and my own mean discriminating intellect
I gained dominion in the city of wisdom
and accordingly my mind expanded naturally.

***

The peak approach to reality, natural perfection,
appeared in the most favored places in the world,
in the great lands of India, China and Tibet,
through the grace of the sages.

Commentaries and precepts, profound and immense,
composed by the best scholars of various persuasions,
defined effective custom, which gradually became sacred,
planting buddha's eternal victory banner.

Depending upon this lineage's wonderful knowledge
and the incomparable grace of my lama,
I have composed The Treasury of Natural Perfection
to explain the vajra-themes of the Great Perfection.

Since these vajra-themes are inscrutable,
eluding my personal experience,
and since I have no talent with words
I have relied upon my masters' explanations.

Like a vine creeping up a great sal tree,
adorning it, attaining great height,
only by the grace of the texts and the lama
have I enhanced these profound and immense themes.

***

With intelligence and health, spreading the wings of intuition,
resplendent in the pure sky of samadhi's clear light,
driven by the dynamic of self-sprung awareness,
the abyss of samsara is crossed in inner space.

Hatched from the egg of unbiased contemplation
the bird of natural perfection on the sovereign approach
spreads its wings of fully-potentiated realization
and soars directly into exalted space.

When the confining shell of body, speech and mind is shattered,
the empty awareness of pure being is optimal brilliant emptiness,
consummate spaciousness is holistic transparence
and the holistic field of all and everything is directly perceived.

In an open, untrammeled, sky-like expanse,
bare empty gnosis is a seamless integrated whole,
unitary inner and outer fields are unchanging empty brilliance,
and the kingdom of sovereign pure being is captured.

The most intelligent yogin, in this lifetime,
receiving the definitive transmission,
pure being, alpha-pure, mental processes inactive,

246

possessing the mind of buddha in his corporeal body,
taught by the lion of men, vanishes beyond.

In the field of utter emptiness is a spacious empty mind,
on top of fundamental bliss is constant mental satisfaction,
in the spaciousness of dissolution is the relief of no-mind,
and the yogin is the all-embracing sky! Ho!

The unthinking natural disposition of pure being open like space,
natural concentration like the uninterrupted flow of a river,
in a single intuition all paths and levels traversed,
this is the dynamic of Samantabhadra! Ho!

In the immaculate sky of self-sprung awareness,
the carefree yogin soars like a great garuda;
absence, openness, spontaneity and unity
are the uncontrived nature of reality! Ho!

In this super-matrix of spontaneous gnostic vision
whatever appears is evanescent gnostic potency,
absent light-form, mere illusory display,
all-inclusive super-emptiness! Ho!

In this buddha-dynamic, nothing moves,
everything self- arising, abiding and vanishing the same,
a space of blissful clarity without extension,
a dynamic dissolving distinction between day and night! Ho!

The empty brilliance of gnosis is changeless pure being,
the timeless purity of samsara and nirvana is the matrix of pure mind,
the images of dualistic perception are the potency of groundless pure being:
realization defies all description and expression! Ho!

When samsara is recognized as groundless—nirvana!
When nirvana is recognized to be mere label—hyperspaciousness!

When nonaction undermines thought—pure being!
Letting things be without ideation—inexpressible!

Without fixation upon any objective—the natural state!
Experience consumed, intellect exhausted—ultimate reality!
The bias of 'yes' and 'no' dissolving—unlimited freedom!
Hope and fear eradicated—pure mind!

In this ultimate definitive essence,
this is my advice to the most talented of future generations:
Follow in our footsteps
and seize the citadel of nonduality.

This encounter with the vajra-space of natural perfection
this best and definitive transmission
this vast reality-matrix of effortless release
this is the final precious samaya commitment.

So stay right here, you lucky people,
let go and be happy in the natural state.
Leave your complicated life and everyday confusion
and in a place of solitude, doing nothing, watch the nature of mind.

This piece of advice is from the bottom of my heart:
fully engage and understanding is born;
cherish non-attachment and delusions dissolve;
and forming no agenda at all reality dawns.

Whatever occurs, whatever it may be, that itself is the key,
and without stopping it or nourishing it, in an even flow,
freely resting, surrendering to ultimate contemplation
in naked pristine purity we reach consummation.

Thus the commentary upon The Treasury of Natural Perfection *elucidates*
the essential reality of all experience—the heart of the teaching.

May the masters' teaching spread far and wide!
May it bring fortune and happiness at all times and places!

Here ends the commentary to *The Treasury of Natural Perfection* by Longchen Rabjampa—The All-Embracing Super-Matrix—a yogin rich in the wealth of great learning in the multitude of Buddhist scriptures who has mastered the sovereign approach. He composed this treatise in the mansion of Kuntuzangpo on the slopes of Gangri Tokar, the White Skull Snow Mountain.

Thrice good fortune!

Endnotes

NB. See Appendix I for abbreviations employed in the notes.

1. See Tulku Thondup (1984), p. 50; Dudjom Rimpoche (1991), p. 494; and Khenpo Tenzin Namdak, "Dark Retreat" transcript, trans. John Reynolds.
2. *Natural Gnosis*, ch. 78 (*Rdzogs chen rang skad smra ba'i le'u*, "The Chapter on the Self-referential Language of the Great Perfection"), pp. 788-9. NLD, pp. 25-6. The 15th line of the tantra (*rdzogs chen rig pa mthong dang ma mthong med*) here reads *mtho dang ma mtho* (neither high nor low; neither extolled nor despised) while the 20th line has been taken as *mthong dang ma mthong*.
3. *The Supreme Source*, ch. 7, p. 25 (all *Kun byed* citations refer to TK). SS p. 141-2. NLD p. 26. The 10th line is interpolated from the tantra.
4. Saraha's *Dohakosha*, quote unlocated. NLD p. 26.
5. *The Junction of the Three Gnostic Dimensions* by the Great Master Garab Dorje: the source of the six works attributed to Garab Dorje is unlocated. Partly quoted in canto 12. NLD p. 27.
6. *The Great Commentary on the Perfection of Wisdom in Eight Thousand Verses* by Haribhadra: quote unlocated. NLD p. 27.
7. *The Supreme Source*, ch. 12, p. 50. SS p. 152. The three types of ritual purity in the brahmanic tradition and in yogatantra (*gtsang sbras dag gsum*), customarily relate to sex, bathing the body and washing clothes. NLD p. 28.
8. *The Supreme Source*, ch. 13, p. 52. SS p. 152 in part. NLD p. 28. Quoted in canto 63.
9. *The Heap of Jewels*, ch. 4, p. 107. NLD p. 29.
10. *The Six Matrixes*, ch. 64, p. 418. NLD p. 29.
11. *The Supreme Source*, ch. 46, pp. 134-5. SS p. 188. NLD pp. 29-30.
12. In *The Precious Treasury of the Way of Abiding* (1998) these four key terms (*gnas bkrol ba*, *'gags bsdam pa*, *chings su bcing ba* and *la bzla ba*) are translated as 'revealing the key point', 'discerning the implications', 'embracing the larger scope', and 'coming to the decisive experience'.

13. *The Heap of Jewels*, ch. 1, pp. 78-81. NLD pp. 30-2.

14. *The Supreme Source*, ch. 5, p. 15. SS p. 139. NLD p. 32. Quoted in context in canto 114.

15. *The Supreme Source*, ch. 5, p. 19. SS p. 139. NLD p. 32. Quoted in canto 9.

16. *The Supreme Source*, ch. 6, p. 18. SS p. 140. NLD p. 32. Quoted in full in canto 99.

17. *The Sphere of Total Illumination*, ch. 54, p. 400. NLD p. 33.

18. *The Supreme Source*, ch. 6, pp. 19-20. SS n/a. NLD p. 34. Also quoted in canto 62 and partly in canto 111.

19. The *Mahayana-uttaratantra* (a basic mahayana text treating the *tathagatagarbha* or buddha-nature) explains it like this: 'Earth rests upon water and water upon air, and air rests upon space; these four great elements have no further base whatsoever. Likewise, the psycho-physical constituents, the elements of perception and the sense-organs, depend upon karma and emotivity. Karma and emotivity depend upon errant perception; errant perception depends upon mental activity; and mental activity is based upon pure mind; the essential nature of mind rests upon nothing at all.'

20. *The Supreme Source*, ch. 49, p. 143. p. SS n/a. NLD p. 34.

21. *The Junction of the Three Gnostic Dimensions* by Garab Dorje. NLD p. 34.

22. *The Supreme Source*, ch. 22 (*Khyung chen*), p. 74. TB ch. 22, p. 87. SS p. 158. See also *The Great Garuda in Flight* trans. Vairotsana, BGB p. 366 and Dowman (2006), vs. 2-4. p. 11-12. NLD p. 35. The tantra and BGB have *gcig las gses* in the 4th line.

23. *Samantabhadra's Mirror of Mind*. NLD p. 35. There are several similar lines on pp. 258-9. On p. 256, however, we read 'The assertion of appearance as mental veils me' (*cir snang sems su 'dod pa nga la sgrib pa yin*).

24. *Natural Gnosis*, ch. 69, pp. 734 and 736. NLD pp. 35-6. The quotation combines two passages from a chapter devoted to refutation of views inimical to Dzogchen.

25. *The Epitome of the Definitive Meaning* (Tantra), text unlocated. NLD p. 36.

26. Variations of interpretation may include: 'everything in nature is made of mental substance', which is false and leads to a cul-de-sac in soteriological intent; 'everything we know is processed by our mental functions and thus can be said to be a product of mind', which is a relative truth and always to be remembered; 'the external world is a projection onto the empty screen of space projected by

mind as the projector', which is a provisional truth useful in destroying attachment to the objects in the sensory fields; and 'there is nothing but mind', 'nothing ever stirs from the nature of mind' or 'pure mind is the essence, nature and manifestation of everything', which are statements basic to the Dzogchen dialectic. In the historical development of Buddhist thought, subsequent to the materialism of the Hinayana which perceived atoms as substantial entities (discrete particles), external phenomena, and material phenomena in particular, are considered to be illusory, and conclusively, in Dzogchen they are given no ontological status whatsoever.

27. *The Sphere of Total Illumination*, chs. 10 and 11 (*Rgyan dang rol ba bstan pa*, "Ornamentation and Display Revealed") p. 318-19. NLD p. 37. The entire definition on page 318 runs: *The defining quality (essence) of potency is its indeterminacy. Its definition is 'elemental potency' (the potency of the elements). Its classification is twofold: it manifests in two ways: either as samsara due to ignorance of gnosis, or as nirvana due to conscious gnosis. Its similes are as follows: it is like the multiple appearances of a single sun, like the never-crystallizing light-rays of the sun, like black aconite or arsenic (both medicine and virulent poison), like camphor (manifesting as either a solid or gas),or like lightening bolts (electricity).* See also Namkhai Norbu & Lennard Lippman (1987: pp. 22-26).

28. *The Supreme Source*, ch. 6, p. 19. SS p. 139. NLD p. 37. Quoted in canto 3.

29. *The Sacred Vase of Gnosis* by Garab Dorje. NLD pp. 37-8. Quoted in part in canto 27, wherein compare the root verse. See also canto 25. In the first stanza the reading from the tantra, *mnyam pa'i klong*, has been preferred to *mnyam pa'i rlung*.

30. *The Sphere of Total Illumination*, ch. 55, p. 401. NLD pp. 38-9.

31. *The Supreme Source*, ch. 9, pp. 33-5. SS p. 146. NLD pp. 40-1. See SS pp. 67-8 and p. 275 n. 146. Quoted in canto 40 and the first verse in canto 66. After this first disclosure of the absence of the ten techniques, under the rubric of the bind of absence the futility of endeavor in the tantric manner is treated in cantos 30, 31 and 32. Canto 47, The Openness of Nondual Action, treats an eightfold tabulation of the techniques. Canto 63 defines atiyoga as realization of their absence, while canto 65 treats the resolution of the ten techniques in openness. Canto 83 considers the ten techniques under the rubric of the bind of spontaneity.

32. *The Junction of the Three Gnostic Dimensions* by Garab Dorje. NLD p. 41. Quoted in canto 2, from which the third line here is derived.
33. *The Copper-Lettered Gem*, text unlocated. NLD p. 41.
34. *The Heap of Jewels*, ch. 2, pp. 86-89. NLD pp. 42-3.
35. *The Heap of Jewels*, ch. 5, pp. 109-112. NLD pp. 44-5.
36. *The Supreme Lamp Sutra*, text unlocated. NLD p. 46.
37. *Free Identity* by Garab Dorje. NLD pp. 46-7.
38. *The Flight of the Great Garuda* by Sri Singha, p. 62. NLD p. 47. Quoted in part in canto 31.
39. *The Great Garuda* by Sri Singha, pp. 62-3. NLD p. 48.
40. *The Great Garuda* by Sri Singha, pp. 57-8. NLD p. 48.
41. *The Sphere of Total Illumination*, ch. 51, pp. 391-2: 'The definition of a *shravaka* ("listener-hearer") is he or she who listens to the teacher's words with his auditory sense and hears their meaning with his intellectual power. Intrinsic gnosis failing to arise from within, he is dependant upon the words of the teacher. The definition of a *pratyekabuddha* ("self-made buddha") is he or she who awakens by himself, by the power of his meditative practice, independent of another's teaching. The definition of a *bodhisattva* is he or she who with perfect renunciation, pristine awareness, compassion and ideal conduct demonstrates them to others. The definition of a *kriya-tantra yogin* is he or she who professes the crucial importance of ritual bathing, chastity and astrology. The definition of an *upa-tantra yogin* is he or she in whom ritual action is dominant and view is secondary. The definition of a *yoga-tantra yogin* is he or she who trains in the four aspects of the four buddha families, purifying his physical, energetic and mental complexes and thus working for others. The definition of a *mahayogin* is he or she who takes the teacher's indications as primary and engages in the yoga of method and wisdom and the three samadhis. The definition of an *anuyogin* is he or she who engages in the reality of uncultivated perfection (the fulfilment stage without the stage of generation). The definition of the *hyper-yogin* of natural perfection is he or she who embraces all the events of existence as nondual timelessly perfected gnostic awareness in the pure dimension of being.'
42. *The Heap of Jewels*, ch. 2, pp. 85-6. NLD p. 49.
43. *The Supreme Source*, ch. 9, p. 115. SS n/a. NLD p. 50.
44. *The Supreme Source*, ch. 46, "The Absence of Any Commitment to Observe", p. 132. SS n/a. NLD p. 50. The context may clarify the meaning: 'The infinite number of vows may be categorized as

physical, verbal and mental: when the suffering of each sensory impression impinges, the body cannot escape its habits, speech cannot express the truth, and our ideas actually oppose the truth— there is no such thing as a flawless idea; in a strait-jacket of physical and verbal commitments it is very difficult to encounter reality.'

45. *The Supreme Source*, ch. 15, p. 60, SS p.153. NLD p.50. Quoted in part in canto 60.

46. *The Supreme Source*, ch. 15, pp. 60-62 (a continuation of the previous quote). SS pp. 153-4. NLD p. 51.

47. *The Six Matrixes*, ch. 1, pp. 396-7. NLD pp. 52-3.

48. *The Great Garuda* by Sri Singha, p. 60. NLD p. 53. Quoted in part in canto 57. In the tantra, in lines 2 and 3 for '*gag, gegs*; in line 4 for *ma spangs, ma yengs.*

49. *The Sphere of Total Illumination,* ch. 41, pp. 370-1. NLD p. 53.

50. *The Sacred Vase of Gnosis* by Garab Dorje. NLD pp. 54-5. The text of the tantra quotation varies slightly from the root verse above. A note is added here in the body of the NLD text, probably inserted by a scrupulous, meticulous editor at a date later than Longchenpa's composition: 'Now, since this scriptural citation is so similar to my root verse, some might think that this is plagiarism, but that is not the case. The opening eulogy in *The Root Verses on the Middle Way* (by Nagarjuna) is borrowed from the *Ratnakuta-sutra*; a few lines from the *Abhidharma-kosha* (by Vasubandhu), like "having the body of its former lifetime", are found in *The Sphere of Total Illumination*; and several lines starting from "O, among the various scriptural traditions..." in Haribhadra's *Minor Commentary (on the Perfection of Wisdom)* feature in his *Illumination of the Twenty Thousand (Stanzas)*. In the same way, in order to inspire some faith in this profound topic, identical expressions are employed and the source is appended as an embellishment.'

51. *The Junction of the Three Gnostic Dimensions* by Garab Dorje. NLD pp. 55-6. Compare the quote from the *Sacred Vase of Gnosis (Rig pa spyi blugs)* in canto 10 which is the source of the three lines in the root verse on the arising, abiding and release of phenomena. Quoted in part in canto 50.

52. *The Great Garuda* by Sri Singha, pp. 60-1. NLD p. 57.

53. *The Sacred Vase of Gnosis* by Garab Dorje. NLD p. 57. Quoted in context in canto 10. Another note follows, probably by the same meticulous editor: 'Since this scriptural source has already been cited, some might think it redundant. However, at this place it is not. It is just as in *The White Lotus*, an extensive commentary on

The Wheel of Time (*Kalachakra Tantra*), where the deity's invocation is quoted thrice, or as in *Candid Speech* (Chandrakirti's commentary on Nagarjuna's *Root Verses on the Middle Way*), where each selection from the *Samadhiraja Sutra* is cited several times.'

54. *The Supreme Source*, ch. 21, p. 72. SS n/a. NLD p. 58.

55. *The Six Matrixes*, ch. 1, pp. 397-400. NLD pp. 58-60. These are not the six matrixes of the tantra named *The Six Matrixes*. These are subsumed in the first chapter of that tantra called "The Matrix Revealing the Total Synchronicity of All and Everything" (*Chos thams cad dus mnyam pa nyid du bstan pa'i glong*). In the penultimate verse in the tantra a line is added: 'Every instance of emptiness is the objective field of Samantabhadra.'

56. *The Great Garuda* by Sri Singha, p. 62. NLD p. 60.

57. *The Supreme Source*, ch. 9, p. 32. SS p. 146. NLD p. 60. This quote forms the basis of the root verse to canto 11.

58. *The Supreme Source*, ch. 48, p. 141. SS pp. 190-1. NLD pp. 60-61.

59. *The Great Garuda* by Sri Singha, p. 62. NLD p. 61. Quoted in canto 15.

60. *The Supreme Source*, ch. 39, p. 115. SS n/a. NLD p. 62.

61. *The Supreme Source*, ch. 47, pp. 138-9. SS p. 189. NLD p. 62. The first three lines comprise the final verse of the quote in canto 122i.

62. *The Supreme Source*, ch. 45, p. 128. SS n/a. See *The Eternal Victory Banner* trans. Vairotsana, BGB p. 363 and Dowman (2006), v. 36, p. 67. NLD p. 62.

63. *The Supreme Source*, ch. 44, pp. 126-127. SS n/a. NLD pp. 63-4. Quoted in parts in cantos 74 and 75.

64. *The Supreme Source*, ch. 41, p. 30. SS n/a. NLD p. 64.

65. *The Great Garuda* by Sri Singha, p. 62. NLD p. 64. Quoted in canto 16.

66. *The Supreme Source*, ch. 22, p. 75. SS p. 159. See also *The Great Garuda in Flight* trans. Vairotsana, BGB p. 367, see also Dowman (2006), v. 10. p. 16. NLD pp. 64-5. The first line is interpolated from the tantra; the last line is unlocated in the tantra.

67. *The Heap of Jewels*, ch. 4, p. 99. NLD p. 65.

68. *The Supreme Source*, ch. 32 (*Nges pa'i tshig bzhi le'u*, "The Chapter of the Four Principles"), p. 97. SS p. 174. NLD p. 65.

69. *The Supreme Source*, ch. 37, pp. 109-10. SS p. 178. NLD pp. 65-6. Quoted in part in canto 74.

70. *The Natural Freedom of Gnosis*, ch. 5 (*Mtshan ma dngos bral gyi le'u ste lnga pa'o*, "Getting Rid of Concreteness"), p. 40. NLD p. 66.

71. *Spontaneously Arising Gnosis*, ch. 70 (*Shes rab kyi dbye ba bstan pa'i le'u ste bdun cu tham pa'o,* "Types of Insight"), pp. 740-1. NLD pp. 66-7.
72. To further the quest for intellectual conviction, regarding the absence of phenomenal and noumenal experience, the logic applied here is that of the Indian Mahayana philosopher Nagarjuna, who demonstrated the unstructured (*nisprapanca*) nature of all experience in his famous *Verses on the Middle Way*. In the Greek philosopher Aristotle's logic, any statement about reality that cannot be expressed in the simple terms of yes/no is logically invalid. It is either yes or no, existent or nonexistent—any intermediate position is categorically excluded.
73. *Samantabhadra's Mirror of Mind*, ch. 3. (*Gol sgrib la bzla ba'i le'u ste gsum pa'o,* "Resolution of Glitches and Veils"), pp. 260-1. NLD pp. 67-8.
74. *The Great Garuda* by Sri Singha, p. 56. NLD p. 68.
75. *The Heap of Jewels*, ch. 5, pp. 111-2. NLD p. 69. Quoted in part in 116. See canto 13.
76. *The Supreme Source*, ch. 53, p. 153, SS n/a. NLD p. 69. See last quote in canto 32.
77. *The Copper Lettered Gem*, text unlocated. NLD p. 70.
78. *The Heart-Mirror of Vajrasattva*, ch. 8 (*Rgyud yongs su gtad pa'i le'u ste brgyad pa'o,* "The Entrustment Chapter", closing lines), p. 386. NLD p. 70.
79. *The Supreme Source*, ch. 9, pp. 33-5. SS p. 146. NLD pp. 70-1. Quoted in canto 11.
80. *The Rampant Lion,* ch. 3 (*Seng ges rang skad smras pa yi le'u ste gsum pa'o,* "The Self-Referential Language of the Lion"), p. 280. NLD pp. 71-2. Quoted in part in canto 86.
81. *The Great Array of Gems*, ch. 4, p. 39. NLD p. 72.
82. *Samantabhadra's Mirror of Mind*, ch. 3 (*Gol sgrib la bzla ba'i le'u ste gsum pa'o,* "Resolution of Glitches and Veils"), pp. 256-7. NLD pp. 72-3.
83. *The Unwritten Tantra*, ch. 1, pp. 218-9. NLD p. 73-4.
84. *The Six Matrixes*, ch. 3, p. 153. NLD p. 74. The tantra has the preferable reading of *gleng gzhi.*
85. *Free Identity* by Garab Dorje. NLD pp. 74-5.
86. *The Transfiguration of the Six Sensory Fields* by Garab Dorje. NLD p. 75.
87. *The Sphere of Total Illumination*, ch. 40, p. 368. NLD p. 76.

88. *The Supreme Source*, pp. 104-5, ch. 35. SS p. 175-6. NLD p. 76-7. The tantra has *lnga po yi* at the end of the fifth line. For the ten absences see cantos 11 and 30. See also *Mdo bcu: Nges par ston pa'i mdo bstan pa'i le'u*: TB Vol. 1, pp. 445.2-450.3.

89. *Synchronicity*, by Garab Dorje. NLD p. 77. Quoted in canto 68.

90. *The Sphere of Total Illumination*, ch. 40, p. 369. NLD p. 78.

91. *The Sphere of Total Illumination*, ch. 40 ("Infallible Revelation of the View of the Great Perfection"), p. 368. NLD p. 78. The quote is found in the tantra as 'Discursive thoughts, neither repressed nor indulged, are like the flickering movement of a goldfish'(*Yid kyi rnam rtog ci 'gyu yang ma phang ma tshol gser gyi nya mo 'gyu*).

92. *The Junction of the Three Gnostic Dimensions* by Garab Dorje. NLD p. 78. Quoted in context in canto 25.

93. *Free Identity* by Garab Dorje. NLD p. 79.

94. *The Great Garuda* by Sri Singha, p. 58. NLD pp. 79-80.

95. *The Great Garuda* by Sri Singha, pp. 59-60. NLD p. 80. Quoted in canto 78. The tantra provides variant readings: in line 2 *'gag* is gegs and *rang gsal* is *rang bsal*; in line 4 *sdam* is *gtams*.

96. *The Unwritten Tantra*, ch. 2, pp. 227-8. NLD p. 80-1.

97. *The Junction of the Three Gnostic Dimensions* by Garab Dorje. NLD p. 81. These verses are the source of the root verses in cantos 54 and 55. In the fifth line the 'six sensory fields' renders *sku drug*.

98. *The Rampant Lion*, ch. 4 (*Seng ge gnyis sbyor gi dgongs pa bstan pa'i le'u*; "The Lion's Teaching on the Dynamic of Union"), p. 295. NLD p. 82.

99. *The Great Garuda* by Sri Singha, p. 60. NLD p. 82. Quoted in context in canto 22.

100. *The Rampant Lion*, ch. 4 (*Seng ge gnyis sbyor gi dgongs pa bstan pa'i le'u*, "The Lion's Teaching on the Dynamic of Union"), p. 296. NLD p. 83.

101. *The Supreme Source*, ch. 13, pp. 51-2. SS n/a. NLD pp. 83-4.

102. *The Supreme Source*, ch. 15 p. 60. SS p. 153. NLD p. 84. Quoted in context in canto 19.

103. *The Supreme Source*, ch. 49, p. 142. SS n/a. NLD p. 64.

104. *The Supreme Source*, ch. 24, p. 79. SS pp. 161-2. NLD pp. 84-5. In the prose commentary to the root verse of this canto 'ignorance' (the absence of gnosis) has been amended to 'gnosis'. Both gnosis and the lack of it are equally bound by pure being (see cantos 87 and 93 and 100), but 'ignorance' appears out of context here.

105. *The Supreme Source*, ch. 6, pp. 19-20. SS n/a. NLD p. 85. Quoted in canto 5.

106. *The Supreme Source*, ch. 38, p. 114. SS n/a. NLD p. 65.
107. *The Transfiguration of the Six Sensory Fields* by Garab Dorje. NLD p. 86. Quoted in context in canto 84.
108. *Matrix of Mystery (Guhyagarbha)*, quote unlocated. NLD p. 86.
109. *The Supreme Source*, ch. 13, p. 52. SS p. 152. NLD p. 86. Quoted in canto 2.
110. *The Supreme Source*, ch. 22, p. 75. SS p. 159. See also *The Great Garuda in Flight* trans. Vairotsana, BGB p. 368; see also Dowman (2006), v. 12. p. 17. NLD p. 86.
111. *The Precious Blazing Relics*, ch. 2, p. 804. NLD p. 87.
112. *The Supreme Source,* ch. 9, pp. 35-6, SS p. 146-7. NLD p. 87-8. The first two lines are the last two lines of canto 11.
113. *Synchronicity,* by Garab Dorje. NLD p. 88-9.
114. *The Junction of the Three Gnostic Dimensions* by Garab Dorje. NLD p. 89. The final couplet is quoted in canto 102.
115. *The Supreme Source*, ch. 9, pp. 33-5. SS p. 146. NLD p. 89. Quoted in cantos 11 and 40.
116. *The Junction of the Three Gnostic dimensions* by Garab Dorje. NLD p. 89.
117. *Synchronicity,* by Garab Dorje. NLD p. 90. Quoted in canto 48.
118. *The Supreme Source*, ch. 6, p. 21. SS pp. 140-1. NLD p. 90.
119. *The Supreme Source*, ch. 10, p. 42. SS p. 147. NLD p. 91.
120. *The Sphere of Total Illumination,* ch. 40 p. 369, with variations. NLD p. 91.
121. *The Transfiguration of the Six Sensory Fields* by Garab Dorje. NLD p. 92.
122. *The Supreme Source*, an abbreviation of the passage quoted in canto 68. NLD p. 92.
123. *The Heap of Jewels*, ch. 3, pp. 90-91. NLD pp. 93-4. The six modes and two media of spontaneity are listed as the eightfold emanation of spontaneity as ignorance in the *Bkra shis mdzes ldan* (p. 214) and alluded to in canto 87 (q.v.): The eight modes of spontaneous emanation: an indeterminate medium emanating like compassion (1); uncrystallizing manifestation emanating like light (2); indeterminate unengaged pleasure emanating like pristine awareness (3); indeterminable inalienable essence arising like pure being (4); all-inclusive equivocal view arising like nonduality (5); nonspecific method arising like ultimate liberation (6); an ultimate doorway into pristine awareness (7); indeterminate, all-inclusive, compassion as the medium of seemingly impure emanation (8): (1. *thugs rje ltar 'char ba'i go ma 'gags pa*; 2. *'od ltar 'char ba'i snang*

ba ma 'gags pa; 3. ye shes ltar 'char ba'i longs spyod ma 'gags pa; 4. sku ltar 'char ba'i ngo bo ma 'gags pa; 5. gnyis med ltar 'char ba'i lta ba ma nges pa; 6. mtha' grol ltar 'char ba'i thabs ma 'gags pa'o; 7. dag pa ye shes kyi 'jug sgo mthar phyin pa; 8. ma dag pa ltar 'char ba'i sgo thugs rje ma 'gags pa). See also Germano (1992) p. 166).

124. *The Supreme Source*, ch. 18, p. 67. SS pp. 155-6. NLD p. 94.

125. *The Supreme Source*, ch. 18, p. 67. SS pp. 155-6. NLD p. 94.

126. *The Supreme Source*, ch. 37, (*Sgom du med pa'i mod dang lung gi le'u ste sum cu rtsa bdun pa'o*), p. 110. SS p. 178. NLD p. 95. Quoted in context in canto 35.

127. *The Supreme Source*, ch. 44, p. 127. SS n/a. NLD p. 95. Quoted in canto 32.

128. *The Supreme Source*, ch. 13, pp. 53-4. SS p. 152. NLD p. 95.

129. *The Supreme Source*, ch. 41, p. 30. SS n/a. NLD pp. 95-6. Quoted in canto 32.

130. *Beyond the Sound*, ch. 2, p. 127. NLD p. 96.

131. *The Supreme Source,* ch. 19, p. 68. SS p. 156. NLD p. 96.

132. *The Supreme Source,* ch. 25, p. 80. SS p. 162. NLD pp. 97-8.

133. From the *Sphere of Total Illumination* ch. 19 (*'Byung lnga mdor bsdus bstan pa'i le'u,* "The Five Elements in Brief"), pp. 333-4 and ch. 20 (*'Byung ba'i mtshan nyid bstan pa dang shar lugs dang thim lugs don dang sbyar nas bstan pa'i le'u,* "Characteristics of the Elements: Their Appearance and Dissolution"), pp. 335-6. 'The "juice" of the elements consists of five "tones" and five "sediments". The five tones are defined as the five aspects of pristine awareness. The five sediments are defined as earth, water, fire, air and space. The elements are described here as gnostic potency and its imagery as samsara and nirvana...The tones of the five elements are the five lights. The sediments are earth, water, fire, air and space. The sediment of the tones are the compositions of flesh and bones. The tones of the sediments are the five colors of the spectrum. They are like the rays of the sun, or rainbow lights shining from a crystal prism...The tone of earth shines forth as a white light, which then appears as sedimental earth...'

134. *The Great Garuda* by Sri Singha, pp. 59-60. NLD p. 98. Quoted in canto 53.

135. *The Six Matrixes*, ch. 3, p. 154. NLD p. 98. See also canto 81. This is the first of a series of Samantabhadra's contemplations quoted in cantos (44), 78, 79, 80, 81, 103, 105 and 106.

136. *The Supreme Source*, ch. 80, p. 209. SS p. 228-9. NLD p. 99.

137. *The Six Matrixes*, ch. 3, p. 155. NLD p. 99. Quoted in canto 105.

138. *The Supreme Source*, ch. 78 p. 205. SS p. 226. NLD p. 99.

139. *Beyond the Sound*, ch. 4, p. 177. NLD pp. 99-100.

140. *The Six Matrixes*, ch. 3, p. 155. NLD p. 100.

141. *The Supreme Source*, ch. 78, p. 205. SS p. 226. NLD p. 100.

142. *The Six Matrixes*, ch. 3, p. 154. NLD p. 100. The penultimate stanza is quoted in canto 104 and the final stanza in canto 78.

143. *Synchronicity*, by Garab Dorje. NLD pp. 101-2.

144. *The Supreme Source*, ch. 80, p. 209. SS p. 229.

145. *The Supreme Source*, ch. 38, p. 112. SS p. 180. NLD p. 102.

146. *The Transfiguration of the Six Sensory Fields* by Garab Dorje. NLD p. 103.

147. *The Supreme Source*, ch. 30, p. 91. SS p. 169. *The Eternal Victory Banner* trans. Vairotsana, BGB p. 359 and Dowman (2006), v. 10, p. 43. NLD p. 104.

148. *The Supreme Source*, ch. 30, p. 91. SS p. 169. *The Eternal Victory Banner* trans. Vairotsana, BGB p. 359 and Dowman (2006), v. 9, p. 42. NLD p. 104. In the third line BGB has *de la bskyod pa med bzhin du* rather than *de las bskyob pa med bzhin du* so that the second sloka could read 'unstirring like space, it is basic sameness'. The tantra reads *de la skyo ba med bzhin du* 'insofar as there is no sorrow in it'.

149. *The Junction of the Three Dimensions* by Garab Dorje. NLD pp. 104-5.

150. *The Sphere of Total Illumination*, ch. 40, p. 368. NLD p. 105. The second stanza is quoted in canto 113 where it is attributed to *The Eternal Victory Banner* trans. Vairotsana: see Dowman (2006), v. 30, p. 52. NLD has *na'ang* rather than BGB *nang* in the third line.

151. *Beyond the Sound*, ch. 2, p. 136. NLD p. 105.

152. *The Rampant Lion*, ch. 3, p. 280. NLD p. 105. Quoted in context in canto 41.

153. *The Six Matrixes*, ch. 4, p. 176. NLD p. 105.

154. *The Six Matrixes*, ch. 4, p. 176. NLD p. 106.

155. *The Beautiful Luck (mahatantra)*, ch. 2 (*Gzhi la 'khrul pa byung tshul bstan pa'i le'u ste gnyis pa'o*, "How Delusion Arises in the Existential Ground"), pp. 213-4. NLD p. 106. See canto 72 and see note 123 for the eight emanations cited in the *Bkra shis mdzes ldan*.

156. *The Transfiguration of the Six Sensory Fields* by Garab Dorje. NLD p. 106.

157. *Synchronicity*, by Garab Dorje. NLD p. 107. Compare the first verse of this quote to the root verse above it and also to the last verse in the quote from *Synchronicity* in canto 82. The first few lines of this quotation appear to be corrupted in the NLD. Readings

from the tantra: for *rlung, klong*; for *'grel pas, bral bas*; *for sa bzhi,
sa gzhi.*

158. *The Rampant Lion*, ch. 5 (*Seng ge stobs ldan gyi lta ba bstan pa'i
le'u ste lnga pa'o*, "Revealing the Vision of the Powerful Lion"), pp.
308-9. NLD p. 109.

159. *The Sphere of Total Illumination*, ch. 88, pp. 453-4. NLD p. 110.
The same tantra (ch. 81, pp. 437-9) clarifies the meaning of the
three 'caverns' or 'cavities' (*sbubs gsum*): 'Classification is threefold:
the jeweline cavern, the cavern of light and the cavern of karmic
propensities. The qualities of the first: immaculate, transparent,
thoughtless and unchanging, the uncrystallizing light of the matrix
of pristine awareness, diffracting imagery in the existential ground
like a crystal prism, the jeweline cavern is the dimension of pure
being. The qualities of the middle one: the dimension of the light of
indeterminate awareness, holding the thirty-two marks of the
sambhogakaya and the five variegated hyper-mandalas brilliant and
resplendent, the cavern of light is the dimension of enjoyment. The
qualities of the last: the four kinds of being by birth, with body-
mind, elements and senses fields, mind and the eight
consciousnesses, this is the cavern of karmic propensities.'

160. *A Concise Commentary upon the Oral Transmission*, text
unlocated. NLD p. 111. See also Patrul Rimpoche's *Tshig gsum
gnad brdegs* Dowman 2003 p. 179.

161. *Free Identity* by Garab Dorje. NLD pp. 111-12.

162. *The Garland of Pearls,* quote unlocated. NLD p. 112. Quoted in
canto 115 and attributed to *Beyond the Sound.*

163. *Free Identity* by Garab Dorje. NLD p. 112. Quoted in context in
canto 14 and in canto 107.

164. *The Supreme Source*, ch. 6, p. 20. NLD pp. 113-4. Quoted in part
in canto 101.

165. *The Supreme Source*, ch. 6, p. 21. SS n/a. NLD p. 114.

166. *The Supreme Source*, ch. 7, p. 22. SS p. 141. NLD p. 114-5.

167. *Beyond the Sound*, ch. 2, pp. 479-80. NLD p. 115. Compare the
quote from *Beyond the Sound* in canto 107.

168. *The Supreme Source*, ch. 6, p. 16. SS p. 140. NLD p. 116.

169. *Beyond the Sound*, ch. 2, p. 479. NLD p. 116.

170. *The Supreme Source*, ch. 6, p. 16. SS p. 140. NLD p. 116.

171. *The Vajra Fortress* by Garab Dorje. NLD pp. 116-7.

172. *The Unwritten Tantra*, ch. 2, p. 227. NLD p. 117. In the fourth line
from the end we assume *bri ba* is in error for *grib*. The last line is
missing in the tantra.

173. *The Supreme Source,* ch. 6, p. 18. NLD p. 118. The third stanza is quoted in canto 3.

174. *The Garland of Pearls,* ch. 5 (*Gnas lugs 'khrul pa rang rdzogs su bstan pa'i le'u ste lnga pa'o,* "Natural Perfection Revealed as Self-perfected Delusion"), pp. 460-1. NLD p. 119.

175. *The Supreme Source,* ch. 6, p. 20. NLD p. 119. Quoted in context in canto 93.

176. *The Stream of Empowering Self-sprung Perfection,* ch. 20, p. 501. NLD p. 120.

177. *The Junction of the Three Gnostic dimensions* by Garab Dorje. NLD p. 120. The first two lines are quoted in canto 66.

178. *The Great Garuda* by Sri Singha, p. 60. NLD p. 121.

179. *The Supreme Source,* ch. 71, p. 192. SS p. 217. NLD p. 121.

180. *The Six Matrixes,* ch. 3, p. 154. NLD p. 121.

181. *The Great Garuda* by Sri Singha, p. 61. NLD p. 121.

182. *The Supreme Source,* ch. 70, p. 190. SS p. 217. NLD p. 121.

183. *The Six Matrixes,* ch. 3, p. 154. NLD p. 121. Quoted in canto 81.

184. *The Rampant Lion,* ch. 4, p. 293. NLD p. 122.

185. *The Great Garuda* by Sri Singha, pp. 59-60. NLD p. 122. Quoted in cantos 53 and 78.

186. *The Supreme Source,* ch. 73, p. 195. SS p. 220-221. NLD p. 122.

187. *The Six Matrixes,* ch. 3, p. 155. NLD p. 122. Quoted in canto 79.

188. *The Great Garuda* by Sri Singha, p. 60. NLD p. 123.

189. *The Supreme Source,* ch. 73, p. 195. SS p. 221. NLD p. 123. The order of the verses is reversed in the tantra.

190. *The Six Matrixes,* ch. 3, p. 155. NLD p. 123.

191. *The Six Matrixes,* ch. 1, pp. 122-5. NLD pp. 123-4. There are two extra verses in the tantra: 'Further, a person who does not follow traces of past tendencies, does not invite future tendencies, and does not rely on the continuity of present tendencies, is called "the timeless gnostic yogin". 'Whoever does not respond to past arrogance, does not waste energy on future arrogance, and does not celebrate present arrogance is "the timeless gnostic yogin"'.

192. *Spoken Word: The Secret Oral Tradition* by Sri Singha. NLD p. 124.

193. *The Rampant Lion,* ch. 4, pp. 293-4. NLD p. 125.

194. *The Heap of Jewels,* ch. 4, p. 100. NLD p. 125.

195. *Free Identity* by Garab Dorje. NLD p. 125. Quoted in context in canto 14 and also in canto 92. Also, see the Garab Dorje quote in canto 51 for the root verse.

196. *Beyond the Sound,* ch. 4, pp. 178-9. NLD pp. 125-6.

197. *The Garland of Pearls,* ch. 5, pp. 339-40. NLD p. 126.

198. *The Garland of Pearls,* ch. 4, pp. 452-4. NLD pp. 126-7. See quote from *Beyond the Sound* at the end of canto 95.
199. *The Supreme Source,* ch. 4, p. 14. SS p. 138-9. NLD p. 127.
200. *The Supreme Source,* ch. 5, p. 14. SS p. 139. NLD p. 127. Quoted in full in canto 114.
201. *Free Identity* by Garab Dorje. NLD p. 127-8. Quoted in canto 14.
202. *The Rampant Lion,* ch. 4, p. 290. NLD p. 128.
203. *The Supreme Source,* ch. 6, pp. 19-20. SS n/a. NLD p. 128. Quoted in cantos 5 and 62.
204. *The Supreme Source,* ch. 6, p. 21. SS n/a. NLD p. 128.
205. *The Supreme Source,* ch. 22. p. 76. SS p. 159-160. *The Great Garuda in Flight* trans. Vairotsana, BGB p. 368; see also Dowman (2006), v. 14. p. 19. NLD p. 128.
206. *The Eternal Victory Banner* trans. Vairotsana, BGB p. 362 and Dowman (2006), v. 30, p. 62. *The Supreme Source,* ch. 30, p. 93. NLD p. 129. We have taken the reading given in canto 85 from *The Sphere of Total Illumination* with *na'ang* at the end of the first line; otherwise we have 'Both outer and inner are the inside of the outside itself' which may not be consonant with the lines following.
207. *The Supreme Source,* ch. 5, pp. 14-15. SS p. 139. NLD pp. 129-30. Partly quoted in canto 3 and canto 109.
208. *Beyond the Sound,* quote unlocated. NLD p. 130. Quoted in canto 92.
209. *The Eternal Victory Banner* trans. Vairotsana, BGB p. 364 and Dowman (2006), v. 44, p. 74. *The Supreme Source* ch. 30, p. 95. SS p. 172. NLD p. 130.
210. *The Eternal Victory Banner* trans. Vairotsana, BGB p. 364 and Dowman (2006), v. 42, p. 72. *The Supreme Source* ch. 30, p. 95. SS p. 172. NLD p. 130. The fourth line appears only in NLD.
211. *The Eternal Victory Banner* trans. Vairotsana, BGB pp. 363-4 and Dowman (2006), v. 41 p. 71. *The Supreme Source,* ch. 30, p. 95. SS p. 172. NLD p. 131-32.
212. *Tantra of Direct Introduction,* ch. 3, p. 103. NLD p. 131.
213. *The Supreme Secret: The Mind of All the Tathagatas,* text unlocated. NLD p. 131.
214. *The Sphere of Total Illumination,* ch. 40, p. 369. NLD p. 131-2, with readings from the tantra. The first three lines are quoted in canto 69 as the last three lines of that quote.
215. *The Supreme Source,* ch. 35, p. 105. SS p. 176. NLD pp. 132-3.
216. *The Supreme Source,* ch. 6, p. 18. SS p. 140. NLD p. 133.
217. *The Heap of Jewels,* ch. 5, p. 111. NLD p. 133. Quoted in canto 38.

218. *Spontaneously Arising Gnosis*, ch. 9, p. 423. NLD p. 133.

219. *The Supreme Source*, ch. 83, p. 216. SS n/a. NLD p. 134.

220. *Spontaneously Arising Gnosis*, ch. 9. pp. 424-5. NLD p. 134-5.

221. *The Supreme Source*, ch. 83, pp. 215-6. SS p. 230. NLD p. 135.

222. *The Supreme Source*, ch. 83, p. 216. SS p. 230. NLD p. 135.

223. *Beyond the Sound*, quote unlocated. NLD p. 135.

224. *Spontaneously Arising Gnosis*, ch. 9, p. 424. NLD p. 135.

225. *The Supreme Source*, ch. 83, p. 216. SS p. 230. NLD p. 136.

226. *Spontaneously Arising Gnosis*, ch. 9, p. 424. NLD p. 136.

227. *Spontaneously Arising Gnosis*, ch. 9. p. 423-4. NLD p. 136.

228. *Beyond the Sound*, ch. 1, p. 443. NLD pp. 136-7.

229. *Spontaneously Arising Gnosis*, ch. 9, p. 423-4. NLD p. 137.

230. *The Right Time* by the master Padmasambhava: text unlocated. NLD p. 137.

231. *The Supreme Source*, ch. 83, p. 216-7. SS n/a. NLD p. 137.

232. *Spontaneously Arising Gnosis*, ch. 9, p. 423-4. NLD p. 138.

233. *The Supreme Source*, ch. 34, p. 101. SS p. 175. NLD p. 138.

234. *The Supreme Source*, ch. 38, p. 112.

235. *The Rampant Lion*, ch. 4, p. 299. NLD pp. 138-9.

236. *The Supreme Source*, ch. 47, p. 137. SS n/a. NLD p. 139-40. The final verse is quoted in canto 31. Note the helpful readings in the tantra.

237. *The Supreme Source*, ch. 15, p. 60. SS p.153. NLD p. 140. See also canto 19.

238. *The Supreme Source*, ch. 42, p. 122. SS p. 185. NLD pp. 140-41.

239. *Samantabhadra's Mirror of Mind*, ch. 2, p. 253. NLD p. 141. See readings from the tantra.

240. *The Garland Of Pearls*, ch. 7, p. 518-9. NLD p. 141.

241. *The Six Matrixes*, ch. 2, p. 140. NLD p. 141.

242. *The Blazing Lamp*, ch. 4, p. 308. NLD pp. 141-2.

243. *The Union of the Sun and the Moon*, ch. 2, p. 185. NLD p. 142.

244. *The Rampant Lion*, ch. 3, p. 277. NLD p. 142.

245. *The Great Array of Gems*, ch. 3, p. 35. NLD p. 142.

246. *Beyond the Sound*, ch. 5, pp. 515-6. NLD pp. 142-3. Neither the commentary nor the tantra are clear in their meaning in the first part of this quote.

247. *The Heap of Jewels*, ch. 1, p. 81. NLD pp. 143.

248. *Beyond the Sound*, ch. 1, pp. 438-9. NLD pp. 143-4.

249. *The Rampant Lion*, ch. 8, pp. 347-8. NLD p. 244.

250. *The Supreme Source*, ch. 29, pp. 89-90. SS p. 167. NLD p. 145.

251. *The Treasury of Abhidharma*, by Vasubandhu, quote unlocated. NLD p. 145.

252. *The Great Garuda* by Sri Singha, p. 54. NLD p. 145.
253. *The Great Array of Gems,* ch. 8, pp. 58-60. NLD pp. 145-6
254. *The Supreme Source,* ch. 83, p. 217. SS n/a. NLD p. 147.
255. *The Supreme Source,* ch. 83, p. 217. SS n/a. NLD p. 147.
256. *The Supreme Source,* ch. 84, p. 220. SS n/a. NLD p. 147.
257. *Beyond the Sound,* ch. 1, p. 443. NLD pp. 147-8.
258. *The Six Matrixes,* ch. 3, p. 157. NLD p. 149.
259. *The Supreme Source,* ch. 22, p. 76. *The Great Garuda in Flight* trans. Vairotsana, BGB p. 369; see Dowman (2006), v. 21. p. 23. NLD p. 149.
260. *Free Identity* by Garab Dorje. NLD p. 149. Quoted in canto 44.
261. *The Transfiguration of the Six Sensory Fields* by Garab Dorje. NLD p. 150.
262. *The Magical Web of Manjushri,* text unlocated. NLD p. 151.

Appendix I
The Tibetan Text and Quotations

The Tibetan title of the root text is *Gnas lugs rin po che'i mdzod*, given in Sanskrit as the *Tathātva-ratna-kosha-nāma*, which may be rendered into English as *The Precious Treasury of Natural Perfection*. This is arguably the most important of Longchenpa's seminal works grouped together as the *Mdzod bdun (The Seven Treasuries)*. This work was composed in the middle of the 14th century in Central Tibet at a hermitage called Gangs ri thod dkar (above Snye phu shugs gseb), still a place of pilgrimage. The title of Longchenpa's auto-commentary is *Sde gsum snying po'i don 'grel gnas lugs rin po che mdzod ces bya ba'i 'grel ba (The Commentary Upon The Treasury of Natural Perfection: An Exposition of the Inner Meaning of the Three Series of Dzogchen Instruction)*.

The root verses seem to be paraphrastic in origin, while the illustrative quotations are overt attributions. The former may be ascribed to Longchenpa himself; the latter may have been drawn from versions of the tantras other than those to which we have access, or alternatively, edited with deep sagacity by the author himself. Whatever the case, in virtually every instance, with some notable exceptions, Longchenpa's version in our opinion is preferable to the tantra sources.

The majority of quotations cited by Longchenpa are drawn from the tantras of the *Rnying ma rgyud 'bum (The Collected Tantras of the Ancients)*. This collection may have been started as a handwritten compendium as early as the 12th century as the *Bairo rgyud 'bum*. A more comprehensive collection was carved in blocks in the 18th century under the auspices of Jigme Lingpa. The three collections available today besides the *Bairo rgyud 'bum* are the *Gting skyes* (Mkhyen brtse) and *Mtshams Brag* editions both printed in Bhutan, which we have utilized, and the edition of the Derge Parkhang.

The most oft-quoted tantra is the *Kun byed rgyal po (The Supreme Source)*, the principal tantra of the Dzogchen Mind Series *(sems sde)*. A compilation of diverse material from the early days of Dzogchen transmission in Tibet, it also includes the five earliest translations of Vairotsana such as *Mi nub pa'i rgyal mtshan (The Eternal Victory Banner)*, also known as the *rDo rje sems dpa' nam mkha' che (The Vast Space of Vajrasattva)*. The *Kun byed rgyal po* has been partially translated by Chogyal Namkhai Norbu and Adriano Clemente (1999) as *The Supreme Source*, which has been a constant source of inspiration (see page references in the notes).

The second most important group of sources from within the *Rnying ma rgyud 'bum* is a group of texts known as the seventeen tantras of the Secret Precept Series *(man ngag sde)*, sixteen of which Longchenpa quotes at least once in the *Gnas lugs mdzod*. The most frequently cited texts belonging to this group are the *Sgra thal 'gyur (Beyond the Sound)*, *Klong drug pa (The Six Matrixes of Samantabhadra)*, the *Seng ge rtsal rdzogs (The Rampant Lion)*, the *Rin chen spungs pa (The Heap of Jewels)* and the *Rig pa rang shar (Natural Gnosis)*. All of these texts—along with the *Kun byed rgyal po* and several others—have been transliterated into the Wylie script by Jim Valby in his digitalized text collection of Nyingma tantras, which we have used by his courtesy to identify and compare cited passages.

Another crucial text from the *Rnying ma rgyud 'bum*, not included amongst the seventeen tantras but quoted many times and quite extensively by Longchenpa, is the *Thig le kun gsal. (The Sphere of Total Illumination)*. It contains a detailed explanation of Dzogchen terminology.

Besides these tantra sources, Longchenpa illustrates his themes most frequently with the revelations of the Knowledge-bearers or Masters of Gnosis *(rig 'dzin*; Skt. *vidhyadhara)*, the early lineage holders. The *Khyung chen (Great Garuda)* by Sri Singha, found in the *Snying thig yab bzhi*, is frequently quoted. The source of the six important texts attributed to Garab Dorje has not yet come to light. Further, Longchenpa includes only two quotes from mahayoga and two from mahayana sources; nothing from the Kanjur and nothing from Bon sources.

Abbreviations and Tibetan Sources

AD   A-'dzom blocks of *Rnying ma'i rgyud bcu bdun*. 3 vols. New Delhi: Sanje Dorje, 1973-7.

BGB   *Bairo rgyud 'bum*. 8 vols. Leh, 1971. See SC.

DCJ   *Bdud 'jom chos 'byung*. Dudjom Rimpoche (1991).

JV   Jim Valby (Jim Valby digitalized collection).

NLD *Gnas lugs mdzod*. Ed. Dodrub Chen: Gangtok, Sikkim, c. 1966 (Adzom Chogar edition).

NTY *Snying thig ya bzhi*. New Delhi; Sherab Gyaltsen, 1975. (From the A-'dzom Chos sgar blocks).

PT   Padma Translation Committee.

SS   *The Supreme Source*. Namkhai Norbu and Adriano Clemente (1999).

SC   Samantabhadra Collection online at the University of Virginia: <hhtp://www.thdl.org/collections/literature/nyingma.php>

TB   *Mtshams Brag* edition of the *Rnying ma rgyud 'bum*. 46 vols. Thimphu, Bhutan: National Library, Royal Government of Bhutan, 1982. See also SC.

TK   *Gting skyes* edition of the *Rnying ma rgyud 'bum*. 36 vols. Thimphu, Bhutan: Dingo Khyentse Rimpoche, 1973-75. See also SC.

The sources of the quotations in the text are listed below according to their classification in the collected volumes of tantras. The titles cited in the endnotes, which open each listing, translate the short Tibetan title of the text. The extended title according to TB (except in the case of *Kun byed rgyal po* where TK has been utilized to conform with *The Supreme Source*) with its translation, is also provided, followed by references in the various collected sources etc, the page references in the NLD, and finally some alternative title translations. (NB. The indices following the TB volume number are derived from the SC index.)

Mind Series Tantras

The Supreme Source: *Kun byed*.

Chos thams cad rdzogs pa chen po byang chub kyi sems kun byed rgyal po: "The Universal Great Perfection of Pure Mind, the Supreme Source".

TK Vol.1/1. (pp. 2-262) 84 chapters (employed only in the annotation of the *Kun byed*).

TB Vol.1/1 (pp. 2-192) 57 chapters.
JV #1, ff.1-200, unknown edition.
Translated in Chogyal Namkhai Norbu and Adriano Clemente (1999).
NLD: 26.4-6; 28.2-4; 28.5-7; 29.6-30.1; 32.4; 32.5; 33.6-7; 34.1-2;
35.2-4; 37.3-4; 40.1-41.1; 50.2, 50.2, 50.2-5; 51.1-7; 58.1-2; 60.6,
6-61.5; 62.1,1-5,5-6; 63.1-64.2; 64.2-4; 64.7-65.1; 65.3-4; 65.6-
66.3; 69.4-5; 70.6-71.2; 76.6-77.2; 83.6-84.1; 84.3-4; 84.4-5; 84.6-
85.1; 85.3-4; 85.7; 86.2-4; 86.5; 87.4-88.2; 89.2; 90.3-4; 91.1-2;
92.6-7; 94.3-5; 94.5-6; 95.1-2; 95.3-6; 95.7-96.1; 96.5-7; 97.6-
98.2; 99.1-3; 99.6; 100.1-5; 102.3-5; 102.5-6; 104.3; 104.4-5;
113.6-114.1; 114.4; 114.7-115.3; 116.1-2; 116.6-7; 118.3-7;
119.6-7; 121.1-2; 121.5-7; 122.3-4; 123.2-3; 127.3; 127.4-5;
128.3-4; 128.4-5; 128.6-7; 129.5-130.3; 132.7-133.1; 133.1-2;
134.1-2; 135.1-2; 135.5; 136.1-2; 137.7-138.1; 138.5-6; 138.6-7;
139.3-140.1; 140.3; 140.3-141.1; 145.2-3; 147.3-4; 147.4-5;
147.5-6; 149.5-6.
"The All-Accomplishing King" (DCJ Vol. II p. 275); "The All-Creating
Monarch" (PT).

Mind Series Transmissions Translated by Vairotsana

The Eternal Victory Banner: *Mi nub pa'i rgyal mtshan nam mkha' che /
Mi nub rgyal mtshan chen po.*
Rdo rje sems dpa' rang bzhin mi nub pa'i rgyal mtshan: "The Nature of
Vajrasattva: The Forever-Unfurled Victory Banner".
BGB Vol. 2, kha, pp. 357-366.
Translated in Adriano Clemente (1999), and in Keith Dowman (2006).
TB Vol.1/1 Ka, pp. 106-113.
JV #26, ff. 89-96, ch. 30 of *Kun byed rgyal po,* unknown edition.
NLD; 129.2-3; 130.6; 130.6-7; 131.1 See also 104.3; 104.4-5; 105.3
"The Total Space of Vajrasattva", Adriano Clemente (1999).
"The Eternal Victory Banner", Keith Dowman, (2006).

The Great Garuda in Flight: *Khyung chen lding ba.*
BGB Vol. 2/53 pp. 366-370.
Translated in Keith Dowman, (2006).
NLD See 35.2-4; 64.7-65.1; 86.5; 128.7; 149.5-6.

Secret Precept Series Tantras

Beyond the Sound: *Thal 'gyur.*
Rin po che 'byung bar byed pa sgra thal 'gyur chen po'i rgyud: "The Great
  Tantra Beyond the Sound: A Fountain of Jewels".
TB Vol.12/1 (pp. 2-173) 6 chapters.
JV #77, ff. 386-530, Volume 10 of TK.
NLD: 96.5; 99.6-100.1; 105.6; 115.4-6; 116.4-6; 125.6-126.2; 130.5;
  135.7; 136.7-137.1; 142.5-143.2; 6-144.1; 147.7-148.3
"The Penetration of Sound" (DCJ Vol. II, p. 261), "Reverberation of
  Sound" (PT); "The Direct Consequence", "Unimpeded Sound"
  (David Germano).

Beautiful Luck (The Great Tantra of): *Bkra shis mdzes ldan chen po'i*
  rgyud.
TB Vol. 12/2 (pp. 173-193) 5 chapters.
JV #64, ff. 207-232, AD.
NLD: 106.4-6.

The Blazing Lamp: *sGron ma 'bar ba.*
Gser gyi me tog mdzes pa rin po che sgron ma 'bar ba'i rgyud: "The
  Beautiful Golden Flower: The Tantra of the Precious Blazing Lamp".
TB Vol. 12/8 (pp. 467-491) 4 chapters.
JV #79, ff. 281-313, AD.
NLD: 141.6-142.1.

Direct Introduction (Tantra of): *Ngo sprod spras pa'i rgyud.*
Ngo sprod rin po che spras pa'i zhing khams bstan pa'i rgyud: "The
  Tantra of the Buddhafields of Precious Direct Introduction".
TB Vol. 12/5 (pp. 280-304) 3 chapters.
JV #69, ff. 77-109, AD.
NLD: 131.2-3.

The Garland of Pearls, *Mu tig 'phreng ba.*
Mu tig rin po che phreng ba'i rgyud: "The Tantra of the Precious Garland
  of Pearls".
TB Vol.12/6 (pp. 304-393) 8 chapters.
JV #68, ff. 417-537, AD.
NLD 112.6; 119.1-4; 126.2-5; 126.5-127.2; 141.4-5.

The Great Array of Gems (Tantra of); *Nor bu 'phra bkod chen po'i rgyud.*
Nor bu 'phra bkod rang gi don thams cad gsal bar byed pa'i rgyud: "The
Tantra of the Great Array of Gems Illuminating the Purpose of Life".
TB Vol. 12/11 (pp. 712-777) 14 chapters.
JV #71, ff. 1-76, AD.
NLD 72.2; 142.4-5; 145.5-146.5.
"The Array of Gems" (PT).

The Heap of Jewels: *Rin chen spungs pa.*
Rin chen spungs pa'i yon tan chen po ston pa rgyud kyi rgyal po: "The
Sovereign Tantra Revealing Great Qualities as a Heap of Jewels".
TB Vol.11/5 (pp. 757-788) 5 chapters.
JV.#82 ff. 73-114, AD.
NLD 29.3; 30.4-32.1; 42.2-43.4; 44.4-45.4; 49.2-5; 65.3; 69.1-4; 93.4;
94.1; 125.3; 133.2-4; 143.4-6.

The Heart-Mirror of Vajrasattva: *Rdo rje sems dpa' snying gi me long.*
Rdo rje sems dpa' snying gi me long gi rgyud: "The Tantra of Vajrasattva's
Heart-Mirror".
TB Vol.12/3 (pp. 193-245) 8 chapters.
JV #81, ff. 315-388, AD.
NLD: 70.1-3.

The Rampant Lion: *Seng ge rtsal rdzogs.*
Seng ge rtsal rdzogs chen po'i rgyud: "The Great Tantra The Rampant
Lion".
TB Vol. 12/10 (pp. 559-712) 13 chapters.
JV #75, ff.245-416, AD.
NLD 71.7-72.2; 82.4; 83.3-4; 105.6-7; 109.1-2, 122.2-3; 125.2-3;
128.3; 138.7-139.1; 142.3-4; 144.4-6.

Spontaneously Arising Gnosis: *Rig pa rang shar.*
Rig pa rang shar chen po'i rgyud: "The Great Tantra of Spontaneously
Arising Gnosis".
TB Vol. 11/3 (pp. 323-693) 86 chapters.
JV #74, ff. 389-855, AD.
NLD 25.4-26.2; 35.7-36.1; 66.7-67.1; 133.6-7; 134.5-135.1; 136.1;
136.2; 136.5-7; 137.1-3; 138.1-2.
"Natural Rising of Awareness" (DCJ Vol. II 275) (PT).

The Natural Freedom of Gnosis: *Rig pa rang grol.*
Rig pa rang grol chen po thams cad 'grol ba'i rgyud: "The Tantra of
Universal Gnostic Liberation".
TB Vol. 11/4 (pp. 699-757) 10 chapters.
JV #72, ff. 1-72, AD.
NLD 66.6-7.
"The Natural Freedom of Awareness" (PT).

The Precious Blazing Relics (The Tantra of): *Sku gdung 'bar ba rin po
che'i rgyud.*
Dpal nam mkha' med pa'i sku gdung 'bar ba chen po'i rgyud: "The Great
Tantra of the Glorious Nonspatial Blazing Relics".
TB Vol.11/6. (pp. 788-815) 3 chapters.
JV #80, ff. 115-151, AD.
NLD: 87.1.

Samantabhadra's Mirror of Mind: *Kun tu bzang po thugs kyi me long.*
Kun tu bzang po thugs kyi me long gi rgyud: "The Tantra of
Samantabhadra's Mind Mirror".
TB Vol. 12/4.(pp. 245-280) 4 chapters.
JV #67, ff. 233-280, AD.
NLD: 35.7; 67.4-68.2; 72.6-73.2; 141.3-4.
"Mirror of Enlightened Mind" (PT).

The Six Matrixes: *Klong drug pa*
Kun tu bzang po klong drug pa'i rgyud: "The Tantra of the Six Matrixes
of Samantabhadra".
TB Vol.12/7 ff. (pp. 394-467) 6 chapters.
JV #66, ff. 111-214, AD.
NLD: 52.3-53.1; 58.4-60.1; 74.6; 98.4-5; 99.3; 100.1-2; 105.7; 106.2-
3; 121.2-3; 121.7; 122.4-5; 123.3-4; 123.4-124.5; 141.5-6; 149.3.
"Six Expanses" (PT).

The Unwritten Tantra: *Yi ge med pa.*
Yi ge med pa rgyud chen po: "The Great Unwritten Tantra".
MB: 11/2 (pp. 298-322) 6 chapters.
JV #83, ff. 215-244, AD.
NLD 73.6-74.1; 80.7-81.3; 117.5-7.

Unclassified Tantras from the Nyingma Gyubum

The Epitome of the Definitive Meaning (Tantra of), *Nges don 'dus pa'i rgyud.*
Rdzogs pa chen po nges don 'dus pa'i rgyud lta ba thams cad kyi snying po rin po che rnam par bkod pa: "The Tantra Epitomizing the Definitive Meaning, the Heart-Essence of All Vision: Jewels in Array".
TB Vol.6/1 (pp. 2-145) 81 chapters.
NLD: 36.1-2.

The Sphere of Total Illumination: *Thig le kun gsal.*
Thig le kun gsal chen po'i rgyud: "The Great Tantra The Sphere of Total Illumination". Attributed to Garab Dorje.
TB Vol. 13/3 (pp. 296-499), 96 chapters.
NLD: 29.4-6; 33.3; 37.1; 37.1-2; 37.2; 38.7-39.3; 53.6-7; 76.2-4; 78.1-2; 78.4; 91.2-5; 105.3; 110.2-6; 131.7-132.1.
"Tantra of the Great All-illuminating Sphere" (JV); "The All-Illuminating Sphere" (PT).

The Stream of Empowering Self-sprung Perfection (Tantra of): *Rdzogs pa rang byung dbang gi chu bo'i rgyud.*
Sku thams cad kyi snang ba ston pa dbang rdzogs pa rang byung chen po'i rgyud: "The Great Tantra Self-Sprung Perfect Power Revealing the Vision of All Gnostic Dimensions".
TB Vol. 11/1 (pp. 2-298) 25 chapters.
JV #73, ff. 235-558, AD.
NLD 120.4.

The Supreme Secret: The Mind of All the Tathagatas (Tantra of): *De bzhin gshegs pa thams cad kyi thugs gsang ba chen po'i rgyud.*
Sang rgyas thams cad kyi thugs gsang ba chen po'i rgyud: "The Great Tantra of the Secret Mind of All Buddhas".
TB Vol.13/17 (pp. 667-681) 6 chapters.
NLD: 131.3-6.

Texts of Sri Singha

The Great Garuda: *Khyung chen.* See The Flight of the Great Garuda.
The Flight of the Great Garuda: *Khyung chen mkha' lding* in the first instance and thereafter *Khyung chen.*

NTY, Vol. V: Bima snying thig (Part III), 2b (Ta), pp. 52-63.
NLD: 47.5-6; 48.1-2; 48.5-7; 53.3-4; 57.1-2; 60.3-5; 61.7; 64.7; 68.5-7; 79.7- 80.1; 80.3-4; 82.6-7; 98.4; 121.1; 121.5; 122.3; 123.2; 145.5.

Spoken Word: The Secret Oral Tradition: *Kha gtam gSang ba'i snyan brgyud.*
Text unlocated.
NLD: 124.6-125.1.
"Spoken Words: The Secret Oral Lineage" (PT).

The Works of Garab Dorje (unlocated)

Free Identity: *Mtshan ma rang grol.*
NLD 46.3-47.3; 74.6-75.1; 79.2-3; 111.5-112.2; 112.6-7; 125.6; 127.7-128.1; 149.6-7.
"Natural Freedom that Underlies Characteristics" (PT).

The Junction of the Three Dimensions: *Sku gsum thug phrad.*
NLD: 27.3-5; 34.4-7; 41.1-2; 55.7-56.3; 78.5; 81.5-7; 89.1-2; 6-7; 104.7-105.3; 120.5-6.
"Direct Encounter with the Three Kayas" (PT).

The Sacred Vase of Gnosis: *Rig pa spyi blugs.*
NLD 37.7-38.6; 54.6-55.1; 57.4-6.

Synchronicity: *Dus gsum chig chod.*
NLD 77.4-5; 88.6-89.1; 90.3; 101.3-7; 107.3-108.1.
"Cutting Through Time", "Cutting Through the Three Times".

The Transfiguration of the Six Sensory Fields: *Tshogs drug zil gnon.*
NLD 75.3-4; 86.1; 92.2-3; 103.2-6; 106.7; 151.1-2.
"Overwhelming the Six Modes of Consciousness with Splendor" (PT).
The Vajra Fortress: *Rdo rje mkhar rdzong.*
NLD: 116.7-117.3.

Mahayoga Tantras

The Magical Web of Manjushri: *'Jam dpal sgyu 'phrul drwa ba.*
TK Vol. 14-16. Unlocated.

NLD: 151.7-152.1.
"The Web of Magical Display of Manjushri" (PT).

The Matrix of Mystery: *Gsang snying*.
Gsang ba'i snying po'i rgyud: Skt. *Guhyagarbha Tantra*.
TK Vol.14, no.187.
TB Vols. 20-1.
NLD 86.2.
See DCJ Vol. II p. 275.
"Heart Essence of Secrets" (PT); "Matrix of Mystery" (HG).

Mayahana Texts

The Great Commentary of The Perfection of Wisdom in Eight Thousand
    Verses: *Brgyad stong 'grel chen* of Haribhadra.
Bstan 'gyur.
NLD: 27.6.

The Treasury of Abhidharma: *Chos mngon pa mdzod* of Vasubandhu.
Bstan 'gyur.
NLD: 145.3

Miscellaneous Unlocated Sources

A Concise Commentary on the Oral Transmission: *Snyan brgyud
    ti ka*.
NLD: 111.3.

Dohakosha of Saraha (Collection of Dohas): *Do ha mdzod* (Saraha).
Bstan 'gyur.
NLD: 26.6-7.

The Right Time: *Dus gnad brtag pa* of Padmasambhava.
NLD: 137.5-6.
Other Titles: "Examination of the Key Points of Timelessness" (PT).

The Supreme Lamp (Sutra of), *Dkon mchog Ta la la'i mdo* (see DCJ Vol.
    II, p. 272).
NLD: 46.1-2.

Appendix II
Index of Similes
Note: indices refer to the canto numbers.

Bird in the Sky
Internal events are like a bird's flight-path in the sky (64); all internal events are like the imprint of a bird in the sky (64).

Brass for Gold
Taking appearances as one's own mind is like mistaking brass for gold (8).

Bubble
The body is ephemeral like a bubble (97).

Candle-flame
Display is like the incandescence of a candle-flame (8).

Children
Immersed in conditioning like innocent children in the playground (20).

Clouds, Mist
All concepts melt away like a mass of clouds evaporating (40); all events arise and fall like clouds emerging in the sky and then dissolving therein (51); the imagery of samsara and nirvana evaporate like clouds in the sky (89); this display is like clouds billowing in the clear sky (97); every experience reverts into gnosis like clouds dissolving in the sky (110); corporeality dissolves like mist evaporating (122i); the elements dissolve like mist evaporating (122i).

Crystal
Gnosis diffracts like the crystal (69); gnosis is like the crystal, its brilliance like the fivefold spectrum within the crystal, and its potential for projection like the propensity of the light to emanate out of the crystal (69); our immaculate nature is like a flawless crystal statue (69);

gnostic awareness, like a crystal prism, contains the fivefold spectrum of natural light (77); the display of gnostic potency, like the spectrum of light appearing in a crystal (82); samsara and nirvana evaporate like colored light retracting into the crystal (89); pristine gnosis laid bare is like a crystal (102); the qualities of gnostic self-expression are like light diffracted in a crystal prism (102).

Dream
Samsara and nirvana appear like dreams in the gnostic scope (12); samsara and nirvana, all gnostic vision, is like dream (94); the miserable states of samsara appear illusory like dream (52); objective appearances are like a woman in a dream mistakenly identified as a former lover (52); potency manifests like dreams arising from the potency of sleep (67).

Emperor, the King
The transmission of atiyoga is like Sumeru, the king of mountains (39); spaciousness governs everything, like an emperor (84); these secret precepts are like an absolute monarch (122i).

Earthen Pot
A conditioned result perishes like an earthen pot (19).

Fish
Thoughts are like fish in a pond (50); every flickering thought is like a golden fish darting in a pond (50).

Fools
Like blind blundering fools they cling to fleeting illusions that inevitably perish (99).

Golden Isle
The matrix is like the Golden Isle (2, 11).

Great Garuda
Hatching from the egg and flying away is like abandoning the corporeal shell in buddhahood (91); the view of natural perfection is like a great garuda soaring in the empty sky (122ii); the carefree yogin soars like a great garuda (127).

House Collapsing
The dissolution of corporeality is like the coalescence of interior, exterior and intermediary space as a house collapses (90).

Lion
We jump through like a lion leaping long and high (90).

Magical Illusion
All experience of the world is like magical illusion (6); appearances are like the eight similes of magical illusion (8).

Mirage
A fool deceived by magical illusion is like an animal pursuing a mirage (17).

Moon in Water, Reflection
Appearances are like the shimmering reflection in water (36); whatever appears in empty gnosis is like the reflection of the moon in water (48); appearances are like reflections in a pellucid lake (54); samsara and nirvana, all gnostic vision, is like the reflection of the moon in water (94).

Old Man
Relieved like an old man basking in the sun (20); deeply satisfied, like an old man, his work done (55).

Rainbow etc
Ornamentation is like a rainbow, or the sun, moon, stars and planets, in the sky (8); like a rainbow shining in the sky having no existence separate from the sky (69).

River, a Flowing Stream
Natural meditation is like a flowing stream (3); hyper-concentration is like a river's strong current (23); concentrated absorption is like a great river's flow (23); nondual pure pleasure is uninterrupted like the river Ganges (23); contemplation is like a great river's flow (79).

Sand-castles
Spiritual exercises are like children's sand castles (31); the creative phase is a childish game like building sand castles (31).
Shadow
Pure vision is with us like a shadow following the body (3).

Sky-walker
He who applies deliberate effort falls straight to earth like a tenderfoot sky-walker (40).

Space, Elemental Space, the Sky (54 instances)
Reality is like the sky (3, 12, 24, 113, 114, 115); pure mind is like the sky or space (3, 4, 9, 30, 61, 80, 83, 106, 114); gnosis is just like elemental space or the sky (9, 21, 99); intrinsic gnosis is pure like the sky (21,115); gnosis is brilliant emptiness like the sky (35, 90, 95, 98, 99); gnosis is infinitely open, like a crystal-clear sky (55); gnosis is empty like the sky (65), our fundamental nature is like space (10); the nature of mind is like the sky (11,30,75); the nature of Samantabhadra is like elemental space (40); atiyoga is like space or the sky (18, 44); nondual perception is open like the sky (46); contemplation is like the sky (91), open-ended like the sky (53), tranquil like the sky (81); total presence is like space (83, 122i); the natural state is like space (84); equanimity is like the sky (84); alpha-purity is like the sky (87); unity is timelessly unstructured like the sky (95); consciousness emerges naturally like the sky (29); the language of biased projection and morally discriminating goal-directed endeavor is like the nonactive sky (35); images are like the sky (65); the body-mind uncontrived like the sky (81); the mind, birthless and deathless like the sky (97); nonjudgmental mind is like space (115); the mind and its field are both pure like the sky, baseless and utterly empty (113); display is nonactive like elemental space (115); view and meditation is like the sky (115); brilliant emptiness is like the sky (122ii); identity is like the sky (122ii); whoever seeks emptiness fails like a blind bird trying to reach the end of the sky (17).

Sun, Sunlight, Sun-rays
Display is like the display of the sun as light (8); timeless expression, original radiance, shines like the sun's rays (29); the sun of reality obscured like the disc of the sun in summertime (38); gnosis is untouchable like the heart of the sun (39); clear-light dawns in the field of reality like the sun in the sky (40); gnosis arises like the sun (46); like an old man basking in the sun (20); the clear revelation of absence is like the rising sun (40).

Vajra
Nondual body and mind is like a vajra (97).

Water and Waves
Display is like water and its waves (50); the play of self-sprung awareness is like water and its waves (104); gnosis is saturated by timeless brilliance like water by wetness (48).

Wish-fulfilling Gem

The mind fulfils all our desires like a wish-fulfilling gem (1); awareness with the speed of light is like the master's fountain of jewels (63); pure mind is like a wish-fulfilling gem (66); the spaciousness of reality is a wish-fulfilling gem (66); the spaciousness of reality is a wish-fulfilling gem (102); the inexhaustible treasure he holds in his hand is like a special precious jewel (120); like someone hankering after the wish-fulfilling gem (74).

Appendix III
List of Tibetan Headings in the Auto-commentary
NB: indices refer to page numbers in the NLD

De-nyid-kyi gnas gsal-bar bya-ba
Prologue

1. Phyag-'tshal-ba (1-2)
   Vajra-Homage
2. Brtsam-par dam bca'-ba (3-4)
   The Promise to Compose

   Bstan-bcos-kyi(s) lus-nyid rgya-cher bshad-pa
   The Concise exposition

3. Rdo-rje'i chings bzhis lus mdor bstan-pa (5-6)
   The Short Exposition of the Four Ineluctable Vajra-Binds

   Yan-lag rgyas-par shad-pa
   The Extensive Exposition

I. Med-pa
Absence

I.1. Med-pa gnad bkrol-ba
The Disclosure of Absence

4. Chos thams-cad dngos-po dang mtshan-ma med-par bstan-pa (7-8)
   The Absence of All Concrete Reality
5. De-ltar med-pa'i dpe don nges-pa (9-10)
   A Definitive Simile for Absence
6. Rig-ngor snang-ba'i chos-can rang-bzhin med-par bstan-pa (11-12)
   Appearances in the Nature of Mind are Inherently Absent
7. 'Di-ltar snang-ba'i chos-rnams lhun-grub rig-pa'i ngang-las g.yos-pa med-par bstan-pa (13-14)

I.2. Med-pa 'gag-bsdams-pa
The Assimilation of All Experience to Absence

I.3. Med-pa chings-su bcings-pa
The Ineluctable Bind of Absence

I.4. Med-par la-bzla-ba
Resolution in Absence

II. Phyal-ba
Openness

II.1. Phyal-ba gnad bkrol-ba
The Disclosure of Openness

II.2. Phyal-bar 'gag-bsdams-pa
Assimilation to Openness

II.3. Phyal-ba'i chings-su bcing-ba
The Bind of Openness

II.4. Phyal-ba'i la-bzla-ba
Resolution in Openness

III. Lhun-gyis grub-pa
Spontaneity

III.1. Gnad bkrol-ba
The Disclosure of Spontaneity

III.2. Lhun-grub-tu 'gag-bsdams-pa
The Assimilation to Spontaneity

III.3. Chos thams-cad ye-nas lhun-grub chen-por bcings-pa
The Bind of Spontaneity

III.4. Chos thams-cad lhun-grub-tu la-bzla-ba
Resolution of All Experience in Spontaneity

IV. Chos thams-cad rang-byung-gi ye-shes gcig-pur bstan-pa
All Experience is Self-sprung Awareness Alone

IV.1. Gnad bkrol-ba
The Disclosure of the Unity of Self-sprung Awareness

**IV.2. Chos thams-cad rang-byung ye-shes gcig-tu 'gag-bsdams-pa
Assimilation of All Experience to the Singularity of Self-sprung
Awareness**

**IV.3. Gcig-pu chings-su bcing-ba
The Bind of Unity**

A Dzogchen Glossary

ka dag : alpha~ original~ primordial~ purity; alpha-pure

ka dag chen po : original hyper-purity

Kun byed rgyal po : the supreme source

kun dpe : the universal simile

kun 'byung : the source, the ubiquitous source

kun 'byung nor bu : wish-fulfilling gem

kun gzhi : experiential~ gnostic~ existential~ ground

kye ma : beware

klong : matrix; expanse

klong chen : super-matrix, vast matrix

klong rdol : bursting forth; efflorescence

dkyil yangs po : boundless center

sku : existential~ dimension, mode, body; = *chos sku*

sku dang ye shes : pure being and pristine awareness

sku gsum : the three (gnostic) ~dimensions ~modes ~buddha-bodies

skye 'gag gi chos : temporal experience

skye med : unborn, unoriginated, unbegun

kho thag gcod pa : to reach conviction, to finally surrender

khyab gdal : all- ~pervading ~encompassing ~embracing; stretching out

khyab dal chen po : integral openness

'khod snyoms : congruent

'khor 'das chos : all experience of samsara and nirvana rnams

'khyil ba : converge, entwine, integrated

'khrul 'khor : vicious circle

'khrul snang : delusive appearances

'khrol du 'jug pa : to give room

gol sgrib : glitches and veils; deviation

gol sgrib med : infallible, flawless

gol sa : place of going astray, deviation

grub bsal med : unproven and irrefutable

grol ba : release, freedom, liberation

grwa zur med : zero-dimensional, without edges or corners

dgag tu med : incessant

dgag sgrub med : without assertion or denial

dge sdig : (conventional) morality, moral duality (virtue and vice), moral conditioning

dge sdig med : in the absence of moral conditioning

dge sdig rgyu 'bras : moral ~causality ~causation ~conditioning

dgongs don : dynamic, purpose

dgongs pa : gnostic dynamic, buddha-dynamic, dynamic; contemplation

'gag : crux, focus, locus, nub, key

'gag bsdam pa : assimilation, integration

'gag med : unimpeded, unobstructed

'gyur 'jug : accessing, to access

'gro drug : six types of beings

'gro 'ong med pa : without moving, neither coming nor going, without variation

293

rgya grol : unrestricted

rgya chad phyogs : unrestricted and impartial; indefinite lhung med openness

rgya ma chad : unrestricted, impartial, unlimited

rgya yan : unconfined, unrestricted, uninhibited, unbounded freedom, unbound

rgyan : ornamentation, beauty

rgyas chod : confirmed

rgyu 'bras : causality, contingency, conditioning, cause and effect

rgyu 'bras dge sdig 'bad rtsol : striving for a positive result

rgyu 'bras med : non-contingent, unconditional, without cause and effect

rgyu 'bras rtsol sgrub 'das : unattainable

rgyu 'bras bya rtsol : rational endeavor, goal-orientation

rgyun chad med : uninterrupted

sgom med : nonmeditation

sgyu ma : magical illusion

sgrims lhod med : not too tight nor too slack

sgra thal 'gyur : beyond the sound

sgro skur : imputation; value judgement (assertion and denial), evaluation

gleng gzhi : discourse, history, association

ngang : space, scope

ngang gis : inhere, is inherent, naturally, intrinsically

nges pa : unequivocal, definite, certain

nges don : definitive meaning

nges med : equivocal, ambiguous, indeterminate

ngo bo : essence, face, nature

dngos po : substance, solidity, concrete identity

dngos med : insubstantial, without concrete identity, lacking any substance, 'nothing is solid', immaterial

snga phyi thog : atemporal mtha' bral

cir (gang du) yang ma grub : nowhere attested

cer mthong : direct~ naked~ perception; 'seeing'

cog bzhag : freely resting, carefree ~relaxation ~detachment

cog bzhag chen po : zero-attachment

gcig pu : alone, unitary, the singularity, unity

gcer bu : naked

bcos med : without artifice, cannot be ~contrived ~improved

cha med : undivided

cha shas spros dang bral : free of ~fragmented structure ~differentiating constructs

chags sdang : emotion

chig chod : immediate, instantaneous

chings su bcing ba : 'the bind'

chub : perfected, comprehended, completed

cho 'phrul : magical emanation

chos : experience, phenomena, events, life, all and everything

chos sku : dharmakaya, pure being

chos dang chos min med : neither sacred nor profane, neither something nor nothing

chos nyid : reality

chos nyid zad pa : experience consummate

chos dbyings : spaciousness, hyperspace

chos med : unreal, nothing

chos zad : phenomena~ experience~ events~ ~consumed ~spent ~consummate

'char : arise, emerge, emanate, issue
'char tshul : mode, inception,
    emanation

ji ltar snang yang : whatever appears,
    no matter how they seem
ji bzhin : just as it is; simplicity
ji bzhin pa : what is already there
'jur sems : anal retention
rjen pa : bare, naked
brjod med : unutterable, inexpressible

nyag gcig : the sole, holistic
gnyis med : nondual
mnyam pa : equality, sameness; the
    same, identical, uniform,
    consonant with
mnyam pa chen po : super~ hyper~
    -sameness; 'great equanimity'
mnyam pa nyid : sameness, equality,
    equanimity
mnyam bzhag : equanimity,
    meditative equipoise, settled in
    sameness
snying po : essence, nature, heart,
    core

ting nge 'dzin : natural~ samadhi
gtan la 'babs/dbab pa : to establish
    conclusively
gtad : focus, target, objective
btang bzhag med : simply being,
    without~ acceptance or rejection~
    biased action; nothing to
    reject/discard or embrace/adopt
rtag chad med : neither eternal nor
    ~temporal ~ephemeral, free of
    eternalism and nihilism
rtog pa : to conceive; thought,
    thinking; construct, concept
rtog tshogs : mental ~constructs
    ~conceptions
rtogs pa : realizing, realization,
    understanding, intuition
lta ba : view, vision

lta ba sgom pa spyod pa 'bras bu :
    view, meditation, action,
    goal/fruition
stong pa : empty
stong pa chen (po) : super~ vast~
    emptiness
stong pa nyid : emptiness
stong gsal : brilliant emptiness, empty
    clarity, empty light
thag gcod pa : utter~ conviction
thig le : seed, nucleus; holistic seed,
    seminal nucleus; sphere; light-seed
thig le nyag gcig : the one~ sole~
    holistic seed
thug phrad : junction, juncture
    (intersection)
thugs : buddha-mind
thugs rje : compassion
theg sman, theg 'og ma : lower
    approaches; gradualist~ gradual~
    progressive~ approaches
thog mtha' med : beginningless and
    endless
thog ma'i gzhi : original~
    primordial~ existential ground
mtha' dbus : extension
mtha' dbus med : zero-dimensional,
    without center or boundary
mtha' bzhi, : four extreme beliefs;
    rigid attitudes/beliefs

dangs gsal ba : pellucid clarity
dam tshig : samaya,
    commitment
dal khod snyoms : congruent
    (homogenous) integration
dus gsum : past, present and future,
    three times, time
dus gsum chig chod : synchronicity
dus gsum sangs rgyas : buddha past
    present and future (Samantabhadra)
de kho na nyid : immediate reality,
    the timeless specificity of reality
de nyid : itself, reality, the nature of
    mind

de bzhin nyid : the *zing* of reality, *tathata*, suchness, reality just as it is, authentic reality

de bzhin gshegs pa'i snying po : pure mind essence

don : meaning, reality

don gyi : actually

don gyi snying po : essential reality, heart-essence, actual essence, core/heart of reality

don gyi rang bzhin : actual function

dran pa : memory, thought, reflection, recollection

dran bsam : ideation

gdangs ba : luminous; luminosity, expression

gdangs gsal ba : crystal clarity

gdams pa : advice, instruction

gdal ba chen po : all- ~pervasive ~embracing ~suffusing

gdod nas dag pa : primordially pure, pure from the beginning, alpha-pure

gdod nas sangs rgyas : primordial buddhahood, primordial awakening

gdod ma'i klong : primordial matrix

gdod ma'i sa : original seat

bdag nyid : identity

bdag tu 'dzin pa : concretization

bde sdug : feeling (happiness and sadness, pleasure and pain); samsara

bde ba chen po : pure pleasure, supreme bliss,

bden med : unreal

'das : superseding, transcending, gone beyond, dissolving

'du bral med pa : inseparable union; 'neither united nor separated', beyond union and separation, never lost nor gained, without anticipation, ineluctable

'du shes : idea, apperception

'dus ma byas : non-composite, unconditioned uncompounded

'dod byung nor bu : wish-fulfilling jewel

rdo rje : vajra, immutable, indestructible, ineluctable, adamantine

rdo rje'i 'gros : vajra- ~dance ~mode ~stance

rdo rje dbyings : vajra-space, the vajra-field

rdo rje snying po'i dbyings : spaciousness of the ~vajra-heart ~vajra-essence

nub pa med pa'i rgyal mtshan : the forever-unfurled (eternal) victory banner

gnad : focus, focal point, key, main thing

gnad bkrol ba : disclosure (of the focal point)

gnas 'gyu : stillness and movement

gnas pa : abiding, being, resting, remaining, existing

gnas pa med : unlocatable, homeless

gnas lugs : the natural state, way of being; natural perfection

rnam rtog : discursive~ thought

rnam dag : immaculate

rnal gzhag chen po : super-relaxation, great natural relief, satisfaction

rnal 'byor pa : gnostic yogin and yogini, authentic yoga

rnal ma'i : fundamental

snang ba : appearance, image, light-form, manifestation, vision

snang ba'i dus nas : 'the timeless moment', in its moment of appearance, at the moment of emanation, right from the start

snang shes nyid : cognition

snang tshul : appearance

snang yul : things arising

snang sems : integral vision

snang srid : the world and its inhabitants, environment and life-

forms, animate and inanimate
snod bcud : matter and energy,
worlds and life-forms, chalice and
elixir

spang blang bral : no preference
spang blang 'khor 'das med : no
preference for samsara or nirvana
spangs thob med : beyond rejection
and attainment
spong len : discrimination, discipline
spongs thob med : ineluctable;
discipline
spyod pa : conduct, behavior, practice
spyod yul : field of action
sprul sku : nirmanakaya, the
dimension of magic
spro bsdu med : neither diffused nor
concentrated
spros : multiplicity, structuring,
elaboration
spros bral : unstructured,
unelaborated; simplicity

phyam gcig : common unity
phyam gdal : equilibrium, equalized,
spaced-out
phyam phyal : untrammeled openness
phyal ba : openness
phyal ba chen po : infinite openness
phyal yas : infinitely open, open to
infinity
phyi nang : outside and inside, inner
and outer
phyogs 'byams : all-suffusing
phyogs med : undirected, nonspatial,
unbiased, spatially indeterminate
phyogs ris med : unbiased and
impartial, the absence of spatial and
temporal distinction, unpatterned,
free of all restriction, unrestricted,
undivided and unbiased,
unrestricted spacetime
phyogs bral : undifferentiated
phyogs su 'dzin : taking sides

phyogs su mi blta : total perspective,
free of any bias
phyogs su lhung med : impartial,
unreified
phra rags : gross~ coarse~ and subtle
'phel 'grib med : neither increasing
nor decreasing
'pho 'gyur : in flux
'pho 'gyur med : without
transformation, without transition
or change; immutable
'phrin las : ideal conduct, buddha-
activity, ritual activity
'phro : project
'phro gnas : proliferating or quiescent
'phro 'du : oscillation
'phro gzhi : projective base

bag yangs : fully receptive
bar med : seamless
bya byed : deliberate action
bya bral : nonaction; nonactive,
inactive; free-form
bya rtsol : goal-oriented endeavor,
deliberate effort, striving, endeavor
byang chub : total presence, total
pure presence
byang chub sems : (bodhichitta) pure
mind
byang chub snying po : the essential
heart of total presence
byar med : nonaction; nonactive,
nonreactive, 'with nothing to do'
byas pa : purposeful action, goal-
directed action
bying rgod : lethargy and agitation,
laziness and excitement,
volatility
byin brlabs : hallowed
byung tshor med pa : without
affectivity
blang dor : discrimination, principled
action
blang dor bya rtsol : directed~
discriminating~ activity

blang dor 'bad rtsol : discipline, struggle for principled action

blang dor med pa : nondiscrimination, without cultivating or rejecting anything, nondiscriminatory

blo : intellect, individual~ ordinary~ mind

blo 'das : intellect ~exhausted ~redundant; no-mind!

blo bral : mindless

blo rab : brilliant; brightest~ broadest~ keenest~ mind

dbye ba med : indivisible

dbye bsal med : all-inclusive, undiscriminating all-inclusive and indivisible

dbyings : spaciousness, field (of reality), hyperspace

'bad rtsol : effort, struggle, activity

'byung 'jug : alternation, strobe-like

'byung 'jug blo : fluctuating mind

'byung tshul : the manner~ mode~ of emanation, emanation

'bras bu : goal (negative), fruition (positive)

sbubs : cavity, hollow, sanctum

ma skyes : unoriginated, unmanifest

ma grub : unattested, indefinable, unproven, cannot be established

ma 'gags : uncrystallizing, inalienable, unreified; unimpeded

ma 'gags rol pa : uncrystallizing display,

ma bsgoms : unaided (concentration), uncultivated

ma nges : uncertain, ambiguous, indeterminate, equivocal

ma bcos : uncontrived, unfabricated, artless

ma byas : unmade, uncreated

ma btsal : unsought, pre-existing

ma rtsol : unattainable

ma yengs : undistracted

ma g.yos : never shifting (from), unstirring

man ngag : secret precept

mi 'gyur : unchanging

mi rtog : unthought, unthinking, nonconceptual

mi gnas : nowhere located, unlocated, unfixed, unlocalized

mi snang : unmanifest, invisible, intangible

mi phyed : indivisible

mi dmigs : unimaged

mi mtshon : unsigned, unindicated

mi g.yo : unmoving

ming tsam : mere label

med pa : absence, nonexistence

med pa gsal snang : brilliant/vivid appearance; image of absence

med pa'i chos rnams : empty phenomena

dmigs pa : imaged

dmigs gtad : an objective, point of reference, focus

dmigs gtad med : nothing to hold on to, untargeted, without ~objective ~ reference ~focus

dmigs med : invisible, unimaginable

dmigs bsam bral ba : indeterminacy

smra bsam brjod 'das : inconceivable and unutterable

btsal bsgrubs : deliberate effort

btsal ba med : not to be found, not to be sought, unwanted, involuntary

rtsal : potency; creativity

rtsa : basis, foundation, source, root

rtsal rdzogs : potentiated; rampant

rtsol ba : effort, striving, diligence, exertion

rtsol sgrub : goal-oriented ~endeavor; spiritual ambition

rtsol sgrub med : without endeavor, effortless, involuntary

rtsol med : the absence of striving

tshogs drug : six sensory fields
mtshan nyid : quality, attribute,
  character, identity
mtshan ma : characteristic, attribute
mtshan ma'i ris : free of all specifics
dang bral
mtshan 'dzin : fixation
mtshan brjod 'das : beyond
  expression, inexpressible, ineffable
mtshon dang mi mtshon med :
  neither signed nor unsigned
mtshon du med : cannot be indicated
mtshon pa'i yul las 'das : beyond the
  specific

rdzogs : perfection; completion,
  wholeness
rdzogs chen : natural perfection, the
  Great Perfection as a school, title etc
'dzin pa : grasping, belief

zhi ba : quelled, assuaged,
  extinguished
gzhi : ground (of being), existential
  ground, base, basis, basic,
  fundament
gzhi bral : with no solid ground
gzhi snang : gestalt ~imagery
  ~emanation; archetypal imagery
gzhi dbyings : the spaciousness of the
  ground; the field as the ground

zang ka ma : pristine, authentic,
  genuine
zang thal : holistic transparence;
  transparent; all-embracing;
  unimpeded; immediate,
  synchronicitous
zang thal chen po : super-
  transparence; transparent,
  translucent
zad : consumed, consummate, spent,
  exhausted,
zad pa'i chos nyid : all-consuming
  reality

zil gyis gnon : outshine, overwhelm,
  transfigure, over-awe
gza' gtad : focus, objective, target
gzugs brnyan : reflections
gzung 'dzin : dualistic perception
  (knower and known,
  subject and object)
gzung 'dzin med : nondual
  perception, the absence of dualistic
  perception
gzeb : trap
bzang ngan : good and bad,
  preference, judgement,
  discrimination
bzang ngan dge sdig 'das : beyond
  moral distinction
bzang ngan spang blang rgyu 'bras
  bya rtsol : morally discriminating
  causal reaction
bzang ngan med : undiscriminating,
  nondiscriminatory
bzang ngan spong len : value
  judgement

'od gsal : clear light

yangs pa : vast; expanse
yid la byed pa : attention
yin lugs : manner of existence
yul : object, (objective) field
yul can : 'the knower' /experiencing
  subject
yul snang : objective field, field of
  appearances, imaged field
yul dbang : sensory field
yul med : nonreferential, unimaged
yul sems : mind and its field, mind in
  its field
yul sems snang ba : dualistic
  appearance
yul sems 'dzin pa : dualistic grasping
ye : ultimate
ye grol : ultimate~ release
ye stong : ultimate~ utter~ emptiness
ye dag : primal purity

ye nas : timeless, primordial; pre-existent, ultimate

ye nas yin pa'i gnas lugs : the timeless state of natural gnosis

ye nas lhun grub : original spontaneity, spontaneously present from the beginning

ye gnas : has always existed

ye bzhin : timeless

ye shes : pristine~ timeless~ primal~ ever-fresh~ awareness

ye sangs : awakened

yeng dang ma yengs med : admitting no degree of focus

g.yo med : never leave, depart, waver from, stir (from)

rang grol : reflexive release

rang ngo : original face, face, nature of mind

rang ngo'i dgongs pa : natural dynamic

rang dag : naturally~ intrinsically~ pure (empty)

rang dangs : self-clarified, naturally unsullied, bright, pellucid, transparent

rang gdangs : self-expression, intrinsic luminosity, luminous self-expression

rang gnas : naturally abiding, indwelling, intrinsic, self-existing

rang snang : gnostic envisionment, auto-envisionment, gestalt imagery, display; self-imaged, self-manifest

rang babs : naturally ~falling ~occurring; adventitious; natural flow

rang byung : self-sprung, self-occurring; spontaneous, natural

rang byung ye shes : self-sprung (pristine) awareness

rang mal : natural disposition, the natural~ original~ state, natural condition

rang gzhag/bzhag : relaxation, natural ease

rang bzhin : nature

rang bzhin bcu : ten techniques; rubric or categories of tantric method

rang bzhin med : insubstantial, absent in reality; inherently absent, evanescent

rang bzhin rdzogs pa chen po : natural perfection, intrinsic natural perfection

rang bzhin gsal ba : brilliant nature, intrinsic clarity, brilliant

rang bzhin bsam gtan : natural~ intrinsic~ concentration

rang yal : (self-) dissolve, melt

rang rig : intrinsic gnosis

rang rig ye shes : intrinsic gnostic awareness

rang shar : naturally-arising, self-arising, spontaneously arising, occurring autonomously

rang sa 'dzin/zin : relax into the natural state, remains in its natural state

rang sar : as it stands, in the natural state

rang sangs : naturally pure, naturally pristine; self-actuating purification, self-dissolution

rang sems : the (ordinary) mind

rang gsal : intrinsic luminosity, natural clarity

rab 'byams : all-suffusing, all embracing

rig ngo : the face of gnosis, the original face, the nature of mind

rig stong : empty gnosis

rig pa : gnosis

rig pa zang ka : authentic gnosis

ris med : indivisible, undivided, indistinguishable

rig 'dzin : mystic, gnostic master

ro gcig : (the) one taste

rol pa : display, play

la bzla ba : resolution; to resolve

lam : path, process

lung : transmission

lus ngag sems : physical, energetic and mental complexes

longs spyod sku : sambhogakaya, the dimension of perfect enjoyment

shar : arise, dawn, happen, start

shar grol : inception and release, release at inception

shar ba : inception; emitting

shar lugs : emanation

shar sa : field of origin, incipient state

shig ge : floating

shes rab : insight (into emptiness)

gshis don : basic meaning

sa bor : disdaining

sangs : awaken, purify, dissolve, clear away

sangs rgyas : buddha, gnostic master

sang rgyas pa : buddhahood

sems nyid : the nature of mind, mind itself

sems nyid byang chub : the pure nature of mind

sems snang : mental image

gsang chen : profound mystery

gsal : shine, radiate

gsal ba : brilliance, clarity, radiance

bsam brjod med : inconceivable and inexpressible, ineffable

bsam gtan : concentrated absorption

bsam dang bral : inconceivable, unthinkable, without plan, without ideation

bsam yul 'das : inconceivable, transcending thought and intention

har sang : awe, fully alert

har sang rgya yan : sudden wakefulness

lhag mthong : heightened insight

lhug pa : left loosely, relaxed; free and easy relaxation, relaxation; relaxed detachment

lhun grub : spontaneity; spontaneous perfection; spontaneously ~accomplished ~arising

lhun grub chen po : super-spontaneity, spontaneous creativity, spontaneous gnosis

lhun mnyam : immanent sameness

lhun 'byams : interfused

lhod pa : loose and easy, relaxed, carefree, slack

'ub chub : consummate fulfilment

'e ma ho : ho!

'ong 'gro : kinetic, variation

Selected English Bibliography

Clemente, Adriano. *The Total Space of Vajrasattva*. Shang Shung Edizioni, 1999.

Dowman, Keith. *The Eye of the Storm*. Kathmandu, Vajra Books, 2006.

-----. *The Flight of the Garuda*. Revised edition. Boston, Wisdom, 2003.

Dudjom Lingpa, *Buddhahood Without Meditation*. Trans. Richard Barron. Padma Publishing, 1994.

Dudjom Rinpoche. *The Nyingma School of Tibetan Buddhism: Its Fundamentals and History*. 2 vols. Trans. Gyurme Dorje and Matthew Kapstein. Boston, Wisdom, 1991.

Germano, D. *Poetic Thought, the Intelligent Universe, and the Mystery of Self: The Tantric Synthesis of Dzogchen in Fourteenth Century Tibet*, unpublished doctoral dissertation, 1992.

-----. "The Funerary Transformation of the Great Perfection", *Journal of the International Association of Tibetan Studies*, no.1 (October 2005): pp. 1-54.

Guenther, H. *Matrix of Mystery*. Boulder, Shambhala, 1984.

Lowe, J. *Simply Being*. London, Vajra Press, 1998.

Longchen Rabjam. *The Precious Treasury of the Way of Abiding*. Trans. Richard Barron with the Padma Translation Committee. Junction City, Padma Publishing, 1998.

Namkhai Norbu and Shane, John. *The Crystal and the Way of Light*. London, RKP, 1986.

Namkhai Norbu and Lipman, Kennard. *Primordial Experience*. Boston, Shambhala, 1987.

Namkhai Norbu and Clemente, Adriano. *Dzogchen: the Self-Perfected State*. London, Arkana, 1989.

-----. *The Supreme Source: The Fundamental Tantra of the Dzogchen Semde*. Ithica, Snow Lion, 1999.

Nyoshul Khenpo. *Natural Great Perfection*. Trans. Surya Das. Ithaca, Snow Lion, 1995.

Reynolds, J. *Golden Letters*. Ithica, Snow Lion, 1996.

Samten Karmay. *The Great Perfection*. Leyden, Brill, 1988.

Tulku Thondup. *Buddha Mind: An Anthology of Longchen Rabjampa's Writing on Dzogpa Chenpo*. Ithica, Snow Lion, 1989.

Tulku Thondup. *The Tantric Tradition of the Nyingmapas*. Marion MA, Buddhayana, 1984.

303